THE TEACHER'S

5
IDEA
BOOK

MAKING THE MOST OF
PLAN-DO-REVIEW

Other Titles in the Series

The Teacher's Idea Book 1: Planning Around the Key Experiences
The Teacher's Idea Book 2: Planning Around Children's Interests
The Teacher's Idea Book 3: 100 Small-Group Experiences
The Teacher's Idea Book 4: The Essential Parent Workshop Resource

Related High/Scope Press Preschool Publications

*Educating Young Children: Active Learning Practices for Preschool
and Child Care Programs*
A Study Guide to Educating Young Children: Exercises for Adult Learners
Extensions—Newsletter of the High/Scope Curriculum
High/Scope Preschool Key Experiences Series:
Creative Representation, Language and Literacy (booklets & videos)
Supporting Young Learners 1: Ideas for Preschool and Day Care Providers
Supporting Young Learners 2: Ideas for Child Care Providers and Teachers
Getting Started: Materials and Equipment for Active Learning Preschools
High/Scope Preschool Classroom Library
High/Scope Preschool Classroom Library Starter Set
High/Scope's Favorite New Titles
Grandpa's Choice Series of Children's Books
Round the Circle: Key Experiences in Movement for Young Children, Second Edition
Movement Plus Rhymes, Songs, & Singing Games, Second Edition,
and accompanying music recordings (cassette, CD)
How Adults Support Children at Planning Time (video)
How Adults Support Children at Work Time (video)
How Adults Support Children at Recall Time (video)
Supporting Children in Resolving Conflicts (video)
Adult-Child Interactions:
Forming Partnerships With Children (video)
The High/Scope Approach to Under Threes (video)
High/Scope Child Observation Record (COR) for Ages 2½–6
High/Scope COR-PC and COR-Mac for Ages 2½–6
High/Scope Program Quality Assessment (PQA)

Available from

High/Scope® Press
A division of the High/Scope Educational Research Foundation
600 North River Street, Ypsilanti, MI 48198-2898
ORDERS: phone (800)40-PRESS, fax (800)442-4FAX
e-mail: *press@highscope.org*
www.highscope.org

THE TEACHER'S

5

IDEA
BOOK

MAKING THE MOST OF
PLAN-DO-REVIEW

Nancy Vogel

HIGH/SCOPE® PRESS

Ypsilanti, Michigan

Published by

High/Scope® Press

A division of the High/Scope® Educational Research Foundation
600 North River Street
Ypsilanti, Michigan 48198-2898
(734)485-2000, fax (734)485-0704
press@highscope.org

High/Scope Press Editor: Holly Barton
Cover design, text design, and production: Judy Seling of Seling Design

Library of Congress Cataloging-in-Publication Data

Vogel, Nancy, 1970-
   The teacher's idea book. 5, Plan-do-review / Nancy Vogel.
      p. cm.
   Includes bibliographical references and index.
   ISBN 1-57379-086-9
   1. Early childhood education--Activity programs--United States. 2. Planning in children--United States. 3. Active learning--United States. I. Title: Plan-do-review. II. Title.

LB1139.35.A37 V64 2001
372.13--dc21   00-053672

Printed in the United States of America
10 9 8 7 6 5 4

Contents

Acknowledgments x

Chapter 1

Introduction to the Plan-Do-Review Process 1

What Is Plan-Do-Review and Why Is It Important? 2

The Components of the High/Scope Daily Routine 7

How the Plan-Do-Review Sequence Fits Into the Daily Routine 9

How Plan-Do-Review Carries Over Into Other Parts of Children's Lives 10

    Throughout the daily routine 10

    Outside of school 11

    Beyond the preschool years 12

What's Ahead in This Book 12

Chapter 2

"What Are You Going to Do Today?" Planning Time 13

What Is Planning Time All About? 14

    Making choices and following personal initiatives 14

    Anticipating actions and events 15

    Expressing intentions 16

    Fostering more purposeful and complex play 17

How to Support Children During Planning Time 19

    Plan with children in intimate settings 19

    Plan where children can see the interest areas and materials 21

    Allow enough time for planning 21

    Provide children with interesting planning games and experiences 21

    Ask children questions 23

    Listen attentively to children's plans 25

    Support nonverbal and vague planners in a variety of ways 26

    Encourage children to elaborate on their plans 29

    Use encouragement rather than praise 32

    Write down children's plans 33

Anticipate that children's ability to plan will change over time 33

What About . . . ? Commonly Asked Questions About Planning Time 43

Chapter 3

Ready, Set . . . Go! Work Time 61

What Is Work Time All About? 65

Engaging in active learning 65

Engaging in High/Scope's key experiences 68

Participating in various types of play 71

How to Support Children at Work Time 80

Offer children comfort and contact 80

Join children on their physical level 82

Observe children, listen to them, and understand what they
are doing 82

Play in parallel with children 82

Join children at their developmental level 82

Label and describe children's actions 83

Look for natural play openings 86

Follow children's leads 87

Take turns with children in their play 89

Extend children's play and learning 90

Ask questions sparingly 94

Encourage children to problem-solve 97

Gather anecdotal notes and observations 103

When Work Time Is Over: How to Support Children at Cleanup Time 105

Give children advance warning that work time will be ending 105

Organize and label materials and containers to enable
children to easily put items away 107

Support children's problem-solving skills 108

Make cleanup time fun and enjoyable 108

Become a partner with children during cleanup 109

Realize that there will be days when not all the materials
will get put away 110

What About . . . ? Commonly Asked Questions About Work Time
and Cleanup Time 112

Chapter 4

Looking Back: Recall Time 131

What Is Recall Time All About? 132

       Thinking back on work-time experiences 132

       Sharing experiences with other children and adults 133

       Beginning to connect planning, work, and recall time 136

       Continuing to reflect on work-time experiences after recall 137

How to Support Children During Recall Time 137

       Provide children with interesting props and games 137

       Ask children open-ended questions 138

       Listen to children's responses 140

       Repeat or rephrase what children say 140

       Interpret nonverbal children's gestures and vocalizations 141

       Make specific comments on what you saw children doing during work time 143

       Write down children's recall accounts 144

       Use encouragement rather then praise 147

       Help children make the connection between their original plans, their work-time experiences, and their recall accounts 148

       Encourage children to carry over their activities to the following day 148

       Anticipate that children's ability to recall will change over time 150

What About . . . ? Commonly Asked Questions About Recall Time 151

Chapter 5

Getting Started: Implementing the Plan-Do-Review Process in Your Program 161

How Do You Begin? 162

       Revise your daily routine 162

       Introduce the plan-do-review process to your children 169

After You Get Going: Maintaining the Plan-Do-Review Process 180

       Meet with your teaching team 181

       Refer to High/Scope resources for assistance 185

What About. . . ? Commonly Asked Questions About Implementing the Plan-Do-Review Process 186

Chapter 6

Involving Parents in the Plan-Do-Review Process 197

Share the Importance of the Plan-Do-Review Process With Parents 198

 Parent meetings 198

 Newsletters 199

 A lending library 199

Encourage Parents to Participate in Planning, Work, or Recall Time 200

 Encourage parents to stay for planning time when dropping children off 200

 Encourage parents to recall with their children when picking them up at the end of the day 201

 Ask parents to make planning and recall games 203

Share Children's Plans, Work-Time Experiences, and Recall Accounts With Parents 203

 Send home representations of children's planning and recall experiences 203

 Videotape or take photographs of children during the plan-do-review sequence 204

 Display children's creations or writing samples 204

 Share anecdotal notes with parents on a regular basis 206

Encourage Parents to Use the Plan-Do-Review Process at Home 206

Chapter 7

Planning and Recall Games and Experiences 207

Props and Partnerships 209

Visibility Games and Tours 214

Group Games 216

Representations 219

Appendix A: Sample Parent Meeting and Overheads 225

Appendix B: Sample Parent Notes Explaining Plan-Do-Review 231

Appendix C: Sample Parent Note Encouraging Plan-Do-Review at Home 237

Appendix D: Sample Planning/Recall Sheets 239

Bibliography 245

Index 247

Acknowledgments

When I first began writing this book I was pregnant with my daughter, Ruth, now 18 months old. As this book goes to print, I am expecting my second child, so it seems as though things have come full circle.

I am grateful to the High/Scope Foundation for giving me this opportunity to write for them. Lynn Taylor, High/Scope's editor in chief, has been nothing but supportive over the last couple of years. Thanks also go to other editorial staff at High/Scope, especially Nancy Brickman for her helpful suggestions in the early stages of this book and Pattie McDonald for formatting the manuscript and putting in all the changes. A huge thank-you to my editor, Holly Barton, whose ideas and suggestions were extremely helpful and whose sweet voice was always so pleasant to listen to on the phone. I also appreciate the High/Scope staff and consultants who shared their ideas, opinions, and expertise, especially Dave Weikart, Chuck Wallgren, Ann Epstein, Mary Hohmann, Michelle Graves, and Beth Marshall.

I thank my entire family for their interest in the progress of my book, their continued support over the last two years, and their endless encouragement—particularly my parents, Marcy and Bob, and my husband's parents, Marsha and Martin. All my love to my husband, Curt, and daughter, Ruth. The two of you keep my world so full of joy and laughter that I can't help but marvel at how truly blessed I am to have you both in my life.

1

Introduction to the

Plan-Do-Review

Process

t's dinner time once again, and you're trying to decide what to prepare for your family. Before you head to the grocery store, you have to make some plans—out of the many (or perhaps not so many) meals your family likes, which one will you make? Which ingredients do you already have and which ones will you need to buy? How about gas in the car—have enough to get you to the store? Will you pay for your groceries with cash, check, or a credit or debit card? (Or will you decide when you get there?!) When you finally get to the store you'll have to make decisions about what brands to buy, what to substitute if you can't find something you need, and which checkout lane seems to be moving the fastest.

When you return home with your groceries and are ready to prepare the meal, you'll likely be actively involved in several steps, including reading the recipe, measuring, stirring, mixing, kneading, heating, tasting, and adding more ingredients. You may run into some problems. Maybe the dough for your dinner rolls is too sticky, so you decide to add more flour. If it's a really big mess, you might throw the whole thing out and start again from scratch or simply pull out the refrigerated, ready-made dough. You may be a person who cleans up as you go along, or maybe you charge through the task and leave the mess to clean up after everyone eats (or recruit family members to do it).

While your family consumes the meal you've worked so hard to prepare, you might review how you made it or which ingredients you used to create a certain flavor. As you taste the chicken you made, you might make a mental note of what you would change the next time you make it—say, putting in less salt and more oregano. Noticing that your children are devouring the new vegetable dish you made, you might decide that you simply must add that recipe to your personal file. Perhaps the pasta dish didn't go over quite so well; you remind yourself to try a different one next time. After the meal is over, you congratulate yourself on another task well done—at least until the next day, when you get to do it all over again!

What Is Plan-Do-Review and Why Is It Important?

What does dinner preparation have to do with plan-do-review? Like adults preparing a meal, children in High/Scope programs engage in a daily process of **planning, working,** and **recalling.** In the classroom, center, or home child care setting, children have the opportunity to choose for themselves what they are going to do during work time that day. Like adults choosing ingredients, children have a rich selection of materials to choose from and endless possibilities for combining them in ways that contribute to their learning and development. To aid in their decision about which of the many activities they will engage in on any particular day, they make a goal or plan ahead of time (as adults do when deciding what to make for dinner). **Planning** encourages children to think through what they want to accomplish and how to go about doing it. This focuses their attention at work time. Put in terms of going to the grocery store for meal ingredients, planning helps children shop purposefully rather than merely stare at the shelves, overwhelmed by so many choices, or make a mad dash from one aisle to the next, pulling all kinds of things off the shelves and putting them in the cart.

Once children have made their plans for the day, it is time for them to begin "making the meal," so to speak. At **work time** they set off to one or more interest areas to put their ideas into action. As they do so, they develop and refine important skills in many areas. For example, as children make a "life raft" from hollow wooden blocks, they explore size, volume, number, and space; learn to cooperate with one another; and exercise their imagination. As they paint a picture of the class's new fish, they discover how to make a representation of a real object. They act out a familiar activity and take on new roles when they serve some "customers" at a fast-food restaurant in the house area. Along the way, they may encounter some difficulties—perhaps there aren't enough hollow wooden blocks to make their life raft, or they can't stop the paint from running down their paper at the easel. Maybe another child is interrupting the restaurant play by flying through the house area in his "airplane." With the help of adults, children are encouraged to find a solution to problems like these that stand in the way of their work-time goals.

Just as adults evaluate their efforts at providing a nutritious, tasty meal for their family, so children have an opportunity after planning and working to reflect on their actions. At **recall time** they are encouraged to share with their peers and with adults what they did during work time, who they played with, and any problems that came up and how they solved them. During this process, they may decide that the next time they build a life raft they could use the Waffle blocks instead of the hollow blocks because there are more of the Waffle blocks, or they may decide they liked the effect of drippy paint and want to use it again the next day.

Planning the dinner-making process gives adults the direction and confidence to complete the task and helps make the process go more smoothly. Afterwards, reviewing what they did allows them to evaluate what worked and what didn't. In a similar way, the plan-do-review process enables children to set their own goal or think through an idea, see it through to completion, and reflect on what they learned from their experience. Children who are encouraged by supportive adults to participate in plan-do-review begin to realize that they can become independent, successful goal setters and achievers. When they consciously think through the details of what they are planning to do, they generally become more purposeful in their actions. While all segments of the High/Scope daily routine are important, the plan-do-review sequence is a significant part of the day and a significant part of the curriculum. In fact, results from *Training for Quality* (Epstein, 1993, p. 159) show that "access to diverse materials and . . . opportunities for planning and recall were the two dimensions of program quality" most important

Overview of the High/Scope Preschool Curriculum

The central principles and guidelines of the High/Scope approach are summarized in the diagram on the facing page: the High/Scope Preschool "Wheel of Learning." (For a full description of each component, see *Educating Young Children: Active Learning Practices for Preschool and Child Care Programs*, by Mary Hohmann and David P. Weikart, High/Scope Press, 1995.) Each component of the wheel is discussed below.

Active learning. Active learning is at the center of the curriculum, as seen in the wheel. Through active learning—acting directly on objects and interacting with people, ideas, and events—children construct their own understanding of the world around them. Children in High/Scope environments are encouraged to follow their own **initiative**—to explore, engage in experiences that are of personal interest, ask and answer questions, set their own goals, solve problems that get in the way of accomplishing those goals, and generate new ideas to test. As they carry out their intentions with the support of interested, involved adults, children naturally engage in **key experiences**—activities that present important learning opportunities in ten key areas of development: *creative representation, language and literacy, initiative and social relations, movement, music, classification, seriation, number, space, and time.*

Whether children are digging in the dirt outside, exploring with eyedroppers and colored water, or dancing with ribbon rings, they are talking with other children and with adults and making choices about what materials to use and how to use them. Adults, in turn, support children in a variety of ways, such as playing as partners with them, helping them solve problems, and providing opportunities for further learning experiences. These **five ingredients of active learning (materials, manipulation, choice, child language, and adult support)** are apparent throughout the High/Scope daily routine and are discussed in more detail in Chapter 3.

Adult-child interaction. The way adults interact with children is a key component of the High/Scope approach because it impacts how comfortable children feel with initiating their own ideas. When adults focus on children's individual interests and strengths and share control with them, children feel encouraged to plan and follow through on activities of their own choosing. Throughout this book a great deal of attention is given to strategies adults can employ that will support children's efforts to construct their own knowledge through interaction with the environment and other people.

Learning environment. High/Scope settings are designed to support active learning. Both the indoor and outdoor settings offer children a wide range of materials that can be manipulated and combined in many different ways—ways that make sense to children and enable them to pursue their own interests. Inside the classroom or home, the play space is divided into several interest areas centered around specific types of play—for example, a block area, house area, toy area, art area, and book area.

Assessment. When adults are closely involved in children's play and activities and make a daily practice of observing them, they learn a great deal about each child's interests and abilities. Assessment in a High/Scope program is based on these daily observations of children. Adults use this information not only to document children's development but also to guide them in providing an environment that meets the physical, social, emotional, and cognitive needs and interests of each child.

Daily routine. The High/Scope daily routine offers children the consistency of a predictable yet flexible sequence of events. The routine is made up of several components: a plan-do-review sequence, small- and large-group times, outside time, transition times, and times for eating and resting, if necessary. These components provide children

with a range of active learning experiences and a balance between adult- and child-initiated activities. Children have opportunities to play indoors as well as outdoors, to participate in both noisy and quiet play. There are times for large-group activities and times when children can choose to play by themselves or with one or two other children or adults. Children also engage in a variety of types of play, including exploratory play, constructive play, pretend play, and games (see pp. 72–79). The daily routine is discussed in detail on pp. 7–9.

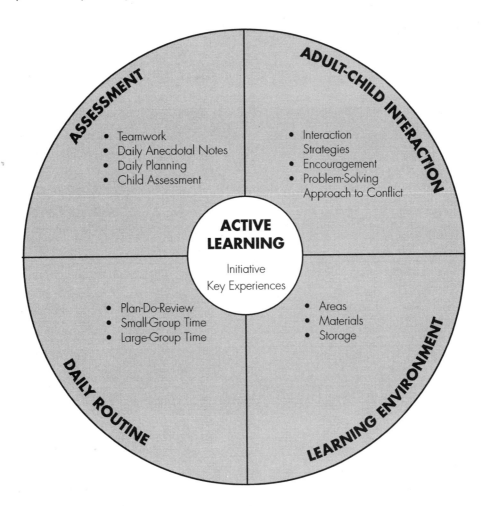

Opportunities to plan and recall and to use a wide variety of materials are vital to children's development.

in promoting young children's development. Because the plan-do-review process is so important to children's development and well-being, this book gives a thorough explanation of the entire process and how to go about implementing it in your preschool classroom or center. Let's begin by looking more closely at the individual components of the High/Scope daily routine and how the plan-do-review sequence fits into this routine. (If you are unfamiliar with the High/Scope Preschool Curriculum, see pp. 4–5 for a brief overview.)

The Components of the High/Scope Daily Routine

Although programs that implement the High/Scope approach vary widely in type of setting, length of day, and so on, they all share the same daily routine components. These components may be arranged in a variety of ways, as we will see in the next section. The plan-do-review sequence is the longest part of the daily routine, totaling between an hour and 15 minutes and an hour and 40 minutes each day. As you read through this list of daily routine segments, note how the names of the segments designate a place or a process rather than a specific activity (for example, *small-group time* rather than *small-manipulative time*).

Planning time (10–15 minutes): Children meet in small groups with an adult so that each child can plan what to do during work time that day. Children's plans come from their own interests and ideas, and they can choose to work with any of the materials in any of the interest areas. Encouraged by supportive adults to expand on their ideas and put their plans into action, children learn to be confident decision makers. They also come to enjoy the opportunity to share their intentions with their friends and with adults who are sincerely interested in their ideas.

Work time (45 minutes–1 hour): This is the "do" part of plan-do-review. Children are busy carrying out their initial plans—interacting with various materials and other children and adults, trying out new ideas, and solving problems that come up. Sometimes children stay with their original plan the entire work time; often they decide to begin another activity. During this time, adults observe children to gain a better understanding of how they think about and interact with the world around them. Adults also play with the children, practicing a variety of support strategies that encourage and extend children's play and thinking. When problems or conflicts arise, either among children or with the materials they are using, adults assist children in coming up with solutions.

Cleanup time (10 minutes): Cleanup immediately follows work time. During cleanup, adults work together with children to return materials and equipment that were used during work time to their appropriate storage spots. They also find a place to put away or display any creations children made during work time.

Recall time (10–15 minutes): In addition to learning how to form and express their intentions, children are developing the ability to think back on and describe significant events. Recall time, the "review" part of plan-do-review, brings closure to the entire sequence. During recall children again meet in small groups, this time to discuss what individual children did during work time and to think about what they learned from their experiences. Children may share problems they faced in carrying out their plans and how they solved them, and they may show their teachers and classmates any projects they worked on or creations they made. Adults show their interest in children's accomplishments by encouraging them to elaborate on their descriptions and to think about how they could extend or modify their plans next time.

Large-group time (15–20 minutes): Children and adults meet together as a large group to play games, sing songs, do fingerplays, tell stories, participate in movement experiences, or play musical instruments. Although many of these experiences are adult-initiated, children are encouraged to contribute their own ideas to the activities as well as learn from the ideas of the other children in the group.

Small-group time (15–20 minutes): Children meet with one adult and 6–10 other children. Adults initiate an activity by choosing, introducing, and making suggestions about the materials the children will use. However, children are not expected to all do the same thing with these materials—instead, they are free to use them in ways that are meaningful to them. As children explore the materials, adults support, guide, and extend their explorations.

Outside time (30–40 minutes): Children and adults play in a natural and open space outdoors. There are opportunities for children to be noisy and physically active as well as quiet and reflective. In addition to the typical playground equipment used in most early childhood outdoor programs, adults offer other play experiences, such as pounding nails into a tree stump, writing on the sidewalk with chalk, or gardening. As during work time, adults observe children, participate in their play, challenge them, and help them solve problems that arise.

Transition times: Children transition from one activity to another throughout the day. For instance, there may be a short greeting time to ease the transition from home to school or a playful activity to move children from large-group time to outdoor time. Because transitions can be stressful for children and adults alike, adults attempt to minimize transitions and make them a relaxed and interesting time of the day for children.

Eating and resting times (amount of time varies according to child or program needs): During snack or mealtime, children and adults share nutritious food and interesting conversation in a relaxed, family-like setting. During rest time, children either nap or engage in quiet play by themselves.

Adult team planning time (20–30 minutes): Classroom team members meet to share their thoughts and observations about how the day went. They also share and record anecdotal notes and make plans for the following day's activities.

How the Plan-Do-Review Sequence Fits Into the Daily Routine

The components of the High/Scope daily routine are flexible and can be arranged in several different ways to meet the needs of your particular program. The plan-do-review sequence, for instance, can occur at the beginning or end of the day, before or after small-group time or outside time. If your program runs all day, the sequence may even occur twice—once in the morning and once in the afternoon. However, the individual segments of the plan-do-review sequence should always occur in a specific and uninterrupted order: planning should always be immediately followed by work time and cleanup time, which should be followed by recall time. Keeping these segments together enables children to begin making the connection between thinking about their ideas, putting them into action, and reflecting on those ideas and actions.

Every program must organize its daily routine, including the plan-do-review sequence, to meet the needs of the children and families it serves. There are a number of program factors to consider as well. If the children in your program arrive at different times throughout the morning, it might make sense to schedule planning, work, and recall time after most or all of them have arrived rather than first thing in the morning, when only a handful are present. On the other hand, if your children are bused to school and all arrive at the same time, you could begin the plan-do-review sequence right away. You may also need to work around the availability of, for instance, outdoor play space or a multipurpose room in your center. When arranging your routine, consider the amount of time you have, children's arrival and departure times, program requirements (such as rest time), and any specific times you must be in a certain place (for meals, outdoor play, "specials," and so on). Then you can begin to work into your schedule the High/Scope daily routine components, keeping in mind the recommended times for each segment and keeping the plan-do-review sequence together.

Of course, you will want to organize the parts of your day in a logical fashion, just as you do in your own personal routine. For instance, during your early morning routine, chances are you don't take care of your personal grooming before you shower or take a shower before you get out of bed. Similarly, you want to plan the children's day so that it flows smoothly, without unnecessary transitions, such as having children remove all their outdoor wear after playing outside and then put it back on again to go home after a brief indoor large-group time. It is important to plan a daily routine that makes sense to children, meets their needs, and is consistent. Following the same routine day after day will give children the sense of security they need to be able to make choices and take risks, which will open the door to exciting learning opportunities.

How Plan-Do-Review Carries Over Into Other Parts of Children's Lives

Children are involved in making plans, carrying them out, and reflecting on them during times other than the plan-do-review sequence. Children often use this process during the rest of the school day, at home, and as they move into formal schooling.

Throughout the daily routine

Following is an example of a group of children playing during outside time. Notice how the children initiate their own informal "planning time" with one another.

> The adult, Darla, is outside with seven preschoolers. In addition to the permanent playground structures, the children can choose to use tricycles and wagons; paintbrushes, paint, and easels that have been hung on the fence; and gardening tools in a small flower garden in a corner of the playground.
>
> Several children are swinging, something they enjoy doing every day for the first several minutes they are outside. As Darla moves around the playground interacting with the children, she overhears a conversation between 4-year-old Sarah and 5-year-old Damon. Sarah tells Damon that she wants to go pull weeds in the garden. Damon says that he will help her and that he thinks maybe the flowers need to be watered. He suggests they fill up the watering can. Sarah seems interested in his idea and says that after he waters the flowers, she should get a turn filling up the can and watering them herself. Darla watches as Sarah goes to the garden and begins pulling weeds and Damon fills up the watering can.
>
> Several children, who are painting at the easel, decide they want to ride the tricycles. As they finish their paintings and hang them up to dry, they talk about playing "cops." They choose one child to be the cop and decide that the others will be people speeding. The cop explains that when he makes a siren noise, the others have to stop and he'll give them a ticket. Another child says that after she gets her speeding ticket, she'll run a red light and the cop will have to give her another ticket. After the children hang their pictures to dry, they run to the tricycles and begin their "cops and speeders" scenario.

Outside of school

Forming a mental image of what they want to do, putting those ideas into action, and then reflecting on those actions becomes such a natural process for children that they continue to use it even outside the school setting. Parents of children in programs that use the plan-do-review process often share stories of their children making plans at home, either for their day at school or for activities they want to do after school or on the weekends. Below are a few examples.

"As soon as Taylor and I get in the car in the morning, he tells me all about what he wants to do while he's at your house. When I pick him up at the end of the day, I ask him what he did that day. Sometimes he tells me about something different than what he had planned in the car, but usually what he did goes along with what he planned. It really helps me feel like I know what he's done at day care."

"It really surprised me the first time my daughter asked me what my plan was for the day. Now it's become a daily ritual between the two of us. She tells me her plan for the day at the center, and I tell her my plan for the day at work. When we get home and have dinner together, we always talk about our day. Even on weekends the two of us will sit down and decide what we're going to do."

"I've noticed that since Jack started attending your preschool, he's more focused when he plays at home. Sometimes he'll tell me what he's planning to do for the afternoon and then go off and get started. When I go looking for him in the basement or in his room, he's usually still absorbed in his activity."

"I just had to share this story with you! Last night, Tatiana was telling us her plan for the evening as we were eating dinner. She told us she planned to watch her new video, play her memory game with her mom, give her baby doll a bath, and have me read her some books. When I asked her when she was going to brush her teeth and go to bed, she told me that wasn't part of her plan!"

These children can't wait to tell their teachers their plan for the day!

Beyond the preschool years

Children who have the opportunity to use the plan-do-review process in preschool will continue to benefit from the experience in elementary school and beyond. They are more likely to continue to use the process (perhaps without even being aware of doing so) to efficiently manage their time, carry out school projects, or engage in their favorite sport. This is the goal of plan-do-review—to enable children to become thoughtful, confident goal setters and decision makers throughout their lives, both in small, everyday tasks and when faced with life-changing decisions. As you read the following chapters and learn how children participate in the plan-do-review process, think about the way the process applies to your own life on a daily basis.

What's Ahead in This Book

Each segment of the plan-do-review sequence will be discussed in depth in one of the next three chapters. In Chapter 5 we'll look at how to actually implement and maintain the plan-do-review process in your program. Chapters 2–5 also answer several questions about the process that are frequently asked by teachers. Since parents are an integral part of their children's education, we'll explore ways to involve parents in the plan-do-review process in Chapter 6. Finally, Chapter 7 will present numerous ideas for planning and recall games and experiences. After reading the information presented here, you will be well on your way to helping children learn to set, pursue, and achieve their own goals!

2

"What Are You Going to Do Today?"

Planning Time

Planning time is the first segment of the plan-do-review sequence and usually lasts 10–15 minutes. The purpose of planning time is to offer children an opportunity to talk to supportive adults and other children about their own interests and intentions, as well as to think through the activities they choose to carry out during the 45–60-minute work time, which immediately follows the planning period.

During planning time children meet with an adult in a small group, usually around a table or on the floor. As children express their plans for the day, some may do so verbally and others nonverbally. A variety of props and planning games (provided by the adult and discussed in detail in Chapter 7) helps keep children interested and excited throughout the planning process. When children have made their individual plans, they leave the planning area and go to the interest area where they want to begin working.

This chapter will explain what planning is all about, why it is important for young children, and how you can use specific strategies to support children during planning time. Also presented are answers to some commonly asked questions from teachers in the field, both those experienced in the plan-do-review process and those just beginning to implement it in their program.

What Is Planning Time All About?
Making choices and following personal initiatives

Too often, both in early childhood settings and in home environments, adults tell children what to do—so much so that children have little control over their surrounding environment or their activities. Children who have few opportunities to make choices may grow up to depend on others telling them what to do, or they may have a difficult time setting goals for themselves and seeing them through. In contrast, children who are given the opportunity to make choices, to think through their intended actions, and to carry out their intentions often grow up to be self-confident, responsible, and able to set and achieve goals. High/Scope's plan-do-review process, as part of a consistent daily routine, enables children to make choices and decisions and to feel a sense of control over their environment.

During planning time children are able to choose activities that are interesting and meaningful to them. Thus, they have the opportunity to follow their *own* interests: "I'm gonna build a tiger cage with all the big blocks." "I want to draw around me and Kenzie and Kyle's hands and see who's the biggest!" "We're lost in the woods, and there's a dinosaur chasing us." Children's own ideas will be meaningful and exciting to them, and they will learn more from initiating and following through on these ideas than from being told what to do ("Today you'll go to the art area and make a turkey using feathers and macaroni." "I want you to go to the house area today, because it's been a long time since you've been there." "Before you go to the block area, go to the writing area and practice writing the letter 'K'"). In addition, children will be more involved in and will concentrate longer on an activity they have planned themselves because they are intrinsically interested in it. Therefore, it is important to accept and encourage children's personal intentions and interests rather than to make choices for them or to divert them from their own goals.

In High/Scope settings, children's own ideas and interests are the basis for work-time activities.

Anticipating actions and events

As children plan, they construct mental images of occurrences that have not yet happened, and they begin to realize that they can act on those images and ideas and carry them out. Children learn that they control their actions, and that through their actions they can achieve their intended goal. Once they realize this, they are motivated to stick to the task at hand until it's finished to their satisfaction. They begin to understand that, ultimately, they are responsible for their own decisions. In turn, this helps them develop a sense of control and become independent and self-confident.

Between the ages of 3 and 6, children develop the ability to identify a goal, formulate an idea of how they will achieve that goal, and then set about working toward it. As 3-year-olds work toward their goals, they tend to solve problems as they occur. As children mature and participate in a

This child is able to anticipate what he will do at work time. Using words and gestures, he expresses his intentions to his teacher and peers.

variety of planning experiences, they will become increasingly able to anticipate problems that may arise and to consider possible solutions even before they get started on their plans.

Expressing intentions

Planning time is an opportunity not only for children to form an idea of what it is they want to do but also to talk about their ideas and intentions with others. As adults ask questions to help young planners think through their ideas, children learn to use more complex language to clarify their plans and add more details. Expressing thoughts and ideas in this way helps sharpen children's thinking process.

Children share their plans in a variety of ways. Although most preschool children communicate their plans verbally, others—particularly those developmentally or chronologically younger—will communicate their intentions through gestures or actions. These children may look toward or point to the interest area where they want to go, touch an object or child they wish to play with, or simply go to an area and begin their play. Whether children express their intentions verbally or nonverbally, however, it is important to recognize and support each child's unique style of communication. (Support strategies for both verbal and nonverbal planners will be discussed later in this chapter.)

Children's initial attempts at verbal plans often consist of a single word or short phrase, such as "Play" or "Go there." Children who make *vague plans,* such as these, usually don't have a clear idea of what it is they want to do, or they may feel that they need more time to make their choice.

You will also hear children making simple or *routine plans.* Routine planners are able to form a mental picture of what it is they want to do. Their plans generally consist of simple phrases indicating where they will begin working or what activity they want to start with: "Play in the toy area." "Be a doggie." "Make a card for my mommy." These children usually begin work time by carrying out the plan they have made.

As children mature and become more comfortable in the learning environment and more confident in themselves as planners, they will start to make more *detailed plans.* Like routine planners, detailed planners form mental pictures of activities they want to do or interest areas where they want to begin working, but their plans are far more complex. Children who offer detailed plans often think through their actions from beginning to end. They often verbalize, step by step, how they're going to carry out their plans: "I'm gonna play some tapes in the music and movement area. I'll use the scarves and the ribbon rings to make up a dance, and when I'm finished makin' it up, I want you to come over and watch me. When I'm done with my dance, you have to clap for me." They may also anticipate obstacles or problems they might run into along the way and generate solutions for solving them.

These changes in the scope and detail of children's planning occur for a variety of reasons. Children typically offer more thoughtful, detailed plans as their interests change and expand, they become more familiar with the learning environment, they move from playing alone or alongside one another to playing in groups, they improve in their ability to form mental pictures and imagine details, and they develop more complex language. Consider Angelica's plans over the course of several months:

September
- During planning time, goes to the toy area and begins playing with the dollhouse and its accessories.
- When it's her turn to plan, she runs to the computer area and begins working on the computer.

October
- *"I wanna go over there."* (Points to the computer area.)
- *"Paint over there."* (Points to the easel.)
- *"I'm gonna play with the babies."*

November
- *"I'm gonna make somethin' for you at the art area."*
- *"Make hot dogs for supper."*
- *"I want you to read me a story today."* (Goes to the book area and brings back a copy of *The Little Mouse, the Red Ripe Strawberry, and the Big Hungry Bear.*)

December
- *"I'm gonna make a picture for my cousin 'cause she's sick."*
- *"I'm gonna look through those books [catalogs] and cut out what I want for Christmas."*

January
- *"I'm going to use the paper over there"* (points to the art shelf) *"and wrap you two presents."*
- *"I wanna play with Justin at the computers. We're gonna play the number game."*

Fostering more purposeful and complex play

Children who are not encouraged to plan their activities tend to be impulsive, acting on their intentions in a random or aimless way. For

Planning Time: An Opportunity for Language Experiences

In an active learning setting, children have many opportunities for expressing their thoughts, feelings, ideas, and intentions. Planning time offers a rich opportunity for children to communicate something meaningful to them. Whether they plan by pointing to an object they want to play with, using a simple phrase about what they will do ("Cut with scissors"), or discussing details ("I'm gonna make a necklace with the red, yellow, and blue beads—twenty of 'em!"), children are encouraged to communicate their intentions to others. As you ask questions to help children think through their ideas, they learn to clarify their plans and add more details.

Planning is also an excellent time to build children's vocabulary and verbal skills. When a child points to an interest area or object, for instance, you can supply a label for what the child is referring to: "Oh, you would like to play with the play dough and cookie cutters today, Josh." This is particularly helpful for younger or nonverbal children as well as those who are learning English as a second language.

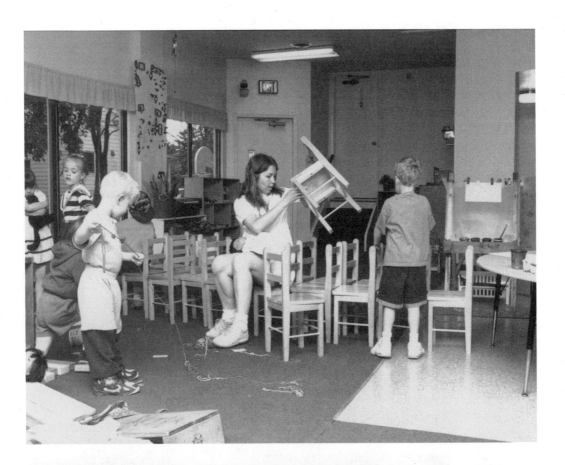

When children plan their activities, they are much more likely to engage in complex and extended play.

example, if you were to walk into a classroom in which there was limited or no planning by children (for example, children were asked where they were going to play but were not encouraged to share the details of what they were planning to do), you might see children flitting from area to area without purpose or playing with materials in very simple and basic ways.

In contrast, when adults encourage children to think through their intentions and to make plans for carrying them out, children's actions become more purposeful. As opposed to routine or repetitive play, children who consciously think through and discuss their plans with someone will engage in play that is more creative, challenging, and productive. In a classroom in which adults encourage children to make plans and think through their actions, you would likely observe children highly involved in their play and incorporating more materials, actions, or ideas.

How to Support Children During Planning Time

Adults take on the role of supporter, facilitator, and encourager during planning time. This section describes ways you can support children during planning time by keeping it a consistent and predictable part of the daily routine, offering a variety of interesting and exciting planning games and experiences, encouraging children to communicate their plans in a variety of ways, and modifying your support strategies as children become more experienced planners.

Plan with children in intimate settings

Planning is a time to share a thoughtful conversation with children about their plans and how they will carry them out during work time. There are several things you can do to provide a predictable, comfortable, and supportive planning environment for children. First, a more intimate setting can be established by creating smaller groups rather than having all the children plan together in a large group. This enables you to respond to each child's plan and helps keep children from becoming bored and restless. To create smaller groups, divide the number of children as evenly as possible among the number of adults in the classroom. Ideally, each adult would have fewer than 5 children in her planning group. More realistically, however, in a classroom with 18 children and 2 adults, for example, each planning group would contain 9 children and one adult. From the first day children plan, the groups should remain consistent—that is, you and your team member should each meet with the same group of children each day (although, as explained below, groups may be restructured later in the year). Placing yourself on the children's physical level will also help to make planning time more intimate— children will sense your respect for and interest in what they have to say.

Although planning time can occur just about anywhere in the classroom—the art area, block area, house area—the place where each planning group meets should stay consistent. If the planning group does move to a

This planning group meets in a cozy area on the floor. All children are actively involved in drawing their plans, and sharing a large sheet of paper helps them notice one another's drawings.

different area of the classroom (or perhaps outside) for the day, gather the group together in the usual place first, *then* move to the new planning spot. Such consistency in the planning group and meeting place helps children feel a sense of security and control.

After several months of meeting in the same planning group, it may be appropriate to move children to a different group. You might notice that several children have developed friendships and have begun playing together during work time, thus you may decide to put those children in the same group so they can plan and recall together. Also, once you have spent several months planning with the same children, you may want an opportunity to plan with a different group. Whenever there is going to be a change in grouping, prepare the children by telling them who will be in each new group.

For example, one teaching team decided to change their planning and recall groups when the children returned from their winter break. By this time in the school year, the adults had observed which children played together during work time and outside time. They decided to place some of the friends in the same groups, anticipating that they might begin making plans and recalling together. To prepare the children for the change, they discussed it at greeting time the last few days before vacation. The teachers also sent a letter to the children and their parents during their time off, informing them which group each child would be in, who the adult in that group would be, and which other children would be in the group. The letter asked the parents to discuss the change with their children and to remind them often about it during their break. When the children arrived back from their winter vacation, the teachers reminded them about the change during greeting time, just prior to planning time.

Plan where children can see the interest areas and materials

Planning time should take place in an area of the room where children can see as many of the materials as possible. This allows less experienced planners to see the materials that are available to them. Although it's probably impossible to see *all* of the materials in the classroom from one particular spot, some places allow better views than others. It's up to you to find such suitable spots. Keeping the shelves and dividers in the classroom low enough for children to see over not only will improve visibility but also will be safer for children (place any taller shelves you may have against the wall). Classroom "tours" during planning time (discussed in more detail in Chapter 7) also provide the children an opportunity to see what's in each interest area. The more familiar the children become with the classroom, the less they will need to rely on actually seeing the materials in order to make their plan for the day. Whenever you add new materials to the learning environment, bring them to the children's attention by encouraging them to look around the classroom for something new at the beginning of the day, by planning a group tour of the classroom as a planning experience, or by discussing the new materials during greeting time or at large-group time, prior to planning time.

Allow enough time for planning

Along with creating a comfortable physical setting for planning, you need to schedule enough time for the process so that children are free to explain the details of their plans without feeling hurried. Children need to know that there will be enough time for you to listen closely to what each child has to say. If children are rushed through planning time, they may push to be first to make sure they get a turn, and they may give a very perfunctory plan because there is not enough time to think through the details. This defeats the purpose of encouraging children to make plans.

Provide children with interesting planning games and experiences

The ultimate purpose of planning time is to allow children to make choices about what they want to do at work time—which interest areas to play in, which materials to use, which activities to engage in, and which children to

Planning props and games may be simple or complex, depending on children's age, planning experience, and interests. At top left, a child tells a puppet what she plans to do at work time. The other two pictures depict representation experiences, in which children either walk to or mark a drawing of the interest areas they'd like to go to.

play with. While keeping your focus on this purpose, you can initiate planning games and experiences that will maintain children's interest and enthusiasm during the planning process.

Children are generally excited about making and sharing their plans with adults and other children, and it can be difficult for them to wait while others are planning. When children are engaged in playing games or using appealing props, however, it becomes easier for them to maintain their interest and enjoyment in the process, and they usually don't mind waiting their turn while other children describe their plans. You can then focus on supporting planners with a variety of strategies, which are described in the rest of this chapter. (A detailed list of planning games and experiences is found in Chapter 7.) It is important to remember that the *props and games* used during planning are different from the *strategies* you employ. While games help hold children's interest while they wait for their turn to plan, it is the interaction strategies you use that will help children better form and express their plans.

Ask children questions

Your role during planning time goes far beyond providing a variety of interesting planning games and experiences. Encouraging children to talk about their ideas is crucial to supporting the development of those ideas.

Asking open-ended questions is one of the easiest and most natural ways to find out what children's intentions are. When we converse with other adults and wish to find out information about a situation, we usually ask questions in order to elicit more details. The same applies to planning with children: We ask them open-ended questions to gather more detailed information about what they wish to do at work time.

"What" questions are direct ways of gaining information about children's intentions: "What do you want to do today, Jenny?" "Chandler, what would you like to use during work time?" "What types of things do you think you might do during work time today, Ian?" Later, as children become more familiar with the plan-do-review process, they will understand the meaning of the word *plan* and will be able to answer questions such as "What's your plan for today, Demarcus?" "I see you've brought some glue to the planning group today, P.J. What do you plan to do with it?" "You told me some of your plan at greeting time, Parvin. Have you thought of anything else you will do?"

In addition to asking *what* children will be doing during work time, finding out *how* a child's plan will be carried out is appropriate as well. Asking "how" questions of more experienced planners might encourage them to look critically at their plans, think about potential problems, and start brainstorming ways they might solve them. Consider the following example:

Rosa: *What's your plan for today, Jasmine?*

Jasmine: *I'm gonna make a kite like the one my brother got for his birthday.*

Rosa: *You're going to make a kite.*

Jasmine: *Yeah. A red and yellow one.*

Rosa: *Hmmm, what do you need to use to make a red and yellow kite?*

Jasmine: *Well, I know I need paper and string and a yellow and red marker and scissors to cut it like a kite.*

Rosa: *I tried to make a kite once, but mine wouldn't stay up in the air. How will you get yours to stay up?*

Jasmine: (Thinks for a while, looking at the art shelf.) *I don't know . . . my brother's kite gots sticks on it. Maybe I need some sticks. Yeah. That's what I'll do. I'll go outside and get some sticks.*

Rosa: *We could ask one of the moms helping in our room today to go outside with you.* (Pauses while Jasmine considers this idea.) *Once you get the sticks, how will you get them to stay on your kite?*

Jasmine: *I could glue them on. Or maybe I'll use tape. Yeah, that's what I'll use. Then I don't have to wait for it to dry.*

Rosa: *You think tape will keep the sticks on?* (Jasmine nods her head yes.) *Okay. Let's ask Kristin's mom if she'd take you outside to look for sticks.*

After these children draw a line from their symbol to the interest area where they'd like to work, the adult follows up with a question such as "What will you do in that area?"

Asking about the children they're going to work with (who) or the area they're going to work in (where) will elicit *some* information from planners, but it generally will be limited. "Who" and "where" questions don't encourage children to think of a plan of action for work time, leaving them without an idea of what to do once they get to their chosen interest area or get together with a certain friend. If you do ask such questions, follow the child's response with another question that will encourage the child to think through the plan more carefully: "What will you do when you get to that area?" "What are the two of you planning to do today at work time?"

Listen attentively to children's plans

Adults in early childhood classrooms often feel they need to be directing the activities and the children, doing most of the talking while children listen and follow directions. However, in programs that incorporate the High/Scope approach, children and adults share control of conversation throughout the day, including during planning. The way you choose to elicit children's plans may vary, but it is important that you listen consistently, carefully, and thoughtfully to what children are communicating. Paying close attention to children's plans—whether verbal or non-verbal, vague or detailed—allows you to understand how much each child is able to imagine and anticipate and how much he or she understands the planning process. Then, taking your cues from the children, you can assist them in making their intentions more detailed or complete; that is, you choose the most appropriate support strategy to try next.

As you listen to children's plans, respect and encourage the choices they make. Otherwise, the purpose of planning time—to encourage children to set their own goals and work toward fulfilling them—is defeated. Adults who are slightly skeptical of or don't fully understand the benefits of the plan-do-review process might find themselves saying things like "Maybe you should go to the house area instead. It's been a long time since you've been there." "There are too

When Children Appear Hesitant or Uninterested in Planning

Generally, children tend to be excited about making plans and sharing them with others. There may be times, however, when you sense less enthusiasm or excitement in the children as they plan. Children may seem to be simply going through the motions rather than giving a lot of thought to their intentions and getting excited about their plans. There is usually an explanation for such a change in children's attitude toward planning. Often planning becomes rather stale and rote because the planning games being used need to be varied or made more interesting for the children. Or perhaps you need to evaluate the toys and materials in your room—are they no longer exciting and challenging for children, and therefore they have lost interest in making plans to use them? Sometimes children make simple or routine plans simply because they are waiting to hear what other children are planning to do. Perhaps the children they usually plan with haven't arrived at school yet, and they're waiting to make a more thorough plan with their friends. In these cases, let children know that you understand their hesitation, and accept statements such as "I want to wait before I plan so I can see where Jin's going" or "I don't know what I want to do yet."

many children in that area right now. You'll need to find someplace else to go." "You've been doing that all week long. Today you should do something else." These types of responses impose adults' ideas on children rather than support children's choices, and there is no point in listening to children's plans if we aren't going to encourage them to follow through on them.

Support nonverbal and vague planners in a variety of ways

There are many strategies that can be used when planning with children who are nonverbal, limited in their verbal abilities, or vague verbal planners. An important factor to remember is that even though some children may not describe in great detail how they plan to carry out their ideas, they are still capable of making plans. It is your job to help these children formulate and express their intentions as fully as possible. Several support strategies can be used when planning with nonverbal or vague planners:

- Interpret children's gestures and actions
- Comment on what children say
- Comment on what children are doing
- Offer alternatives

These strategies are discussed next, along with examples that illustrate each strategy.

Many children plan by pointing or gesturing to an object that they would like to use or to a place in the classroom where they'd like to go. Be sensitive to this way of communicating by **interpreting children's gestures and actions** rather than suggesting activities you think the children would like to do or "should" do. Consider the following example:

Laura: *What would you like to do today during work time, Mark?*

Mark: (Looks around the room at the various interest areas; sees some children who are finger-painting with shaving cream. He smiles.)

Laura: *You see the children in the art area using the shaving cream.*

Mark: (Points to the children.)

Laura: *You're pointing to the children who are finger-painting.*

Mark: (Leaves the planning group and walks quickly to the art table. He puts his hands in the shaving cream.)

Laura: (Follows Mark to the art table.) *It looks like you want to finger-paint. Why don't you get a smock, and I'll help you roll up your sleeves.*

Vague planners may be unsure of their plans or of the planning process. After asking an initial question, such as "What do you want to do today?" or "What's your plan for work time?" simply **commenting on what children**

say may elicit more details from them. In using this strategy you follow the children's leads, leaving the children in control of the conversation. Another way to encourage children to share in the planning conversation is to narrate or **make comments on what children are doing.** The following example illustrates how a child is able to successfully communicate her plan because the adult uses this strategy.

Jennifer: *What do you want to do today, Marianna?*

Marianna: (Barks several times, then pants.)

Jennifer: *You're barking like a dog.*

Marianna: (Barks again, then whimpers and makes a sad face.)

Jennifer: *You seem like a sad dog.*

Marianna: *Lost.*

Jennifer: *You're a dog that's lost?*

Marianna: *Come find.*

Jennifer: *You're a lost dog, and you want me to find you.*

Marianna: (Nods and barks.)

Jennifer: *I'll finish planning with the other children, then I'll come looking for you, doggie.*

There may be times when, for whatever reason, children don't respond to any of these strategies. You may want to **offer alternatives** when this occurs. Instead of getting frustrated with the children and giving up on helping them plan, suggest some choices you think the children may be interested in, based on their interests and recent activities.

Yelena: *What's your plan for today, April?*

April: (Starts to giggle and climbs onto the adult's lap.)

Yelena: *Have you thought about what you'd like to do during work time?*

April: *I don't know.* (Giggles some more.)

Yelena: *You seem awfully giggly today.*

April: (Giggles some more and plays with the adult's hair.)

Yelena: *How about I finish planning with India and Darius, then I'll walk with you around the room and you can decide what you want to do.*

April: *Okay.*

Yelena: (Finishes playing the Hula-Hoop planning game with the other two children, stands up, and walks around the room with April, holding her hand.)

April: (Enters the house area, takes some dishes off the shelf, and puts them on the table. Reaches for the telephone.)

Yelena: (Remembers that April enjoyed planning with the telephone a couple of days ago. Reaches for the other telephone and begins dialing it.) *Ring. Ring. Ring.*

April: (Picks up her telephone and answers it.) *Hello.*

Yelena: *Is this April?* (Waits for a response.) *Hi. This is Yelena. What's your plan for today?*

After the other planners in this group have placed their bear counters on the drawing of the interest area they will go to, this child stays to elaborate on his work plans with the adult.

April: (Speaks in a high voice.) *I'm gonna set the table, then get ready for my baby's birthday party.*

Yelena: *Oh. It's your baby's birthday today?*

April: *Yes. She's one year old. I'm going to bake her a cake.*

Yelena: *Mmm, a cake!*

April: *Yes. A strawberry one.*

Encourage children to elaborate on their plans

During planning, adults often focus on those planners who are nonverbal or vague, trying to gain a clearer picture of their plans. In doing so, they may inadvertently spend less time conversing with planners who are more elaborate in the description of their intentions. It is equally important to practice the same supportive strategies with these planners, encouraging them to give even more details or to think through their plans more thoroughly. In addition to the strategies that have already been mentioned, there are some other strategies that are effective with more detailed planners. These include encouraging the children to talk about **space and materials, details of their plans,** and **the sequence or order in which they want to carry out their plans,** and reminding children about **activities they have previously been involved in.**

Encourage children to discuss materials and space

Discussing materials children are going to use or the space in which they are going to carry out their plans may help children anticipate and think through solutions to problems that may interfere with their intentions. As mentioned previously, asking questions like "How are you going to do that?" or "What materials do you need to make that?" will encourage children to think more carefully about the details of their plans.

Emelia: *What are you going to do in the woodworking area today?*

Luis: *I'm going to make a race car that I can use to race with Michael.*

Emelia: *Have you thought about how you're going to make your race car?*

Luis: *Well . . .* (Thinks for a moment, looking over to the woodworking table.) *I guess I need a piece of wood for the car part and then some wheels.*

Emelia: *Do you know what you'll use for the wheels?*

Luis: *Maybe those things in the art area will work.*

Emelia: *What things are you thinking about?*

Luis: (Goes to the art area and returns with several spools.) *These things.*

Emelia: *Oh, the spools. Those are pretty big. Do you think they'll fit on your car?*

Luis: *I guess I'll need a big piece of wood.*

Emelia: *How will you get the spools to stay on the car?*

Luis: *I can use some nails and the hammer.*

Emelia: *You think nails will work?*

Luis: *Yeah. That should do the trick! I want to paint it, too.*

Emelia: *It looks like there are lots of children using the paint in the art area right now.*

Luis: *That's okay. They'll be gone by the time I'm ready to paint.*

Emelia: *Do you think you'll get everything on your race car done today?*

Luis: (Shrugs and thinks for a moment.) *Well, maybe I'll paint it tomorrow.*

Ask children about the details of their plans

In addition to conversing about space and materials and asking questions to help solve potential problems, talk about the specifics of children's plans with them. This helps children plan step by step how they will accomplish certain tasks. Children may overlook these steps if the details of their plans are not elicited and discussed by supportive adults.

Lynn: *What's your plan for today, Rachel?*

Rachel: *I'm going to draw a picture.*

Lynn: *Oh, a picture.*

Rachel: *Yeah. A picture of my family.*

Lynn: *You've got a big family.*

Rachel: *I know. I got a mom, a dad, a sister, a brother, another brother, a baby in my mommy's tummy, a dog, three cats, and a rabbit.*

Lynn: *That's even more than I thought! I don't think I ever saw your rabbit.*

Rachel: *Well, we just got him. His name is Oreo, 'cause he's black and white.*

Lynn: *So, you're going to draw your bunny black and white?*

Follow up children's representations of what they plan to do by asking open-ended questions about the details of their plans.

Rachel: *Yeah. And I'm gonna make my dog black, 'cause he's black. I'm gonna make my one cat brown, and the other two all different colors.*

Lynn: *I'm wondering how you're going to draw your new baby in your mommy's tummy.*

Rachel: *Well, you can't really see the baby yet, but I'll draw my mommy really big.*

Lynn: *Your mommy looks really big?*

Rachel: *Oh yeah! She's even bigger than my daddy now!*

Encourage children to talk about the order in which they will carry out their plans

The concept of time is an abstract one, but most preschoolers are able to anticipate, remember, and describe a sequence of events. Encouraging children to think about and describe their plans in sequence helps them sharpen their ideas and organize their plans.

Lily: *You circled a lot of areas on your planning sheet, Ryu.*

Ryu: *That's because I'm going to a lot of areas today.*

Lily: *What are you going to do in all of those areas?*

Ryu: *Well, I'm going to listen to* Goodnight Moon *on that thing in the book area.*

Lily: *The tape recorder?*

Ryu: *Yeah. I'm gonna play the painting game at the computer.*

Lily: *What are you going to do in the block area?*

Ryu: *I'm gonna build a thing like they got at Sea World for the fish to swim in.*

Lily: *An aquarium?*

Ryu: *Yeah, a 'quarium. I also want to look at the new ant farm we got.*

Lily: *How are you going to keep track of everything you want to do?*

Ryu: (Thinks for a moment.) *I'll put numbers by where I circled the areas on my paper. Like this.* (Writes a *1* next to the block area, draws a small ant on his paper and places a *2* next to it, then writes a *3* next to the computer area and a *4* next to the book area.)

Lily: *So, first you'll go to the block area to build an aquarium, then you'll go look at the ants, then you'll use the painting game at the computers, and last you're going to listen to the* Goodnight Moon *book on tape. Is that right?*

Ryu: *Yeah. And I'll carry around my planning sheet, so I know what comes next!*

Remind children about activities they have previously been involved in

As children become more familiar with the plan-do-review sequence, you will begin to see their plans being carried out over several days. Reminding children about previous plans they made or their recent work-time experiences may help encourage them to build on their plans from one day to the next.

Rick: *What are you going to do in the toy area today?*

Brant: *I'm going to build with the Tinkertoys.*

Rick: *I remember you built a helicopter with the Tinkertoys yesterday.*

Brant: *Yeah. Today I'm going to make a bigger one, with the propellers at the front and the back.*

Rick: *Two propellers this time. I remember that you also fit some of the people inside your helicopter yesterday.*

Brant: *Yeah. And today I'm gonna make a place for the helicopter to land.*

Rick: *How are you going to do that?*

Brant: *I need to make a big "X" on the floor.*

Rick: *What will you use for that?*

Brant: *I think I'll use some tape.*

Use encouragement rather than praise

All of the adult support strategies described so far convey to children that you are genuinely interested in listening to and learning more about their ideas and intentions. Another way to assure children that their plans are valued is to encourage, rather than praise, their ideas. Consider the following adult response.

Miranda: *What's your plan today, Jake?*

Jake: *I'm gonna build a tractor in the block area.*

Miranda: *Great idea. That sounds like a super plan!*

Miranda probably felt that her praise of Jake's plan was motivating and encouraging for him. However, since Jake was making a plan based on his own interests, he was already intrinsically motivated to carry it out. What he needed from the adult was not empty, vague praise but simply validation of his ideas and a sense of confidence that he would be able to make his plan work.

Note also how, by praising Jake's idea, Miranda learned only that he wanted to build a tractor. She did not discover whether he had thought through the details or steps of his plan. Jake probably did not have as clear of an idea of how to carry out his plan as he would have if Miranda had supported him by asking for more details ("How are you going to build your tractor?" "What kinds of things will your tractor do when it's finished?") or if she had responded with comments that kept the conversation flowing.

Another drawback to praising children as they plan is that it tends to encourage children to compete with one another for the adult's praise, as illustrated in the following example.

Julia: *What's your plan for today, Aisha?*

Aisha: *I'm going to paint a rainbow.*

Julia: *Oh, that sounds pretty! What are you going to do, Aubrey?*

Aubrey: *I'm going to paint a rainbow, too, but I'm going to make flowers under mine.*

Julia: *Beautiful!*

Children who hear other children getting praised for their ideas may try to outdo one another in order to please us, the adults. They begin to rely on our praise, and if they don't receive it, they question whether or not their ideas are good enough. Eventually they may stop taking risks and trying new things, focusing instead on what they think we want them to do. Thus, their intrinsic motivation to make plans and carry them out is lost.

An alternative to praise is encouragement. The strategies mentioned in this chapter are useful for encouraging children to develop and follow their own intentions, which are meaningful to *them*. Instead of having children rely on adults to judge their ideas and their work, the goal is to help children learn to evaluate their own efforts, deciding for themselves whether or not a particular idea was carried out to their satisfaction. Encouraging children to do this will give them the confidence they need to be successful planners and doers.

Write down children's plans

One final way to encourage children and show them that you value their ideas is to write down their plans. For example, if children trace an object they plan to use during work time or draw a picture of what they want to do, they might dictate something for you to write on their paper. You might also encourage children who are interested in print to begin "writing" their own plans on paper. Children's plans can also be written formally as a way of documenting how their plans become more detailed and complex throughout the school year. Documented plans can be used to illustrate the plan-do-review process with children's parents. (This will be discussed in greater detail in Chapter 6.)

Anticipate that children's ability to plan will change over time

As mentioned earlier, preschoolers are beginning to form mental pictures of events or actions that have not yet taken place. They are increasingly able to think about and verbalize what they want to do without having to actually see the materials that are available or the other children they may want to work with. As this ability to anticipate actions continues to develop, children's plans will include more details. Thus, the goals that 3-year-olds establish will be less sophisticated than those of 5-year-olds. The amount of planning experience children have had will also determine the level of sophistication of their plans.

Be aware of the way children's planning abilities are changing, and modify your support strategies and planning games accordingly. In the following example of a preschool classroom, you will see how the teaching team implemented planning during the course of the school year. Highlighted throughout the scenario are some plans that were made by 3-year-old Max. As you read, notice how Max's plans became more complex as the year progressed. Also note how the adults adapted the planning process, including the support strategies they used and the games and experiences they chose, to meet the needs of the children as they became more confident in their ability to plan.

Planning through the year: One teaching team's experience

The first month

Team members Diane and Steve originally began implementing High/Scope's plan-do-review sequence in their program in the middle of the school year after being introduced to the idea during a staff inservice. They then attended an extensive workshop on the plan-do-review segment of the daily routine over their summer break, and they felt confident about implementing it more thoroughly in their program for the upcoming school year. A few weeks before the children were scheduled to start school, Diane and Steve sat down together to reflect on their summer workshop experience. They reviewed the successes and frustrations of their implementation of the High/Scope approach the previous school year, then discussed their plans for the upcoming year based on the new information and ideas they had gained from the training.

The first thing they wanted to do was to offer a chance for the children in their program to visit the classroom with their parents before the first day of school. This would give the children an opportunity to explore the various interest areas and materials that would be available to them when they started school, without feeling overwhelmed by all the excitement of the first day. Steve and Diane agreed that planning time would be a more meaningful experience if the children had already had a chance to explore some of the materials. Diane and Steve knew that they had several returning children, who would already be familiar with the classroom, but they felt that those children would benefit from an early visit as well since some of the interest areas had been moved and there were some new materials in the classroom.

Diane and Steve would be working in their classroom and participating in staff inservice meetings for 2 weeks prior to the children starting school, so they felt this would be a good time to schedule the classroom visits. They shared their idea for the visits with their coordinator, reviewed their schedule, created enough time slots for parent and child visits, and shared the responsibility of calling parents to make appointments. They suggested to parents that they bring a list of questions with them to their visits, which would last about 20 minutes each. Most of the parents were able to find a time that fit in their schedule. They seemed pleased with the opportunity for their children to become familiar with the classroom and the teachers as well as with their own chance to speak individually with the teaching team. Diane and Steve agreed that the individual classroom visits would not replace the home visits they usually conducted during the first couple of months of school; they simply viewed the classroom visits as another valuable contact opportunity with parents and children.

When Max arrived with his father, Doug, Steve and Diane introduced themselves, and Max hid behind his father's leg. Diane and Steve suggested that Doug take some time to explore the room with Max and see what materials interested him. They agreed that once Max felt a little more comfortable in his surroundings, they could focus on any questions Doug might have.

Max quickly left the security of his father's leg. He explored several toys in the toy area, dumping out puzzle pieces and watching the sand timers made from plastic one-liter bottles. He moved to the block area, where he pushed several wooden cars across the carpet, pulled several unit blocks from the shelf, and dumped the dollhouse pieces onto the floor. Next he headed toward the easel. He stayed in the art area for a while, exploring the paint at the easel and mixing colors on the newsprint that had been set out. Doug talked for a few minutes with Diane while Steve went over to interact with Max, who would be in Steve's group for planning and recall time. Before Doug and Max left, Diane and Steve helped Max put away the toys he had played with. This gave them an opportunity to show Max how the materials in their classroom were labeled and stored.

After all the classroom visits were over, Diane and Steve agreed that although the children had had an opportunity to explore the interest areas and the materials in the classroom, the two of them still needed to keep their planning experiences extremely simple for the first week of school. On the first day of school, Steve and Diane divided the class into two planning groups. Steve led his group on a walk through the classroom. When they entered each interest area, Steve would say something like "This area is called the house area. I see dishes, telephones, and babies here." As they made their way around the room, Steve allowed the children to stay in an interest area that appealed to them rather than finish the tour with the group. He listened carefully during the walk as the children who had attended the school last year talked about what they were planning to do in the different areas.

When they approached the art area Steve said, "Here's the art area. I see play dough, markers, paint, and glue." Max immediately left the planning group and began painting at the easel, as he had done when he had visited the classroom earlier. Steve recognized that this was Max's way of expressing his plan, and he said, "Max, you must have remembered the paint from when you were at school before. Let me help you get a smock so the paint doesn't get on your shirt." He showed Max where the smocks were, then finished his walk with the two remaining children.

When Diane and Steve met at the end of the day, they talked about how their respective planning times had gone. Steve decided that since his planning time had gone so well he would repeat the activity the next day, but this time he would encourage the children to talk about what they saw in the interest areas. He might say something like "Now we're in the block area. I see cars. What do you see?" He thought the children would be excited about this game, and even those who didn't participate verbally would still benefit from hearing others say the names of the materials. He also felt that this game would give the returning children a chance to show the new children some materials that they enjoyed working with. Steve and Diane also agreed that since many of the children were new to the idea of planning, they would both try to interact with as many children as possible during work time and comment on their choices: "Hassan, I see you decided to work with the computer in the computer area." "Trisha, you chose to use the markers and paper in the art area."

The next day when Steve led the children into the toy area, he said, "This is the toy area. I see puzzles. What do you see?" Max responded, "Toys," and headed for the Duplo blocks. Steve said to Max, "You found the Duplos to play with today."

By the end of the first week, Diane and Steve were very pleased with how well planning time was going. They were especially excited about how the more experienced planners (who had been in their program the previous year) were helping the new children by showing them where materials were kept, telling them the names of the interest areas, and playing with them once they had chosen materials to work with. The two adults felt that listening to the more experienced planners was helping the new children understand the concept of making a plan more quickly.

On the last day of the first week, Steve had the children meet at their planning table, then go find something they wanted to work with that day. Steve gave all the children a large plastic basket to put their materials in and told them to bring it back to the table and show him what they had chosen to play with. Max went to the toy area and brought back a puzzle and sand timer to show Steve. Steve asked, "What did you find to play with today?" Max replied, "Puzzle." Steve said, "You found the puzzle and the sand timer. Where did you find those?" Max pointed and said, "Over there." Steve replied, "You're pointing to the toy area. So, you're going to play with the puzzles and the sand timers in the toy area?" Max smiled, said "Yep," then left for that area.

During the second week of school, Steve explained to Diane that although he was pleased that the children were becoming familiar with the names of the interest areas and seemed to be comfortable in the classroom, he was concerned that their plans were repetitive and still very basic. Diane reminded him that they had learned in their training that new planners tend to repeat their plans because they like the comfort of repetition and because they enjoy doing things that are familiar to them. They're often very anxious to start their work time, and they sometimes plan quickly so they can begin playing right away. Steve and Diane decided that they would continue to take their cues from the children, encouraging a little more conversation at planning time but still supporting those children who simply wanted to get started with their work time.

The two adults continued to implement planning experiences that were very concrete and involved having children either touch the object they wanted to work with or go to an interest area where they wanted to work. Some of the games the children played included looking through "binoculars" at an area or object that interested them; taking one end of a long piece of yarn or string (the other end held by the adult) to an area or an object they wanted to play in or with, then coming back to tell the group what they were going to do; and bringing the materials they wanted to use to the planning group, then placing them on the area card (that matched the interest area sign) where they were planning to work.

The third month

By this time in the school year, Diane and Steve noticed that the children were very excited about the planning process. Some children arrived at their planning groups with a plan already in mind, and many of the children's plans were more detailed and purposeful. Steve and Diane decided that since the children had a clear understanding of the planning process, they would begin using the word *plan* when inquiring about the children's intentions for work time. Diane and Steve were now able to implement planning games that were a little more abstract than the previous ones they had used. By this time, the children were familiar enough with the classroom and the interest areas that they no longer needed to see an object before they knew what they would do with it. They were developing the ability to anticipate and describe what they were going to do, what object or materials they needed, where they would play, and who their companions would be. Steve and Diane were thrilled with the growth the children had shown, and they felt reassured about their decision to implement planning time into their routine.

Following are some examples of planning games that Steve implemented with his group, and Max's more detailed plans. One day the group sat in a circle around a Hula-Hoop that had been marked in one place with a piece of tape. Steve began by chanting "What will you do at work time, work time? What will you do at work time today?" While he chanted the children passed the Hula-Hoop through their hands, and when he stopped the chant the children stopped moving the hoop. The child whose hand on or closest to the piece of tape talked about his or her plan. Then the group began the game over again. When it was Max's turn, he said, "Gonna build a car." Steve asked, "What are you going to use to build your car?" Max thought and then replied, "The big blocks and steering wheel."

During their team planning time one day, Diane and Steve talked about the children's increased interest in the telephone in the house area, which had been donated. They wrote a note to parents, asking if anyone had an old telephone they were no longer using at home or at their workplace. Two parents responded to their request, and within a couple of days they had several telephones to add to the house area. Steve decided to use those telephones as planning props. He placed several on the planning table. Some children chose simply to call each other and talk, just as they did during work time, and others talked to Steve about their plans. Here's a conversation that occurred between Max and Steve.

Max: (Pushes buttons on his telephone.)

Steve: *Hello? Is this Max? What's your plan for today, Max?*

Max: *Gonna be a mailman.*

Steve: *You're going to be a mailman?*

Max: *Yep. And take stuff to people.*

Steve: *What kind of stuff are you going to take?*

Max: *Letters.*

Steve: *Where are you going to get the letters?*

Max: (Pauses.) *Could you make 'em?*

Steve: *You want me to write some letters so you can take them to people?*

Max: *Yep.*

Steve: (To the other children at the table.) *Is there anyone here who can help me make letters for Max to deliver to people?* (One child says yes.) *Max, Trina said she'll help me write some letters for you.*

Max: *Okay. I gotta make my mailman truck.* (He leaves for the block area.)

Another planning experience that Steve tried involved a planning "road." Ahead of time, he took a piece of butcher paper several feet long and drew six equal sections on it (one for each interest area in the room). In each section he drew an interest area symbol that matched the sign representing that area. For planning time, Steve gave the first child a steering wheel and told her to "drive" to an interest area on the planning road where she'd like to work. She did so and explained her plan, then gave the steering wheel to another child to plan. Here's what happened when Max got the steering wheel.

Max: ("Drives" the steering wheel from one side of the planning road to the other and back again.)

Steve: *Max, can you drive to the area where you'll work today?*

Max: *I did.*

Steve: *That's a lot of areas. What's your plan?*

Max: *Be a mailman again.*

Steve: *I've noticed that when you're a mailman, you go to a lot of the areas to deliver the mail.*

Max: *'Cause that's what us mailmans do.*

Steve: *Have you decided how you're going to get the mail to deliver today?*

Max: *My mom gave me some.*

Steve: *You were really thinking ahead, weren't you?*

Another planning experience that both Steve and Diane tried involved a wipe-off planning board. They made this board on a piece of heavy tagboard, drawing the interest area symbols on the left side of the board, then covering the board with plastic laminate. Children used wipe-off markers to write their names, draw their symbols, or make a mark next to the interest area in which they were going to work. Then they were encouraged to talk about what they were going to do there. For another planning experience, Diane and Steve used a tape recorder, microphone, and blank tape. The children talked into the microphone to record their plans for the day. Yet another planning game extended the earlier activity of going to an interest area and bringing back an object to work with. This time the children used a pencil and a piece of paper to trace around the object after they brought it back to their table.

Diane and Steve felt like they were spending a lot of time preparing planning props and games to use during planning time, but they agreed that if they covered the things with plastic laminate, many of the props and games could be used for years to come. They found a storage shelf in their classroom where they could store all of their planning and recall props and games.

The sixth month

Around the fourth month of school, after the children returned from their winter break, Diane and Steve decided that it was time to change the planning groups. By this time, some children had formed friendships during work time and other parts of the daily routine. The adults wanted to make sure that children who played together at work time were able to be with each other during planning time and recall time. Max was moved to Diane's planning group to be with his friends, Carter and Trina.

By the sixth month, the children were settled into their new planning groups and were including their friends in their plans. Steve and Diane noticed the children adding even more details to their plans, often including several complex steps. The children's enthusiasm for planning time had grown, and most chose to stay and talk about their plans with the adult and the other children rather than run to an interest area to begin work time right away. Diane and Steve had worked very hard at varying the materials and interest areas in their classroom to accommodate children's changing interests throughout the year. They also introduced new planning games but found that while the children did enjoy new experiences, they seemed to prefer expanding on familiar games. The two adults agreed that although the props and games seemed fun for the children, the children's real enjoyment and excitement was in actually making and explaining their plans. Because the children's plans were becoming more detailed and Diane and Steve were encouraging more thought and discussion, planning time was lasting several minutes longer.

During one particular planning time, Diane gave each of the children a piece of paper and a pencil and asked them to draw a picture of what they were going to do during work time. Following is the conversation she had with Max, Trina, and Carter.

Diane: *Max, tell me about your plan for today.*

Max: *I drawed a movie place.*

Diane: *Like a movie theater?*

Max: *Yeah. A movie theater.*

Diane: *What's your plan for the movie theater?*

Max: *Trina and Carter and me are gonna run the movie theater, like we did before.*

Diane: *I remember you lined up the chairs like seats in a movie theater yesterday.* (Pauses for a response, but Max is thinking). *Does your theater sell food?*

Trina: *Yeah. We sell popcorn and candy and nachos.*

Max: *Yeah. You can be in charge of that.*

Diane: *What's your job, Max?*

Max: *Me and Carter gotta make tickets, then we gotta get the chairs right.*

Carter: *Yeah. We gotta make tickets first.*

Diane: *What will you use to make tickets?*

Carter: *Paper and scissors.*

Diane: *What time does your show start?*

Max: *Five seven.*

Diane: *That's pretty soon! You'd better get busy.*

Another planning game Diane tried involved giving each child a puppet and encouraging children to talk with one another or with Diane about their plans for work time. On another day, Diane made a map of the classroom on a large sheet of paper. She used symbols to designate where the interest areas were and drew other parts of the room, such as the door, sink, and bathroom. The children "walked" toy people to the place on the map where the children wanted to go that day, then they described what they would do in that area. A third idea Diane tried was to encourage the children to give clues to what they were going to do during work time. The rest of the group then tried to guess the child's plan based on the clues. She encouraged children who were going to work together to take turns giving clues. Diane also tried a planning experience that she had tried earlier in the school year but which was too abstract for the children to understand at the time. She encouraged the children to pantomime their plan, and then she and the other children guessed the plan. The children understood the game by this time in the year, and they were very creative with their gestures.

The last month

Diane and Steve decided to change the planning groups once again after the spring break. They kept together many of the children who were planning and working with one another but felt that some minor changes to the groups might add some variety. By the end of the school year, they hadn't noticed many significant changes in the way the children were planning, although planning time was still an exciting part of the day. They did notice that the children's plans were still increasing in complexity and detail. Many of the children's plans were so detailed that when they carried them out during work time, they stayed involved in their plan for the entire 50-minute period. They also noticed children explaining their plans in sequence: "First, I'm going to work at the water table, then I'm going to the house area to fix fish sticks and corn for dinner, and last I'm going to go to the art area to draw a picture of my kitty."

As they reflected on their implementation of the plan-do-review sequence at the end of the school year, Diane and Steve were intrigued with the way the children's plans had developed and how planning had affected the children's play during work time. They had seen more purposeful and complex play than they had ever seen before, and they attributed it to the fact that the children were planning their actions ahead of time, expressing their own intentions, and making their own choices. They had seen this happen to some extent the year before, but to see the progression from September to June was especially exciting for them. Steve and Diane felt that the time that they spent problem-solving with each other and supporting each other daily as a teaching team was extremely valuable as well.

What About . . . ? Commonly Asked Questions About Planning Time

Whether you've been using High/Scope's plan-do-review sequence in your program for several years or you're still thinking about incorporating it into your daily routine, you'll probably have many specific questions about this portion of your day. In this chapter and the next three chapters (which discuss work time, recall time, and implemetation issues), we've provided answers to questions that are commonly asked by professionals who are in the field and who are either implementing or beginning to implement planning time, work time, and recall time in their daily routine.

After children have made their plan, do they have to wait and listen to all of the other children's plans before they can begin their work time?

Generally, once children (or pairs of children) share their plan with you, they are free to move on to the interest area where they have chosen to carry out their plan. You can then support the next child as he or she is planning and continue in this way until each child has made a decision. Children are generally very enthusiastic about carrying out their plans and are anxious to begin their work time. It is unrealistic to expect young children to wait until everyone has planned before they can begin their work.

As happens at other times in the daily routine, during planning time there is usually a child who gets to go first while the others have to wait. Be sensitive to this issue and look for ways to vary the order in which children plan. One suggestion for objectively choosing which child will plan is for either you or a child to pull a child's name, symbol, or photograph out of a bag. The child who is chosen then plans. After that child has planned, he or she can pull the next child's name from the bag before leaving the

As these children finish sharing their individual plans with the adult, they leave the group to start work time.

planning group. Another idea is to play a game similar to "Spin the Bottle." Gather all the children in a circle and spin a bottle. When the bottle stops spinning, whomever it is pointing toward is the first child to plan. Before that child begins work time, he or she spins the bottle to see who will plan next. Additional planning games and experiences are described in detail in Chapter 7.

Do all of the children plan every day?

Yes. For all of the reasons discussed earlier in this chapter, it's important to hear all of the children's plans for work time and to support them while they share these plans. To facilitate this, keep the planning groups small. With a smaller group, you will be able to focus more on each individual child and not feel as if you have to rush through each child's plan in order to hear the next child. Another key factor in listening to each child's plan is allowing enough time in the daily routine for planning.

If you cannot get the planning group size down to where it is possible to hear each child's plan daily (for instance, you are the only adult in the room), there are several strategies you can try. Perhaps you can have a volunteer parent or grandparent help out with one group while you plan with the other. (If you do this, be sure that the volunteer understands and is comfortable with the planning process.) Another strategy that works especially well when children are used to the planning process and have friends in their planning group is to have children share their plans with a partner. When planning in pairs, one child is the supporter, listening to the other child's plan

Sometimes plans are secret, meant only to be shared with an adult!

and asking questions about what that child is going to do. When the planning child is finished, he or she becomes the supporter and listens to the other child's plan. Providing props, such as telephones, puppets, or walkie-talkies, encourages two children to share their plans with each other. If you have children plan in pairs, however, and you are the only adult in the room, try to listen to as many children's plans yourself as possible. For instance, you might want to divide the class into two groups; have one group plan in pairs while you plan individually with the other group, then switch groups the next day.

What do I do if a child says he doesn't want to make a plan?*

This is typical at the beginning of the year because many children are unfamiliar with the classroom and the routine. This is one reason it is important to start out with planning and recall games and experiences that are very simple and that help children become more familiar with the materials and the classroom. For example, if Tasha is having trouble planning, you might simply take her hand and walk around the room with her, looking at and exploring the materials available. If any interest is shown, you could then label the child's plan, saying "I see you've made your plan to play at the water table, Tasha." You may also ask a child to point to where he or she would like to work or to find an object in the room to play with.

---

*This answer appeared in a similar version by Warren Buckleitner and Susan M. Terdan in *Supporting Young Learners 1* (pp. 270–271), by N.A. Brickman and L.S. Taylor (Eds.), 1991, Ypsilanti, MI: High/Scope Press.

Another way to look at this situation is to consider that *it's impossible not to make a plan*. One particular child, Moira, crawled under the table and stayed there for all of work time for the entire first week of school. After talking with her mother, the teachers found out that at home the child was talking about the things she saw at school. Her "plan" was to observe, and the teachers tried to label it for her: "Your plan is to rest under the table and watch what is going on in the classroom." Only after she became more familiar with the materials and the people in the room did Moira come out from under the table. She was soon interacting with the other children. As this incident illustrates, it's important not to force a child into planning something he or she isn't really interested in doing. This could interfere with the child's emerging ability to make and follow a plan.

It's suggested that once I've heard a child's plan, he or she is free to go to an interest area and begin work time. If this is the case, how am I supposed to assist in solving conflicts between children or help support children who are beginning their work time?

If you have taken the time to discuss in detail children's plans and have supported them in thinking through what they're going to do, which children they're going to work with (if any), and what materials they're going to use, children will be focused on carrying out their plans when they begin their work time. They may not need much support in getting started. As explained earlier, the planning process leads to more involvement and concentration in children's play.

Conflicts can be excellent opportunities for children to engage in problem solving. Often, adults need to be with the children to support them in the problem-solving process, and sometimes conflicts arise while they are still planning with other children. Some of the conflicts that occur at the beginning of work time can be avoided, however, with careful consideration and planning on the teaching team's part.

Conscientious planning and assessment of your learning environment is crucial. One of the most common conflicts at the beginning of work time occurs when two or more children want to use the same material. To avoid this conflict, be sure to provide several of the same materials for children to use. Also, add plenty of materials that are interesting and appropriate for the developmental abilities of your children rather than have just a couple of interesting or novel materials that all the children are interested in. Arranging your learning environment in a way that encourages children to be independent will also increase their ability to begin work time on their own. If children can get started on activities themselves it will cut down on the number of requests often heard while part of the group is still planning, such as "Could you hang up my easel painting?" "Will you get that toy out of your cabinet for me to play with?" "Will you lift me up so I can reach the sink?"

Another conflict that occurs in some classrooms as work time begins relates to setting limits on the number of children who can participate in a particular interest area at one time. For example, a teaching team may decide that only four children are allowed in the block area at the same time. There are four hooks at the entrance of the block area, and children hang their name tags on the hooks when they go into the area. Once the hooks are full, no more children are allowed in the block area. Conflicts may arise when, for instance, two or more children approach the block area at the same time and there is only one hook empty. This type of situation can be avoided by not limiting the number of children in an area, an issue that will be discussed in more detail in the next chapter.

Of course, you can't always predict or prevent conflict situations, and there may be times when, in the middle of planning time, you're needed to help solve a conflict. In this situation there are several options. First, if you have a teaching team member, and she is available, she may be able to help solve the conflict while you continue with your planning group. If you're the only adult in the classroom, or if your team member is still planning with her group of children, you will need to try some other ideas, especially if you think the conflict will take a long time to resolve. If a parent or other adult is volunteering in the classroom and is familiar with the basic planning process, that person may be able to take over your planning group for a few minutes. Another possibility is to combine the few children left in your planning group with the other adult's planning group, or have the remaining children in your group plan with a partner while you assist the children having the disagreement. If you cannot leave your planning group, you may be able to bring the children who are involved in the conflict situation over to your planning group and have them sit on either side of you, offering them comfort and contact. After you are finished planning with the other children you could then attend to the conflict. However, this might be difficult and distracting to you and the children who are planning if the children who are involved in the conflict are highly emotional or physical. The suggestions discussed here may not be optimal ones, but they may work depending on the particular situation. Ultimately you'll have to do what your teaching instincts tell you, taking into account the severity of the conflict and the children who are involved in the conflict. (For more specific information on the conflict resolution process, see pp. 100–103.)

Do children have to carry out their plan, or can they change it?

Children are free to change their plans during work time if they wish, just as adults occasionally change the plans *they've* made. As adults, we are constantly making plans and modifying or changing them throughout our day. Whether or not we follow through with our plans depends a great deal on outside factors that may distract us from our original intentions. For example, Francesca, a mother of two, had intended to spend the day running errands.

She had planned to drop the children off at school, then go to the dry cleaners, the bank, the mall, and the grocery store. She had also planned on cleaning out one of her closets that afternoon. When Francesca's 7-year-old daughter woke up with a fever and a cough that morning, though, she realized that her daughter would have to stay home from school. Francesca had to modify her plans for the day. Instead of running errands, she scheduled a trip to the doctor's office as well as the pharmacy. Francesca decided that she would call a neighbor to drop her son off at school, then after taking her daughter to the doctor's office she would come home and clean out her closet while her daughter rested. After spending an hour shuffling through old photographs in her closet, she decided that instead of cleaning the closet she really needed to put all of her family photos into an album. She spontaneously changed her plan from cleaning the closet to working on a photo album, something she had been meaning to do for the last year and a half and a task she knew she would enjoy more.

Obviously, we adults don't always make changes in our plans for a particular day. Many times we follow our plan for the day without interruption. The same is true with children. They may follow through with their plan for the entire 50-minute work time, or they may make a plan and then decide to change it after 5 minutes. Consider the following example.

> During planning time, Jessica explains to her teacher that she is going to the art area to draw a picture and write a note to her father. She immediately goes to the art area and gets paper, an envelope, markers, and tape from the shelf. She also notices some new scraps of colored paper that the teachers have recently added to the art area. Jessica begins exploring the paper scraps by taping them together and making a long chain. Chen, who is also working in the art area, suggests that Jessica make a bridge with her paper chain. For the next 35 minutes, Jessica and Chen add on to their paper chain, making it about 9 feet in length. When they finish, they tape the chain to the sink and several shelves and chairs in the art area. Jessica and Chen clean up the art area and go over to the water table together. The adult who had listened to Jessica's original plan to draw a picture and write a note to her dad has observed these interactions between Jessica and Chen. She has overheard the two of them talking about how they are going to "make the bridge really long and hook it onto the art area," and realizes that they were discussing their new plan together. The adult understands that although making a chain was not Jessica's original plan, it was a valuable and worthwhile experience.

By understanding and accepting that children will sometimes change their plans, you will be better prepared to support the children in whatever they decide to do. When you notice that a child has changed his or her plan, try moving over to that child and finding out more information about the new plan. This is not a necessary step, as we will address with the next question, but it is a way of learning in more detail what the child's intentions are and how he or she is planning to carry them out. The child may invite you to join in carrying out the new plan as well.

If children change their plan, do they have to tell an adult?

No. As discussed in the previous question, it is natural for children to change their minds about what they want to do and to make new plans. Sometimes children will follow through with their original plans but they are done in only 15 minutes, in which case they must then decide what to do next. Whatever the motivation for making new plans, throughout work time children will be moving from one activity to another, changing interest areas, modifying their plans, exploring new materials, and finding new friends to play with. It would be impossible for you to listen to and support all of the children's new or modified plans in addition to supporting their play and activities during work time.

Generally during planning time, the plans children discuss are for where they're going to go and what they're going to do *first*. They then leave the planning group and begin work time. When working with a less experienced planner, you may want to observe as the child begins work time to see if he or she seems to understand the connection between stating a plan and following through with it. If the child does begin to carry out his or her plan, you may wish to approach the child, make a statement such as "I remember during planning time that you said you were going to come to the block area and play with the ramps and cars," and possibly stay with that child for a while to support his or her play. If the child doesn't begin to carry out the intended plan, you might approach the child and say something like "It looks like you've changed your plan from the block area to the toy area. You found the beads to play with instead of the ramps and cars." Again, you may wish to stay with that child and support his or her play.

Even with more experienced planners you want to be aware of where the children are during work time, what they're doing, and whether or not they are following through with their plans. If you notice children who seem to have changed their plans, you could approach them to find out their new plans or simply observe them to see what they will do next, as the adult did with Jessica and Chen. It is not necessary, however, to feel that you have to listen to and be aware of all of the children's new plans before they carry them out.

How do you plan (or recall) with children who are nonverbal or have limited language skills?

Keep in mind that your main purpose during planning (or recall) is to find out what the children want to do during work time and to help them figure out how to carry out their intentions. Be sensitive to the verbal abilities of the children in your classroom and initiate planning activities that can be used by children with a wide range of language skills.

Children with limited verbal skills can communicate their plans in a number of different ways:

- Simply beginning their activity
- Pointing
- Bringing an object they want to play with to the planning group
- Taking the adult (and the rest of the planning group) to an area in which they want to play or to an object they wish to use
- Touching an object from a choice of several in front of them
- Gesturing how they want to use a particular object
- Touching an interest area sign from a choice of several in front of them
- Drawing a picture of where they want to go or what they want to do

By observing children not only at planning time but throughout the day, you will become aware of how individual children communicate their intentions. This will help you to respond in an appropriate way to those children whose verbal skills are limited. Try some of the strategies that were discussed on pp. 26–29, such as interpreting children's gestures and actions, asking an

These children use a picture board of the class's interest areas to choose the materials they want to play with.

initial open-ended question, narrating what you see and commenting on what the child says, and offering alternatives when the child doesn't respond. Keep in mind, too, that children are often sensitive to one another's methods of communication, and the other children in your planning group may be able to assist you in figuring out what a particular child is trying to communicate.

The following are some examples of supporting and encouraging planners with limited verbal abilities.

Planning experience: Several toys collected from each interest area have been placed in the middle of the planning group's circle.

Abby: *What would you like to do during work time today, Kia?*

Kia: (Puts her arms in the air, then pats her legs.) *Da da da da.*

Abby: *Can you show me what toy you'd like to work with?* (Points to the toys on the floor.)

Kia: (Picks up a block.)

Abby: *Would you like to work with the blocks in the block area?* (Points to the block area.)

Kia: (Hits the block on the floor several times, then picks up the play dough.)

Abby: *You've got the play dough now. Is that what you want to work with?*

Kia: *Da da da da.* (Puts her hands up in the air, then pats her legs several times. Smiles.)

Abby: *You seem excited about the play dough. What are you going to do with the play dough today?*

Kia: (Pounds the play dough on the floor, then hits it with her fists.)

Abby: *You're pounding the play dough.* (Gestures as if she's pounding.) *I wonder if you'd like to use the clay hammers that are in the art area with your play dough. Let me show you where they are.* (Stands up and takes Kia's hand. They walk to the art area together.) *Here are the hammers.*

Kia: (Pulls the basket of hammers off the shelf, takes the play dough and the hammers to the table, sits down at the table, and begins pounding.) *Da da da da.*

Abby: *It looks like you've decided to work with the play dough and hammers today!*

Planning experience: The teacher and children form a "planning train" and move around the room so the children are able to see the interest areas and materials they can choose from. Children leave the train as they see something that interests them.

Takara: (Leads children from the house area into the art area.)

Nicholas: (Begins to paint with the brushes at the easel.)

Takara: *Nicholas, do you want to work at the easel today?*

Nicholas: (Nods his head.)

Takara: *Is there anyone you want to work with today?*

Nicholas: (Points to a child standing in the line of the train.)

Takara: *You'd like to work with Dominic today? Dominic, would you like to paint at the easel with Nicholas?*

Dominic: *Okay.*

Nicholas: (Reaches for Dominic's hand and leads him over to the easel.)

Planning game: The children and teacher have formed a circle. The teacher plays music while the children pass a beanbag around the circle. When the music stops, the child who has the beanbag explains his or her plan.

Safiya: (Holds the beanbag that's been passed to her.)

Catherine: *Safiya, what would you like to do today?*

Safiya: *Ball.*

Catherine: *You want to play with a ball?*

Safiya: *Ball.*

Catherine: *Which ball do you want to use?*

Safiya: *Ball.* (Points to the toy area.)

Catherine: *You're pointing to the toy area. I'm not sure which ball in the toy area you're talking about.*

Safiya: *Ball.* (Again points to the toy area.)

Trevor: *She played with the marble game yesterday in the toy area.*

Catherine: *Hmm. Safiya, why don't you show me the ball you'd like to play with today.*

Safiya: *Ball.* (Stands up, walks to the toy area, and pulls the marble game off the shelf.)

Catherine: *You're going to play with the marble game today!*

The only thing the children in my group want to do during planning time is play with the props or games I've chosen. What do you suggest I do?

While it's important to choose interesting props and games to use during planning time, it's equally important to remember the purpose of this part of the daily routine, which is to encourage children to make work-time choices.

If the planning activities you've chosen become extremely complex and time consuming, the focus will be on the activities themselves rather than on supporting children's plans. Try to keep your planning games simple enough that they do not distract children from making their plans. Remember, you should only spend about 10 to 15 minutes for planning time, even less if your group is very young or is new to the process.

We know that the first thing children do with an object they've never encountered before is to explore it. They will want to feel, manipulate, shake, taste, and listen to it and see what it can do before they will be able to use it for a purpose. Before you use a prop, material, or game for planning, introduce it to the children during small- or large-group time, work time, or outside time, giving children ample opportunity to explore the material before they are expected to use it for planning. Otherwise, you run the risk of having children more interested in exploring and playing with the materials than planning with them.

I get so frustrated with the children who always plan to do the same thing during work time. Should I allow them to make the same plan day after day, or should I encourage them to try something else?

It's okay for children to routinely make the same plans day after day. Consider the following analogy. Think of the hobbies we adults have, such as reading, working on craft projects, exercising, or baking. We spend so much time pursuing these hobbies because they are activities we have chosen to do ourselves, therefore we are intrinsically motivated to continue engaging in them. There are reasons we choose and continue to stay involved in our hobbies. Having a hobby allows us to do something that interests us, and we find a certain amount of enjoyment in doing the activity. When we are engaged in it we generally experience feelings of control, success, and competence. Whenever we have some free time, whether in the evening, on the weekend, or during a vacation, we quite often choose to pursue our favorite hobby.

Keeping this in mind, think about why a child might choose, during planning time, to do the same thing day after day. Planning time gives children an opportunity to express their choices and to be able to do what motivates them intrinsically. Children experience satisfaction, enjoyment, success, and a feeling of competence when engaged in an activity of their own choosing, just as adults do when they are engaged in their hobbies.

Although children might routinely plan the same thing each day, their plans will develop and change as time goes on. Using an adult as an example again, let's think of a woman who plans to exercise each evening. She might make variations in her exercise routine from night to night. One evening she may decide to walk for an hour, the next night she follows along with an exercise video, and the next she might choose to lift weights. Likewise, 5-year-old Matthew might make a plan each day to build a house in the block area. One day Matthew might build the house with blocks, the next three days he might add props to his house and invite some friends over for dinner, and after that he might role-play with his friends about his house being on fire, with them playing the firefighters.

Certainly it's appropriate to offer children ideas that may extend their plan and their play, but these suggestions should always be based on the children's interests. If we discourage a child's routine plan, we take away the child's opportunity to pursue his or her own interests, and planning time becomes adult-directed. Instead, it should be a time that is child-initiated, offering children a chance to experience enjoyment, success, control, and greater learning opportunities.

I started planning with my 3-year-olds last week, and they just don't seem to understand what's going on. I don't feel like it's worth continuing. Am I doing something wrong?

Probably not! It's not at all uncommon for children—particularly younger preschoolers—to take a while to understand the plan-do-review process. If it's the beginning of your school year, the children may simply be too excited about exploring their new room and all the interesting materials to want to take the time to plan their explorations. There may also be children who feel nervous about being in a new place, and it could take some time before they are ready to share their plans with others. If it's the middle of the school year and planning time has just been introduced, the children may not understand why suddenly they have to talk about what they want to do before they can do it.

Understand that when children first begin planning, they may not plan in a conventional way—that is, verbalize what they want to do. They may simply start their work time, or they may point or use gestures to communicate. With these children, you can interpret their actions for them: "You want to paint today, Sasha." "Luke, I see you found a book to read." These statements give young and inexperienced planners the language to describe their plans, and eventually they will be able to use words to express their ideas. When they do begin to verbalize their plans, their statements will likely be very simple ones, such as "Play blocks." "Art area." "Go there." or "Crayons." As children grow older and have more experience with the planning process, their plans will become more complex and detailed. Also, keep in mind that some children will understand the process of plan-do-review before other children and that their plans may become more detailed sooner than others. Children develop at their own pace in all areas, and the process of planning is no exception.

To make planning time easier for the children to understand, keep your planning games and experiences simple and concrete. Visibility games, which allow children to see the choices that are available to them, are especially helpful to young or new planners. It is much more concrete for children to see and touch objects and demonstrate what they will do with them than it is for them to form an image of a material in their heads and verbalize what they're going to do with it. One effective visibility game is to walk with the children around the classroom and show them what's in each interest area. When they see something that interests them, they can leave the rest of the group and begin their work time. Be sure to comment on their plan: "It looks like Rashaad is going to play with the train in the block area!" "Corinne, you found the two dolls you played with yesterday." You might also collect several objects and materials from each interest area and bring them to your planning group. Again, children can choose something that interests them, and you can talk about where in the room they might find that object or material. As children become more familiar with the classroom and more experienced with the planning process, you could have each child take a basket or a paper bag to an interest area and bring back something that he or she would like to explore during work time. You may want to ask children some questions about what they plan to do with their chosen object, but remember that some children will be more willing and able to discuss their plans than others. It's essential to support children at their own level of development.

After your children plan and have moved on to work time, watch to see if they are following through with what they said they would do. Note which children flit from one interest area to another and which children are able to independently follow through on their plans. Observing the children in this manner will give you clues as to how to interact with and support each child. For example, if you notice a child going from one place to another during work time and having difficulty getting started on a plan, you might go over to that child, place yourself on the same physical level, and simply play alongside the child, imitating what he or she is doing. Having you nearby may provide the support needed to focus his or her attention on an activity. Talk about the child's plan and what he or she is doing, possibly suggesting ways to continue the plan or extend it further. By paying close attention to children as they are beginning work time, you may realize that more children understand the planning process and are able to get involved in their activities independently than you had originally thought. Planning time will take some time to implement successfully, but when the children finally understand the process it will have been well worth the effort and persistence.

What do you do about planning (or recalling) with mixed-age groups or a group of children with a wide range of developmental abilities?

Planning with children who have a wide range of developmental abilities doesn't have to be that much different than planning with a group of children whose abilities are similar. The important thing is to be sensitive to

Children with a wide range of verbal abilities participate in this planning experience, in which they show the group an object they plan to use at work time.

how each child plans. You can generally use the same planning game or experience for all of the children in your group; however, you may need to modify the types of questions you ask, depending on children's individual levels of development. Expect that the level of detail in children's plans will vary from child to child. Consider the following planning-time scenario.

Planning experience: The adult, Molly, has collected several old cameras that have no batteries or film. The children take a picture of the interest area where they'd like to play, an object they want to use during work time, or a child they'd like to play with.

Molly: (Pulls Chantelle's photograph out of a bag.) *Chantelle, can you take a picture of what you'd like to do today during work time?*

Chantelle: (Picks up a camera from the middle of the table, and takes a picture of the computer area.)

Molly: *What are you going to do in the computer area today?*

Chantelle: *I'm gonna play the bunny game with Christopher.*

Molly: *It looks like Christopher is already waiting for you over there.*

Chantelle: (Puts the camera on the table and moves to the computer area.)

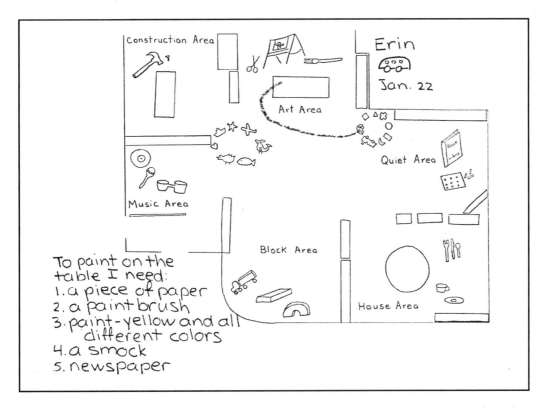

A planning map (see Chapter 7, p. 221) can be used in a variety of ways—from simply marking the areas where children will work to detailing what they need to carry out their plans.

Molly: *Let's see whose turn it will be to plan next.* (Pulls Patrick's photograph out of a bag.)

Patrick: (Runs to the block area and begins taking the train tracks and train off the shelf.)

Molly: (Watches Patrick, understands that he is new to the program, and decides to go work with him and talk about his plan when she's finished planning with the other children.) *It looks like Patrick is excited about those trains and train tracks in the block area. Let's see who will plan next.* (Pulls out Liu's photograph). *Liu, what's your plan for today?*

Liu: (Takes a picture of her friend Sarah, then a picture of the house area.) *Me and Sarah are going to the house area, and we're gonna put on the hats and the shoes and the dresses and we're gonna cook.*

Sarah: *Yeah, and we're gonna make soup and hot dogs and cake for dinner. And I'm gonna be the mom and Liu's gonna be the big sister.*

Molly: *It sounds like you two are going to be busy over there today! What kind of soup are you fixing?*

Sarah: *Chicken and stars.*

Molly: *Mmm, that's one of my favorite kinds of soup. Can I come over and have some soup and hot dogs when you're finished cooking them?*

Liu: *Yep, and you can be the neighbor.*

Molly: *Okay. I'll see you in a little bit.* (Pulls Akito's photograph out of the bag.) *Akito, what's your plan for today?*

Akito: (Takes a picture of the toy area, followed by the art area, the bathroom, the back of the shelf in the house area, the book area, and the music and movement area.)

Molly: *That's a lot of areas! Can you choose the first place you want to work today?*

Akito: (Still taking pictures of different places throughout the room. Discovers the button that opens the door for the film.)

Molly: *You really seem to like taking pictures with the camera. Would you like to do that for a while?*

Akito: (Smiles.)

Molly: *There are only two more pictures in the bag. I wonder who will be next.* (Pulls out the photograph of Kory.)

Kory: (Picks up the camera from the table and takes a picture of the art shelf.)

Molly: *I see a lot of things on that shelf. What are you going to use today?*

Kory: (Takes a picture of the glue, scissors, envelopes, paper, and magazines.)

Molly: *What are you going to do with all of those things?*

Kory: *I'm gonna make a surprise for my mom. Will you help me write a note to her?*

Molly: *You're going to write a note for her?*

Kory: *Yeah. It's her birthday today.*

Molly: *I'd be happy to help you. Just let me know when you need me.*

Kory: *Okay.* (Leaves for the art area.)

Molly: *I wonder whose picture will be next.* (Smiles at Victoria.)

Victoria: (Giggles.) *It's my turn!*

Molly: (Pulls out Victoria's picture.) *What's your plan for today, Victoria?*

Victoria: *Guess.*

Molly: *I have to guess what you're going to do today?*

Victoria: (Giggles some more.) *Yep!*

Molly: *Will you give me a clue?*

Victoria: *It's kind of messy, and you can't get it on your shirt or else your mom will get mad at you.*

Molly: *Do you have to wear a smock when you do it?*

Victoria: *Yep, and you go like this when you do it.* (Moves her arm up and down and side to side.)

Molly: *Are you going to paint at the easel today?*

Victoria: *How did you guess my plan?*

Molly: *Your clues helped me guess what you were going to do.* (Puts the bag with the photographs on the shelf behind her.) *I think I'm going to go see what Patrick is doing.* (Moves over to the block area where Patrick is playing with the train and train track, and asks if she can play with him. She begins talking to him about what he's doing.)

3

Ready, Set...Go!

Work Time

Work time immediately follows planning time in the plan-do-review sequence. It usually lasts between 45 minutes and an hour, depending on the makeup of each particular group of children as well as program schedules and time constraints. Work time is naturally followed by cleanup time, which will also be discussed in this chapter. To get a better idea of what happens during a typical work time, let's take a look at one preschool class with 2 adults and 17 children, who range in age from 3 to 5 years old.

The adults, Cathy and Nancy, have just finished planning with the children, and the children are already busy in the various interest areas of the classroom. Cathy moves to the house area and discusses with Katie and Elizabeth their plans for work time. Katie tells Elizabeth that she wants her to be the mother, and Elizabeth agrees. Katie begins using the electric blender (the cord is cut off), which the adults recently added to the house area, while Elizabeth gives one of her babies "diarrhea medicine."

Mitchell and Tanisha wear safety goggles as they use screwdrivers and pliers to take apart old appliances that have been donated by parents of children in the program. Marlon enters the area and immediately begins working with a screwdriver. Tanisha reminds him that he has to wear his safety goggles if he's going to work at the "take-apart table."

John is alone at the water table, playing with the water wheel. He spies some markers on the nearby art table. He picks up the yellow marker, places it in the water, swirls it around and around, and watches as the ink turns the water yellow. Then he takes the yellow marker out of the water, picks up a red marker, swirls it around, and watches the red ink bleed into the water.

Sunil moves to the computer area by himself, where he turns on the computer and the monitor. Once the computer is ready he clicks the mouse on his symbol and name, which allows him to begin the program. As he plays the pirate treasure hunt game, he calls his friend Dewayne over to see what he's done.

Allison, Danae, and Angelica are sitting next to one another in the house area, using the markers to "paint their fingernails." Rebekah begins doing karate moves near the girls, and Allison immediately joins her. Danae calls Nancy over to the area to see what Rebekah and Allison are doing. Nancy finishes taking pictures with the instant camera, which she will use for her group's recall later, comes over to the house area, and begins watching the karate play.

She observes that although the girls are kicking their legs and moving their arms in a punching manner, they are not touching one another and are being careful not to hurt anyone. Nevertheless, she feels she'd better stay nearby until the karate play ends. Angelica joins in the karate play as well, and the three girls take turns doing a karate move, backing away when it's time for someone else to have a turn.

Joshua, Andrew, and Dewayne take the cars from the block area off the shelf. The three boys discuss which cars they want to use and end up shouting at one another. Cathy approaches to see what the problem is, but by the time she arrives to assist in resolving the conflict, the boys have already solved it. They build a "road" with the unit blocks, then proceed to race their cars on it.

Meanwhile, the karate play has ended in the house area, and the girls begin painting Nancy's fingernails and toenails. Angelica, Rebekah, and Allison tell Nancy to pretend she's been in a car accident and that they're the doctors. They continue their play by putting Band-Aids on Nancy's arms and feet and beanbags on her legs for "ice packs." They tell her that she also has the chicken pox, and they use the markers to make dots on her arms and legs. Nancy steps out of her role as a patient to ask if the marks they're making will wash off. Rebekah shows Nancy the marker and says, "Yep. See, it says 'washable.'" Katie joins the girls' play and begins making chicken pox marks on her arms and legs, too.

Elizabeth has continued her play in the house area but is no longer the mother. Danae joins her, and the two girls line up the chairs in rows of two, all facing the same way. They gather all the food and dishes, and Elizabeth uses the ice cream scoop and play dough to fix "ice cream" for herself and Danae. They sit down in the front row to eat their "food" and watch a "movie."

Marlon lines up several hollow blocks from the block area along the edge of the book area, explaining that he is making a "home." Cathy observes his actions for several minutes, writing down an observation to share with Nancy at their team planning time. Marlon tells Cathy to bring him more hollow blocks, and he adds them to his line. Andrew continues to build a block road, which is now extending from the block area into the book area. Marlon tells Andrew that he can't make his road go that way because it's going to run into his home. Cathy encourages the two boys to resolve their conflict, and they decide that Andrew will use some of the curved unit blocks to make his road turn before it reaches Marlon's home. When Marlon is finished building, he uses a long unit block as his "leaf blower" and walks around the perimeter of his home, making a humming noise.

Dewayne, Rebekah, and Sunil have moved from their previous areas into the art area, where they are using the paint and paintbrushes to paint their hands. Once their hands are covered, they slap them on pieces of blank construction paper. They laugh at one another's painted hands, then compare their handprints, talking about whose are the biggest, the smallest, and so on.

Nancy and Cathy notice that there are only 5 more minutes until cleanup time, and they sing a song together that alerts the children that work time will soon be ending. Cathy helps the children in the art area clean the paint from their hands and arms, and she encourages them to wipe off the table where they were working.

Angelica, who has moved from the house area into the art area, is painting at the easel. Louis is on the other side of the easel, and they move from one side to the other, looking at each other's work. When Angelica finishes painting, she removes her painting from the easel and hangs it up on the drying rack with clothespins. She goes to wash her hands. Louis also removes his painting from the easel and calls Angelica over to help him hang it up. She doesn't respond, so he calls for Cathy. When she doesn't hear him, he tries to unclip a clothespin but is unsuccessful, so he takes his painting to a nearby shelf and places it on top to dry.

Nancy and Cathy turn off the lights and say, "Guess what time it is!" They begin playing a tape with the cleanup music on it. This signals to the children that work time is over and cleanup time has begun. The children begin putting away their materials and preparing for the transition to recall time.

As you can see, work time is a busy and enjoyable time of the day for both children and adults. It is the "do" part of the plan-do-review sequence. During this time, children are actively involved in carrying out the plans they made during planning time, creating new plans, conversing with one another and with adults, constructing knowledge of the objects and events around them, and solving problems as they interact with materials and other children. Adults, too, are busy, supporting children's play by talking with them about what they're doing, listening to and observing them as they play and solve problems, joining in children's play while allowing children to retain control of the play, and using their observations to introduce materials and ideas that build on children's interests and extend their explorations. In addition, adults are continuously monitoring all parts of the room to ensure children's physical and psychological safety. They also write down observations of what the children are doing and saying.

In the illustration above, the adults understood that as the children in their classroom played and interacted with one another during work time, they were developing important intellectual, social, emotional, physical, and language skills. The teachers felt comfortable supporting the children's active learning, knowing that they were engaged in many of High/Scope's key experiences.

Some adults may not feel comfortable with some aspects of a High/Scope work time. Some of you might wonder, for example, why Allison, Angelica, and Danae were allowed to use the markers for painting their fingernails. Some might feel uncomfortable with the karate play that was occurring in the house area and question the teacher's decision to allow it to continue. Others of you might think, "I have so much work to do. I can't spend that much time playing with the children" or "Even if I did have time to play with the children, there is no way I would let them make 'chicken pox' marks on me with markers!"

In order to understand work time, it is helpful to know what children do during this part of the daily routine and why work-time experiences are important. Observing and understanding what children are learning as they explore, play, and solve problems during work time will help you understand why High/Scope teachers interact with children the way they do. You can then explore your own personal comfort level with various interaction strategies and look for areas in which you are willing to modify your approach to working with young children. This chapter will explain how work time provides children with many opportunities for learning and exploration and will offer you some suggestions for supporting children's work-time experiences.

What Is Work Time All About?

Children are doing much more than "just playing" at work time—they are initiating active, hands-on explorations; engaging in a number of key experiences; and participating in several different types of play.

Engaging in active learning

Active learning is at the center of the High/Scope Curriculum (see the High/Scope Preschool "Wheel of Learning," p. 5). Although it is woven throughout the daily routine, it is especially evident during work time. What is active learning? It is a **physical activity,** in which children act on a variety of objects in their environment to test their ideas or answer their questions. It is also a **mental process,** in which children interpret the effects of their actions in order to develop a more complete understanding of the world.

Active learning happens when these five ingredients are present: **materials, manipulation, choice, language from children, and support from adults.** Let's take a look at how these ingredients come together to make work time an exciting, child-initiated active learning experience.

Materials

During work time, children need a variety of materials to work with. These include everyday objects, natural and found materials, tools, messy materials, heavy and large materials, easy-to-handle materials, and the child's body itself (for example, for using different body movements and the singing voice). In the scenario at the beginning of this chapter, children were using screwdrivers, paint, an electric blender, markers, water, beanbags, computers, wooden blocks (unit blocks and large, hollow blocks), ice cream scoops, play dough, and many other materials. Toys and materials should be interesting and meaningful to the children and should be appropriate for a wide range of developmental levels.

Manipulation

Children act on and manipulate materials in ways that make sense to them. After children have made a plan for work time, they use the classroom materials to help them carry out their intentions. For example, children pound, cut, fit materials together, stir, shake, squeeze, glue, stack items on top of each other, pour, saw, paint, and write. Think back once again to the example at the beginning of the chapter and consider how the children manipulated various materials in the classroom.

Choice

Children are motivated to explore and learn when given the opportunity to make their own choices and pursue their own interests. In an active learning setting, children make many different choices throughout the daily routine, especially at work time. For instance, they choose which materials to use and how to use them in order to carry out the plans they have made. They decide which interest areas to go to, who to work with, how to carry out their plans once they get started, how long to stay involved in their activity, and when to end their activity and move on to something else. Although the classroom materials are arranged into various interest areas (art area, house area, book area, etc.), children are free to move these materials around and combine them in order to try out their ideas and achieve their goals. Adults support children's individual interests, enable them to initiate their own activities, and follow children's leads when interacting with them.

Language from children

If you observed a classroom in which adults rather than children were in control of the activities, you would be likely to hear the adults' voices more than children's. Some adults believe that children acquire knowledge from

Work time is full of opportunities for children to exchange ideas with one another, such as discussing the parts each will play in a role-play scene.

what they are told by adults; thus, the adults do most of the talking while children are expected to listen and learn. However, in an active learning classroom children are encouraged to discuss their own ideas and actions with other children and adults. Using language is a way for children to make sense of the world around them (as well as a way for them to solve problems), so it is important to encourage children to explore and ask their own questions rather than expect them to answer a lot of our questions.

Support from adults

As mentioned earlier and illustrated in the example at the beginning of this chapter, adults are actively involved in supporting children throughout work time. They work closely with children; play with them as their partners; enter into the spirit of playfulness; follow children's leads; extend children's play and learning; watch them as they play; document their own observations; and encourage children to solve problems, offering assistance as needed.

Many early childhood educators believe that they are providing an active learning experience simply by offering materials for children to handle and explore. While manipulating materials with intention *is* essential, without the other ingredients mentioned (choice, language from children, support from adults), it does not constitute active learning. All five active learning ingredients must be present in order for children to construct their own understanding of the people, materials, ideas, and events around them.

An active learning environment presents rich opportunities for children to explore their world.

Engaging in High/Scope's key experiences

As children explore and manipulate the materials available to them during work time, they naturally engage in High/Scope's **key experiences,** which are "creative, ongoing interactions with people, materials, and ideas that promote children's mental, emotional, social, and physical growth" (Hohmann and Weikart, 1995, p. 5). Children engage in key experiences as they pound with a hammer, take turns with another child on the swing, move their bodies in time to music, or describe their new pet to an adult. The key experiences are arranged in 10 major categories: creative representation, language and literacy, initiative and social relations, movement, music, classification, seriation, number, space, and time (see complete list on facing page).

Although children engage in various key experiences throughout the entire daily routine, there are a multitude of opportunities to do so during work time because of the wide variety of materials and activities available. Consider the following example of two 4-year-olds, Monique and Simone, playing together in the art area during work time. Note the key experiences they engage in as they play.

> During planning time, Monique and Simone decide they want to play together in the art area and use the dry-erase markers and boards (**initiative and social relations**—*making and expressing choices, plans, and decisions*). When they arrive in the art area,

High/Scope Preschool Key Experiences

Creative Representation
- Recognizing objects by sight, sound, touch, taste, and smell
- Imitating actions and sounds
- Relating models, pictures, and photographs to real places and things
- Pretending and role playing
- Making models out of clay, blocks, and other materials
- Drawing and painting

Language and Literacy
- Talking with others about personally meaningful experiences
- Describing objects, events, and relations
- Having fun with language: listening to stories and poems, making up stories and rhymes
- Writing in various ways: drawing, scribbling, letterlike forms, invented spelling, conventional forms
- Reading in various ways: reading storybooks, signs and symbols, one's own writing
- Dictating stories

Initiative and Social Relations
- Making and expressing choices, plans, and decisions
- Solving problems encountered in play
- Taking care of one's own needs
- Expressing feelings in words
- Participating in group routines
- Being sensitive to the feelings, interests, and needs of others
- Building relationships with children and adults
- Creating and experiencing collaborative play
- Dealing with social conflict

Movement
- Moving in nonlocomotor ways (anchored movement: bending, twisting, rocking, swinging one's arms)
- Moving in locomotor ways (nonanchored movement: running, jumping, hopping, skipping, marching, climbing)
- Moving with objects
- Expressing creativity in movement
- Describing movement
- Acting upon movement directions
- Feeling and expressing steady beat
- Moving in sequences to a common beat

Music
- Moving to music
- Exploring and identifying sounds
- Exploring the singing voice
- Developing melody
- Singing songs
- Playing simple musical instruments

Classification
- Exploring and describing similarities, differences, and the attributes of things
- Distinguishing and describing shapes
- Sorting and matching
- Using and describing something in several ways
- Holding more than one attribute in mind at a time
- Distinguishing between "some" and "all"
- Describing characteristics something does not possess or what class it does not belong to

Seriation
- Comparing attributes (longer/shorter, bigger/smaller)
- Arranging several things one after another in a series or pattern and describing the relationships (big/bigger/biggest, red/blue/red/blue)
- Fitting one ordered set of objects to another through trial and error (small cup—small saucer/medium cup—medium saucer/big cup—big saucer)

Number
- Comparing the numbers of things in two sets to determine "more," "fewer," "same number"
- Arranging two sets of objects in one-to-one correspondence
- Counting objects

Space
- Filling and emptying
- Fitting things together and taking them apart
- Changing the shape and arrangement of objects (wrapping, twisting, stretching, stacking, enclosing)
- Observing people, places, and things from different spatial viewpoints
- Experiencing and describing positions, directions, and distances in the play space, building, and neighborhood
- Interpreting spatial relations in drawings, pictures, and photographs

Time
- Starting and stopping an action on signal
- Experiencing and describing rates of movement
- Experiencing and comparing time intervals
- Anticipating, remembering, and describing sequences of events

they take the boards and markers from one of the shelves and bring them to the table. As Monique chooses the purple marker, she explains to Simone that her daddy is going to paint her room purple because it's her favorite color. As the two girls begin making marks on their boards, Monique describes more details about her new purple room to Simone (**creative representation**—*drawing and painting;* **language and literacy**—*talking with others about personally meaningful experiences*).

Simone uses the markers to draw "two dinosaurs eating flowers," and explains that "the mommy dinosaur is eating the big flowers and the baby is eating the small flowers" (**seriation**—*fitting one ordered set of objects to another*). While Simone is drawing dinosaurs, Monique is looking at the interest area signs and copying the names of the areas—art area, block area, toy area, music area, computer area, and house area—onto her marker board (**language and literacy**—*writing in various ways*). When she finishes writing the names of the interest areas, she looks at what she has written and discovers "they all got the same letters . . . a-r-e-a!" (**classification**—*exploring and describing similarities, differences, and the attributes of things*).

Simone gets up from her chair to get an eraser from the shelf. She bends over and walks to the shelf with her hands on the floor— "just like the dinosaurs walk"—and looks under her arm toward Monique. "Hey, Monique," she says. "You look funny right now!" Monique joins Simone on the floor, and they move around the classroom on their hands and feet, laughing at how everything looks different upside down (**movement**—*moving in locomotor ways;* **space**—*observing people, places, and things from different spatial viewpoints*). Several minutes later, they return to the art area, put their dry-erase markers and boards away, and move to the computer area together.

In only a 15-minute period, and in only one interest area, Simone and Monique were engaged in at least eight key experiences. Imagine the number of key experiences occurring in a 45–60-minute work time in a class with 18 children! As you can see from the example above, the key experiences are not "objectives" to be "taught" to children—rather, they spring naturally from children's interactions with the people and materials around them. When the classroom is filled with a variety of exciting, open-ended materials and staffed with supportive adults, there are many opportunities for children to experiment, invent, construct, explore, and pretend. There are also opportunities—for example, during small- and large-group time—

for adults to introduce activities centered around key experiences that children don't seem to encounter or engage in during other parts of the day.

Work time also offers children many opportunities to learn how to play with and communicate with one another—important social skills that are illustrated in the following work-time scenarios.

> Kyrston has been watching Joey and Martin play with the fire trucks in the block area for several minutes. He asks them if he can have a truck when they're finished, and they both say sure. He continues to patiently watch them play with the trucks for about 10 more minutes, waiting for one of them to grow tired of the play and move to another area. Finally Joey decides to leave the block area, but as he leaves he gives his fire truck to his best friend, Billy. Kyrston immediately begins to cry. Martin sees this and offers Kyrston his fire truck to play with instead.

> Jonah, Callie, and André are in the house area together. Jonah and Callie are each holding a baby doll and sitting at the table looking at menus. André comes over to them, pulls out a pad of paper from his pocket and a pencil from behind his ear, and asks what they want to eat. They give him their orders, which André scribbles down. He goes over to the stove and comes back with "sandwiches," "potato chips," and "cookies." Callie gives her baby a bottle, then tells André that she'd also like something to drink. He writes that down, goes over to the shelf, and returns with the rest of her order.

When children have the opportunity to learn how to develop friendships, work cooperatively with others, and deal with social conflicts in their early years, they build a foundation for successful, satisfying relationships as adults.

Participating in various types of play

Work time is centered around children's play and explorations. During this time children engage in several different types of play, depending on their age and developmental level as well as on their interests on any particular day. Later in this chapter we will discuss several support strategies that will make work time a more meaningful time for you and the children in your program. Having a clear understanding of how children play and the benefits they gain from their play will help you choose the most effective support strategies to incorporate during work time.

Exploratory play

You will frequently see children squeezing, shaking, tasting, smelling, splashing, pounding, or poking various materials in the classroom. Children are naturally curious about new items, and they use all their senses to discover more about the properties of objects and what they can do. Through *exploratory play*, children construct knowledge and begin to form an understanding of the objects in their environment. Consider the following examples.

Three-year-old Nedra's plan for work time was to play with the play dough and cookie cutters, and she has just arrived at the art area. One child is painting and two others are gluing toothpicks onto pieces of cardboard. As Nedra approaches the play dough container, she sees the two children who are using the glue, something she's never used before. She watches how the glue oozes out of the bottle and forms puddles on the cardboard as the children squeeze it. She looks around the art area, finds the other glue bottles on the shelf, and chooses her own bottle to use.

After she's found a piece of cardboard, Nedra turns the glue bottle over and squeezes it, but nothing happens. She asks her teacher for help, and her teacher refers her to Jack, one of the boys who is gluing. He helps her open the cap, then she turns the glue bottle over and squeezes it. After several squeezes, Nedra examines the puddle of glue that has formed on the cardboard by cautiously putting her finger in it. She rubs her finger around in the puddle in a circular motion, discovering that it is slippery, wet, and cold. She takes her finger out of the glue, cautiously licks it, wipes her tongue and finger on her shirt, then squeezes more glue, forming an even larger puddle. She puts the bottle down and this time puts her entire hand in the puddle, feeling the soothing sensation. She rubs her hand around in the glue, and quickly adds her other hand. She stands at the table for several more minutes, rubbing her hands together and spreading the glue on the backs of her hands, then up her forearms.

As Nedra rubs the glue over her skin, she begins to realize that the once soft and soothing material is becoming sticky. She presses her hands together and pulls them apart several times, each action requiring more effort. When she places her hands on the cardboard, it sticks to her. She decides to add new glue to the puddle, and quickly discovers that once again the glue feels soft and slippery. She continues this activity for about 20 minutes, washes her hands and arms at the sink, then moves to a new interest area.

When children engage in exploratory play, they manipulate materials to find out what they are like and what they can do. The girls above discover that beans, though solid, can flow from one container to another like water. The children below experiment with sticking a variety of objects into play dough.

Five-year-old Tyler's plan was to play in the toy area and use the Legos to make a boat. He spends about 15 minutes using the Legos, fitting them together to form a recognizable boat. He then looks on the shelf and sees the gears building set, a toy he's never seen or played with before. He takes the gears out of the box, noticing that they fit easily onto the base piece. After he has placed several gears on the base, he tries turning one and discovers that they all move at the same time. Tyler adds more gears on the opposite corner of the base and turns the same gear he turned before, but discovers that the new ones he added aren't turning. He wonders if they're not turning because they're not touching each other, so he adds a few more in the middle to make them all touch. This time Tyler is successful in making all the gears spin together by turning just one.

The children in both of these examples were engaged in exploratory play. Nedra and Tyler were primarily interested in discovering the properties of the novel materials they had found. In the process of her explorations Nedra discovered that the glue was sticky, but it may take several more similar experiences with glue before she begins to understand that its main purpose is to hold things together. Tyler, although engaged in constructive play (explained in more detail in the next section) when he was building his boat with the Legos, became involved in simpler exploratory play when he began experimenting with the gears set and learning how that particular toy worked. This experience gave him a clearer understanding of the purpose of the gears building set, and during his next encounter with the toy he may engage in constructive play with it.

There is no specific age at which children play with materials in an exploratory manner. In fact, even we adults explore materials that are new to us. The next time you're shopping in a store that sells various types of gadgets or new inventions, pay attention to your own behavior and that of other adults. Watch how others will pick up a gadget and explore it, much in the same way a preschooler would, to see what its purpose is. When you add a novel material to your learning environment, you will see children of all ages explore its properties before they combine it with other materials or use it in a more constructive manner.

Constructive play

Once children have explored the functions and properties of a particular material, they will begin playing with it in a more goal-oriented fashion. This type of play, in which the children's intentions are to make, build, or arrange something, is called *constructive play*. Consider the following examples of children engaged in this type of play.

Constructive, or goal-oriented, play takes many forms, such as making jars from clay, making a Valentine from a variety of art materials, and measuring a friend's head to make a hat!

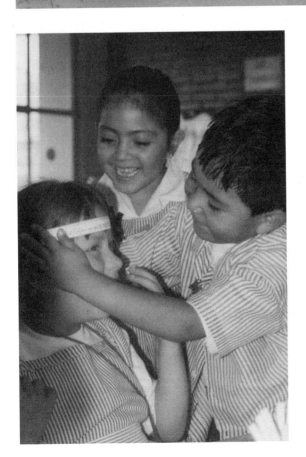

Kelly, who is 4 years old, has made a plan to go to the art area and wrap a present that she made at home for her friend Elise. When she gets to the art area she collects scissors, tape, and newsprint paper from the easel. She places the bead bracelet she made for Elise in the middle of the paper and begins folding and refolding the paper around the bracelet. She wraps the masking tape around the package until the paper is no longer showing, then cuts the tape with scissors. Next, she takes the present and a pencil over to Elise's cubby and copies Elise's name onto the package. She returns to the art area, where she gathers three paint containers from the easel, places them on the table, and proceeds to cover the entire package with red, purple, and orange paint.

Five-year-old Demetrius is in the toy area, looking through the container of seashells. He finds several large conch shells, lines them up in a row on the floor, and counts them. Next he finds several very small angel wing shells and lines up the same number of these, parallel to the conches. Finally, he finds several tulip shells (smaller than the conches but larger than the angel wings) and lines them up between the other two rows of shells. When he finishes lining up all the shells, Demetrius finds a box of shoelaces and places one shoelace around each set of shells (the large, medium, and small).

Three-year-old Chase and 4-year-old Alexander have made a plan to go to the block area and make a "sidewalk." They carry the large, hollow blocks over to the classroom door and line them up on the carpet near the door. When they run out of hollow blocks, they use the unit blocks to continue building their sidewalk. By the time they are finished with their project, the sidewalk extends from the door, through the block area, and into the house area. After walking on it themselves several times, they invite the other children in the classroom to "come take a walk on our sidewalk!"

Although constructive play is often thought to occur only in the block, construction, or woodworking areas, constructive play can actually take place anywhere, just as exploratory play can. When children have a particular goal in mind—whether it's to build a hospital in the block area, put together a marching band with instruments from the music area, or paint a castle in the art area—they are engaging in constructive play. In the three examples above, the children were all involved in constructive play. While their activities were very different from one another's (wrapping a present, sorting seashells, and building a sidewalk), they all had definite goals in mind.

I am reminded of how adults, too, engage in constructive play and the entire plan-do-review process as my husband, Curt, and I undertake a home improvement project. As we work on our basement over the weekends, Curt and I are essentially involved in constructive play (although it usually feels more like work than play).

Before we were able to get started on building the rooms in our basement, we were involved in a planning stage that lasted several months. During this period, we decided that we would build two rooms—an office and a workout room. We asked ourselves such questions as "How much do we want to spend on this project?" "Whom do we need to call to get a building permit?" "How large do we want to make the rooms?" "What type of ceiling do we want to put in these rooms?" and "What are we going to do about heat?" After answering these questions and many others, we were ready to draw up the plans and make a list of materials that we would need for our project. After a couple of trips to the home improvement store (which proved both lengthy and expensive), we were ready to get started.

Just as children who are involved in constructive play have a particular goal in mind, so do Curt and I as we build the two rooms in our basement. And just as children occasionally pause to look at what they've done and consider how to solve problems that arise, so do we. Whether we're framing our walls, adjusting ductwork in the ceiling, installing electrical wiring, or mounting the drywall, we consistently evaluate the job that we're doing. When we run into unexpected obstacles, we brainstorm ideas until we are able to come up with an effective solution to the problem. We realize that modifications to our plans are necessary in order to successfully complete our goal. Similarly, children's plans will often need to be modified as they evaluate their work and solve the problems that arise during their constructive play.

Pretend play

Pretend play occurs frequently in preschool classrooms. As illustrated in the examples that follow, children engage in *pretend play* when they use one object to stand for another or when they take on the role of someone or something else (a baker and salesperson, a ship's captain, a mother). Children's assumed roles and their imaginative play often focus on people or situations that are real or meaningful in some way to them. Through this type of play, children attempt to make sense of their world and seek some control over events they have seen or taken part in, such as feeding a baby, chasing a "bad guy," or fixing a car. Imaginative play is also a rich opportunity for social interaction and language experiences.

Pretend play doesn't always happen in, and shouldn't be limited to, the house area. In fact, children engage in pretend and imaginative play in every interest area of the classroom and often outside as well. Below are some typical pretend play scenarios.

In the art area, Holly is using a rolling pin, cookie cutters, and play dough. After rolling out the dough, she presses the cookie cutters in it, making "cookies" of various shapes. She places them all on a plate from the house area and walks around the room selling her cookies for $5 apiece.

Sitting on a pile of blocks and holding a steering wheel in his hands, Nolan is the captain of a "ship." His "passengers" are sitting on several hollow wooden blocks that have been arranged behind him. His ship is sinking, and he uses a unit block to talk to the "rescue guys" on his "walkie-talkie." Nolan goes to the book area, gathers several pillows, and brings them back to the passengers, telling them that they will have to use these "floating things" when they fall into the water.

Carmen is in the house area, preparing for her "daughter" Sophie's birthday party. Carmen uses a variety of pots and pans as well as several small manipulative toys to make Sophie's "strawberry cake." As she does this she picks up the telephone and uses a pen to mark her next "doctor's appointment" on a nearby calendar. She puts plates and cups on the table and places "candles" (plastic pegs) on Sophie's "cake" (a foam pegboard), then sings "Happy Birthday."

Games

Children often enjoy playing a variety of games during work time. These games may be simple or complicated; traditional games that someone has taught them or new games the children have created themselves. A game may be played by an individual child or by a whole group of children.

Group games offer children an opportunity to cooperate; negotiate; compete in an enjoyable, nonthreatening environment; and improve their physical or cognitive skills—all in an entertaining way. Consider the following examples of children involved in various games during work time.

Brynn, Alyssa, and Tamara (all 5 years old) have set up several plastic buckets in a line on the floor and are tossing beanbags from the music and movement area into the buckets. The three girls have placed a piece of tape on the floor, which they have to stand behind when they toss the beanbags. They make a rule that the person tossing the beanbags has to start with the closest bucket before she can work her way toward the farthest bucket. They also develop a scoring system in which the closest bucket is worth one point, the second, two points, and so on. As they take turns tossing and realize how difficult it is to reach the farthest bucket, the girls develop more rules, such as "Each player gets three tries" and "It's okay to step over the piece of tape on the floor when you try to toss the beanbag in the last bucket."

Three-year-old Nathan has found a memory game on the shelf in the toy area that is just like one he has at home. He asks his teacher, Donita, if she will play with him, and she agrees. Nathan mixes all of the cards on the floor, puts them face down in rows, then tells Donita that he gets to go first. They play the game following the traditional rules, just as his parents have taught him.

Carlos has been in the toy area putting various puzzles together for several minutes of work time. He reaches for the sand timer that's on a nearby shelf, turns it over, dumps out a puzzle, and quickly begins putting the puzzle back together, frequently glancing at the timer. When he finishes the puzzle and sees that the sand is still flowing in the timer, he thrusts his hands in the air and says "Yea! I'm the winner!!" He waits for the sand to run through, turns the timer back over, then repeats his game several more times.

This discussion of what children do at work time shows the variety of activities that take place during this part of the day and their importance to children's learning and development. For children to gain the most benefit from their play and explorations, they need observant, involved, and supportive adults. The next section more fully discusses how you can interact with children during work time to enhance their play.

How to Support Children At Work Time

Recall that in order for active learning to take place, all five ingredients—materials, manipulation (with intention), choice, child language, and adult support—must be present. Adult involvement in children's play is often overlooked, but in preschools that incorporate the High/Scope Curriculum adult support is just as important as the other four ingredients of active learning.

Work time is not a time of the day to work on bulletin boards, write lesson plans, do paperwork, write notes to parents, or take care of other "teacher responsibilities." Nor is it an opportunity to simply sit back and relax while the children have "free play," getting involved only when children need help or are arguing. Work time is an opportunity to actively interact with children—playing with them, following their leads, extending their play and learning, observing them, and documenting what you see and hear children doing and saying. These and other support strategies are described in detail in this section. How you decide to support children during work time will depend on your observations of children's needs and interests and on the types of play occurring in the classroom, which is why so much attention was previously given to the various types of play young children engage in.

Offer children comfort and contact

Sometimes children need immediate or ongoing attention and acknowledgment from you. There are many different reasons for this, and children express their need for such support in a variety of ways. For example, children

The Art and Science of Teaching

Perhaps you have heard the teaching profession referred to as both an art and a science. To illustrate the difference between the two, High/Scope trainers sometimes ask workshop participants to think of significant people who have touched their lives in some way. When asked to write down the specific characteristics or traits that make these individuals special, participants use such descriptors as *patient, good listener, good sense of humor, caring, loving, giving of themselves, creative, stable influence, provided a sense of security, playful,* and *kind.* It is explained to the participants that these types of traits are part of the "art" of teaching, and that it's very difficult for someone to teach an adult how to possess these attributes.

In contrast, the supportive teaching strategies that are taught in High/Scope workshops and discussed in this chapter constitute the "science" side of teaching. They are concrete strategies that can be learned and refined with some practice, techniques that will help you to be more supportive of children's needs and interests. While this science of teaching is important in creating an appropriate environment for youngsters, it cannot substitute for the art side of teaching. As you're reading about, learning, and incorporating the interaction strategies suggested here, always keep in mind your own special characteristics with which you can touch the lives of the children you come in contact with.

might appear apprehensive or nervous about a certain situation and need your reassurance. Some children might move from one interest area to another without engaging in play or carrying out their plans; they may need you to stay near them and offer some direction. Some children seek almost constant acknowledgment; such children need assurance that you do care and are aware of their efforts or needs. At times, you may notice children watching the play of others, wanting to join in but unsure of how to do this or too shy to ask. These children, too, need your encouragement and support.

Be aware of children's cues that let you know they are in need of your presence or reassurance. At these times you may want to use some of the specific interaction strategies that will be mentioned later, but sometimes children simply need a smile, a hug, a reassuring look, a lap to sit on, or a hand to hold. Simple acknowledgments ("I see, Waneta!" "You're still feeling sad about your dog, Christian") or nurturing physical contact may be just what children need to feel reassured that they are in a safe, secure, caring, and loving environment.

Sometimes children need a bit of adult encouragement to start an activity or join in play with other children.

Join children on their physical level

Many adults use this support strategy without even consciously thinking about it. If you are not used to practicing this strategy, make an effort to put yourself on the children's physical level. This frees children from having to "look up" to you and frees you from "looking down" on the children. In order to get on the children's physical level, you may have to kneel, squat, sit, or even lie on the floor. If you are not already doing so, wear clothes that are comfortable and easy to move around in so that you are able to focus your full attention on the children.

Observe children, listen to them, and understand what they are doing

Before you enter children's play silently observe them in action and listen to them as they play. These observations will help you understand the type of play children are involved in and how best to support them in their play. You may feel that you are not "teaching" children what they need to learn if you are simply observing and listening to them. You may also be concerned about the reaction of other teachers—those not familiar with this particular strategy—who walk into your classroom and see you "simply watching" the children. It's important to give yourself permission to quietly observe children at play and to understand that by doing this you will be able to choose appropriate and supportive interaction strategies.

Play in parallel with children

As you place yourself on a child's physical level and observe what he or she is doing, you might begin playing alongside the child with similar materials. Your actions should be similar to the child's and should not distract the child from what he or she is doing. For example, if a child is snipping an envelope with scissors, you might snip other nearby materials, such as construction paper, magazines, or wallpaper scraps.

This strategy is often effective with children involved in exploratory play. They will often notice your actions and initiate a conversation or interaction. As you parallel-play with children, you will find many opportunities to use other support strategies mentioned in this chapter, such as labeling and describing children's actions, taking turns with children, and extending their play and learning.

Join children at their developmental level

In addition to putting yourself on the children's physical level, interact on each child's developmental level as well. To do this you will need to be aware of where each child is functioning. It's particularly helpful to understand the various types of play that were mentioned earlier. As you consider the following illustration, think about the different types of play the child and the teacher are engaged in.

Three-year-old Rena is in the art area using the play dough. She pounds the play dough flat, presses her fingers in it, then picks it up, squeezes it through her fingers, and pounds it some more. As she plays, Rena tells a story and sings a song about what she is doing. She repeats the sequence with the play dough several times, continuing her talking and singing. Rena's teacher, Jacqueline, comes over and kneels next to her at the table. She asks Rena, "What are you making? I'm going to make a snowman today." Jacqueline picks up some play dough and begins rolling the dough into three balls of different sizes. She then stacks the balls on top of each other, forming a snowman. As she talks to Rena about all the snow outside, she adds eyes, a carrot-shaped nose, arms, a scarf, and a hat to her snowman. When Jacqueline is finished she says to Rena, "Look at the snowman I made!"

Although Jacqueline's intentions were good (she worked alongside Rena with the play dough rather than introduce another play activity) and she did support Rena by getting on the same physical level, she did not consider the level or type of play Rena was involved in. Rena was clearly involved in exploratory play. She was pounding, poking, and squeezing the play dough, learning about its properties and functions as she explored it. Jacqueline, however, chose to use the play dough in a constructive manner herself. She had a particular goal in mind—to form balls and make a snowman. Because Rena was not "making" anything, Jacqueline's opening question ("What are you making?") was irrelevant to what Rena was doing. It would have been more appropriate and much more validating to Rena for her teacher to have first observed her to see how she was playing with the play dough, then joined her in exploring the play dough in the same way (playing in parallel, as explained earlier).

Label and describe children's actions

As you watch children closely during work time, comment from time to time on their actions. Labeling and describing what children are doing is a simple, effective way to validate children's actions and to offer support and encouragement. This strategy is illustrated in the following examples.

Ellen is in the block area playing "cops" with two children. Manuel comes over to Ellen to show her what he has been working on in the art area.

Manuel: *Look at what I made.* (Shows Ellen his paper, which has collage materials attached with glue along with several letters and numbers written in marker.)

Ellen: *I see you used some buttons and Styrofoam on your paper.*

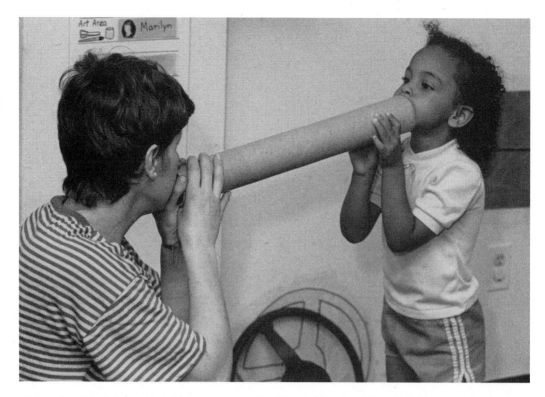

*Your role as participant in children's play may involve simple turn taking, as above, or role-playing in an elaborate imaginative scene, below. In role-play situations, you might extend children's learning by making comments or asking questions: "I noticed when we visited the barber shop the other day, there was a man getting a shave **and** a haircut. I wonder if Rafael wants a shave, too?"*

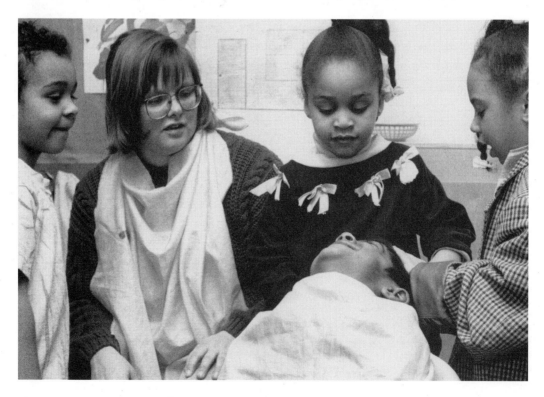

Manuel: *Yeah. I glued them on.*

Ellen: *You used a lot of glue. There's some dripping down there.*

Manuel: *Lots of glue'll make 'em stick better.*

Ellen: *It looks like you wrote something with a red marker.*

Manuel: *Yeah. It's a note to my baby sitter. It says "Your dog is mean."* (He points to the letters as he "reads" the note.)

Three-year-old Shannon is at the easel exploring the paints for the first time. Her teacher, LaTrish, kneels next to her, watching Shannon's actions.

Shannon: (Dips the paintbrush in the yellow paint cup and brushes the paint on her easel paper.)

LaTrish: *You're painting with the yellow paint.*

Shannon: (Dips the paintbrush in the red paint cup and dabs the brush on her paper.)

LaTrish: *You're making dots!*

Shannon: (Smiles at LaTrish. Dabs the brush in the red cup and brushes it over the yellow paint on her paper.)

LaTrish: *Look at that! You made orange paint on your paper.*

Shannon: (Looks at the paint cups, then at her paper. She dips her brush in the red cup and the yellow cup, mixing the two colors, and brushes the paint on her paper. She smiles at LaTrish again.) *I make orange!*

LaTrish: (Smiles back at Shannon.)

In both examples, the adults simply described the children's actions: "You used buttons and Styrofoam on your paper." "You're making dots!" In the first example, this strategy encouraged Manuel to continue describing his collage and to talk about the details of it. In the second example, the teacher's comments caused Shannon to look more closely at her painting and notice that she had mixed two colors to make a third.

Describing Children's Actions

Labeling children's actions as they work may at first seem stilted, unnatural, and potentially irritating to children. True, if someone were to stand next to an *adult* and describe each move he or she made, the adult probably would get annoyed with the other person. For example, if you were fixing dinner and someone was watching and describing exactly what you were doing ("You're adding the margarine." "You're chopping up the vegetables." "Now I see you're stirring the rice"), it would be irritating. However, children typically don't seem to mind such remarks. Their response is usually positive, because having adults show interest in them and their activities makes them feel important and valued. Labeling children's actions also gives them a model for language and helps them understand that activities can be described meaningfully to others. If you sense that children *are* becoming irritated when you use this strategy, simply try supporting these children in a different way.

Look for natural play openings

Once you have observed what children are doing and saying and noted the types of play they are involved in, you can decide whose play you are going to enter as well as how and when you are going to enter it. Look for natural play openings, when children might be receptive to a participant joining them—for instance, when they are engaged in parallel play, in a role-play scene, or in moving to music. When you do decide that it's appropriate to enter a child's play, you can wait for the child to initiate a conversation and then respond accordingly or initiate a conversation yourself by making a comment or observation on the child's activity. Both of these strategies allow you to enter a child's play in a way that is nonthreatening to the child and respectful of his or her activities. They also validate the child's actions and encourage him or her to continue the activity or add to the play. Take a look at the following examples of adults entering children's play.

Damon, 4, is busy at the rice table during work time. His teacher, Anita, has been watching him fill various containers with his right hand and pour the rice over his left hand and arm. Each time he pours the rice, he moves higher and higher up his arm. He switches to filling the container with his left hand and pouring the rice over his right hand and arm. Anita approaches the rice table and kneels beside Damon. She picks up a container similar to the one he is using and, without saying anything, begins to imitate his actions. After a few minutes he says to Anita, "I'm goin' to my grandma's house today." They talk about Damon's grandmother and their plans for the afternoon as they both continue to play with the rice.

Valerie has been observing two girls, Brae and Sunny, working in the house area together. She hears them discussing the "soup and pudding" they're fixing for dinner, and she watches as one stands at the stove, stirring the ingredients in the soup, while the other puts bowls, spoons, and cups on the table. Valerie approaches the house area, squats down so she's on their level, and says to the girls, "That soup sure smells good!" Brae invites Valerie into the house area and offers her some soup while Sunny adds another bowl, spoon, and cup to the table.

Amir is in the art area using rubber stamps and ink pads. His teacher, Brad, has been playing with clay along with two other children in the art area and has been watching Amir use the stamps. In addition to making marks on his paper with the rubber stamps, Amir has been putting his fingers on the ink pad and making fingerprints on his paper. Each time he adds a fingerprint, Amir lifts up his paper to inspect what he's done. Brad moves his chair toward Amir and says, "I wonder what my fingerprints would look like if I tried that." Amir tells him that he can use the ink pad but needs to get his own piece of paper. Brad does so, then makes several fingerprints on his paper. After inspecting his teacher's fingerprints Amir tells him, "Yours sure are big!"

Generally, it's more natural and less disruptive to join children when they are exploring, pretending, or playing games than when they are involved in constructive play. This does not mean, however, that you can never play along with children in their constructive play. If children want your participation and feel that you can help them achieve their intended goals, or if they need your assistance with a problem, the children will invite you to play with them, and you can then follow their lead. There may be times when you and the children choose not to say anything at all to one another during play. There may also be times when you initiate a conversation and the children don't respond. Just because there is limited or no conversation during children's play does not mean that positive interactions are not occurring. The next few strategies discussed are effective whether or not there is any verbal communication.

Follow children's leads

The phrase "follow children's leads" has been mentioned several times in this chapter, so let's take a closer look at what it means. When you follow children's leads, you enable them to be in control of the play situation or activity. You step out of your "teacher role" and become an equal partner with children. This of course does not mean that you allow children to do something that is unsafe or harmful. Certainly you need to step back into the teacher role to prevent a harmful situation from occurring. These situations aside, when you play with children encourage them to use initiative and to create their own ideas for how to do something or what to do next. By respecting children's choices and encouraging children to follow through on them, you validate their ideas.

To contrast the results of following children's leads with those of directing children's play, consider the following two examples. In the first, the adult follows the child's lead and enables her to retain control of the play episode. In the second scenario, the adult remains in control of the activity.

Adults are sometimes surprised at where they end up when they follow children's leads—like in a "beauty salon"!

Five-year-old Elana is in the house area with her teacher, Constance. Elana suggests to Constance that the two of them play house and that she will be the mom and Constance can be her dog. Constance agrees and immediately gets down on her hands and knees and begins barking and panting like a dog. Elana says to her, "Oh, you must be very hungry. I'll get you some dinner." Constance barks excitedly while Elana fixes her "dog food" and puts it in a dog dish. While Constance is "eating," Elana goes to the art area and finds some yarn for a "leash." When she returns, she tells Constance that it's time for her walk. Constance again barks excitedly while Elana cuts a long piece of yarn. When Elana begins to tie the yarn around Constance's neck, Constance steps out of her role as a dog and explains to Elana that it's dangerous to put things around people's necks because it could choke them. She asks Elana if she can think of anywhere else to attach the yarn, and Elana suggests tying it to Constance's wrist. Constance agrees that this would be a safer place to tie the leash, and she immediately steps back into her role as the dog. She lifts her "paw" and Elana ties the yarn loosely around her wrist. Elana tells Constance, "Okay, let's go for your walk," and she leads Constance around the classroom.

In the art area, 4-year-old Alora is drawing with markers on cellophane paper. She notices that the lines she is drawing do not show up very well, so she puts her marker down and tries another one. Her teacher, Melissa, approaches and tells Alora that markers don't write on that kind of paper. She gives her a sheet of white drawing paper instead. Alora begins contentedly drawing on the paper, and Melissa says, "Hey, I've got an idea. Let me show you what you can make." She takes the marker from Alora, draws a circle, then says, "See if you can make a circle." Alora draws a circle, then continues with what she was drawing before. Melissa says to her, "Now try this," and draws a triangle on Alora's paper. Alora draws a triangle, then puts the cap back on the marker. She tells Melissa that she's going to go to the block area, and she leaves the table.

In the first example, the adult let Elana decide for herself what she would do in the play scenario and what Constance would do. Constance stepped out of the dog role Elana had assigned to her only to inform Elana about a dangerous situation. By letting Elana be in control and initiate what would happen next in the play scene, Constance showed Elana that she respected her ideas. This encouraged Elana to continue and extend her activity. Over the next couple of weeks, this "dog play" developed to include several other children, and it became a very complex and involved play scenario.

In the second example, Melissa interrupted Alora's play in a couple of ways. Alora was in the process of discovering for herself that markers write differently on different surfaces. However, when Melissa *told* her that markers don't write on cellophane and offered her a different type of paper, Melissa took away Alora's chance to discover that detail for herself (no doubt thinking that she was being helpful). Then, when Alora began drawing on the paper, Melissa once again took control by dictating what Alora should draw. Rather than encourage and support Alora in her own choices, Melissa discouraged her and eventually caused Alora to lose interest in her chosen activity.

Take turns with children in their play

As you become a partner with children in play and share control with them, you will find many opportunities to take turns with children as they play. In order to understand this type of support strategy, consider the following example. Also note how the adult incorporates other strategies, such as getting on the child's physical and developmental level and playing in parallel with the child.

Jason, 4 years old, is on the floor in the toy area, playing with the small table blocks. He has sorted out all the cubes and is stacking them on top of one another. He stacks them as high as he can, then watches as they fall over onto the floor. His teacher, Marie, has been watching this and decides to join him in his play. She sits down next to him. She continues to watch him as she chooses her own blocks and stacks them in the same manner as Jason. Jason also continues stacking his cubes on top of one another and finally places a cube on top that makes his stack rock back and forth. Marie says to him, "That sure is getting wobbly." Jason says "I know!" and laughs as they fall down. Jason gathers all of the cubes in front of him and starts to stack them again. Marie takes one of the cubes, looks at Jason, and places it on top of the cube he just put down. Jason smiles, then stacks another cube on top of hers. They continue this turn-taking game, looking wide-eyed at each other when the stack starts to sway. When it falls over, they repeat the game.

Extend children's play and learning

As you observe children's play and enter into their activities, you will often see opportunities to help extend children's ideas and expand their current play. This can be done by **suggesting new ideas within the context of the play** that's occurring and by **gently challenging children's thinking and reasoning.** In order to use these strategies successfully, it's important that you have taken the time to observe the children's activity, are familiar with the type of play that's occurring, and respect children's responses to your suggestions. That is, if you find that your suggestions detract from children's original intentions or that children do not respond to your ideas, continue to follow the children's lead rather than impose your own ideas.

Offer new ideas within the context of ongoing play

You can build on children's play episodes by offering suggestions based on the children's interests and the play that is occurring. Consider the following examples that illustrate this strategy.

Tiffany and Jemani have been working in the house area for the past couple of days, planning a birthday party for their friend Haley. Each day during planning time, Tiffany and Jemani discuss more tasks they need to complete in order to prepare for the party. The activities they have chosen include making paper-chain decorations with paper strips and staplers; collecting some of Haley's favorite toys and books from the interest areas and wrapping them with decorated newsprint paper, tape, and yarn; painting pictures for her at the easel; and using cookie cutters to make "cookies" out of play dough.

Today during work time their teacher, Shay, is helping them "bake cookies" for the party. As the two children work with Shay, they decide that they will bring Haley and a few other children to the house area when their cookies are finished baking. Shay mentions that whenever she goes to a party, she always receives an invitation that tells where and when the party will be and who it is for. She asks if any invitations have been sent for Haley's party. Jemani's eyes open wide and she screams, "Tiffany, we forgot the imbitations!!" Tiffany looks surprised, throws her arms up in the air, and runs to the art area to get paper and markers, saying "We got to make the invitations!!"

When Tiffany returns to the house area, she asks Shay how to write the words *invitation, 11:00, house area,* and *Haley.* Shay writes the word *invitation* and shows Tiffany and Jemani how to write *11:00* so they can copy it onto their papers. She asks the two if they know where they can find the words *house area* and *Haley* somewhere in the classroom to copy on their own. During the remainder of work time, Jemani and Tiffany copy Haley's name from the symbol on her cubby and the words *house area* from the sign that is hanging in the house area. As they finish writing their invitations, Shay tells them that work time will be ending soon, and they decide to wait until the next day to have the party.

Tara and Benjamin are in the book area, sitting side by side on the beanbag chairs that were recently added to the classroom. They have spent about 20 minutes taking turns "reading" *The Very Hungry Caterpillar,* by Eric Carle. Their teacher, Suzette, notices their interest in the story and remembers that she has a puppet that goes along with the story. The puppet is a green sock with eyes sewn on to make it look like the caterpillar in the book. To accompany the puppet, there are felt pieces in the shape of the different foods the caterpillar eats in the story, as well as a felt cocoon and butterfly like the ones shown at the end of the story.

Suzette finds the puppet in her storage cabinet and brings it to the book area, where Tara and Benjamin are still involved in the story. She waits in a nearby beanbag chair until Benjamin has finished with the last page. She introduces the puppet and the other props to them, and the children are immediately interested. Suzette stays with them as they "read" the story once again and as they use the puppet and the felt pieces to act out the story.

Suzette moves to another interest area to support other children, and she glances over to the book area several minutes later. By this time, Tara and Benjamin have both taken turns working the puppet and have moved on to another book. She returns to the book area with a storage container and suggests that the two place the caterpillar puppet and the accompanying pieces in the box, since they are finished playing with it. She also suggests that they may want

One way to build on children's curiosity and encourage them to explore objects further is by making "I wonder…" statements, such as "I wonder what happens when I put the magnifying glass farther away from my eye."

to make a label for the storage container and the shelf, but Tara and Benjamin decide that they want to go to the block area instead. Suzette accepts their decision and writes herself a note to make a label for the puppet box after the children leave for the day.

Gently challenge children's thinking and reasoning

In addition to offering new ideas within the context of ongoing play, you may see opportunities to extend children's play and learning by gently challenging their thinking and reasoning. Young children think and reason differently than older children and adults do, and you may want to occasionally introduce your preschoolers to new ways of looking at materials and events. Realize, however, that they may not be developmentally ready to understand more complex concepts that you try to present. When this occurs, accept the children's viewpoint and understand that given time and opportunity to experience concepts for themselves, and with your continued support, children will eventually develop a more mature way of thinking and reasoning. The following examples illustrate this support strategy of challenging children's thinking. Note that in the second example, the child is not ready to understand the concept the adult is trying to illustrate, and she accepts this as appropriate for this child's level of development.

Keegan and Sydney are sitting on the floor in the house area, playing with acorns Sydney collected at outside time. Sydney divides the acorns, one at a time, between herself and Keegan. They each end up with 14. They spend a few minutes playing and arranging their acorns in different ways on the floor.

Their teacher, Maggie, has been observing the two children and writes an anecdotal note about how Sydney divided the acorns evenly between herself and Keegan. Maggie approaches the house area and sits on the floor next to the two children. She comments that Keegan has piled his acorns together, while Sydney has formed a large circle with her acorns. Keegan looks at Sydney's circle of acorns and says to her, "Hey . . . you got more than me!" Sydney responds, "No, I don't. We each got the same." Maggie wonders aloud how they could find out if they have the same number, and the children suggest counting them.

Keegan: *1, 2, 3, 4, 5, 6, 7, 8, 9, 10, 11, 12, 13, 14.* (He lines up his acorns in a row as he counts.)

Sydney: *1, 2, 3, 4, 5, 6, 7, 8, 9, 10, 11, 12, 13, 14.* (She also lines up her acorns in a row.)

Maggie: *You each have 14.*

Keegan: *Yeah. We got the same.*

Maggie: (Asks both children) *Can I move your acorns?*

Sydney and Keegan: (Both nod their heads.)

Maggie: (Spreads Keegan's acorns across the floor and puts Sydney's in a pile.) *Now who has more acorns?*

Keegan: (Smiles.) *I do!*

Sydney: (Looks frustrated.) *No, you don't. We each got the same. See?* (She counts her acorns and puts them in a row, then counts Keegan's acorns and puts them in a row as well.)

Maggie: (Rearranges the acorns once again, this time putting Keegan's in a pile and spreading Sydney's out across the floor.) *Now who has more acorns?*

Keegan: (Looks at the acorns and thinks for a moment.) *Nobody's got more. We got the same!*

Sydney: (Smiles.) *That's what I said!!*

Three-year-old Sean is in the block area building a tower, using small blocks on the bottom and larger blocks on top. His teacher, Ann, is playing next to him. As Sean adds more blocks to his tower, it falls over. He has tried several times to make it higher and is becoming increasingly frustrated.

Ann: *You seem upset, Sean.*

Sean: *My tower keeps falling over!*

Ann: *Your tower won't stay up, huh? I wonder why it keeps falling.*

Sean: *Yesterday I built a really big tower with lots of blocks, and it didn't fall down!*

Ann: *I see. When you used lots of blocks, it didn't fall down.*

Sean: *Yeah. I need more blocks, but Chelsey gots 'em all. See, her tower stays up!*

Ann: *Chelsey has the blocks you need, and her tower is not falling over. Hmmm. I wonder what Chelsey did to keep her blocks from falling over.*

Sean: (Looks at Chelsey's blocks.)

Ann: (Pauses for a moment.) *It looks like Chelsey put her big blocks on the bottom of her tower. I wonder what would happen if you put the big blocks on the bottom of your tower.*

Sean: (Shakes his head.)

Ann: *You don't think it would stay up?*

Sean: *No. 'Cause I need those blocks.* (Points to Chelsey's blocks.)

Ann: *Should we go ask Chelsey if she'd let you use some of her blocks?*

Sean: *Yeah.*

Ask questions sparingly

Several years ago, a woman attending a High/Scope training shared a story with her training group. She explained that the two kindergarten teachers from her school were conducting their annual spring screening. A 5-year-old girl who was very excited about entering kindergarten arrived with her mother. In the room where the screening was taking place, one of the teachers asked the little girl a series of standard screening questions, such as "What color is this?" "What shape is this?" "Do you know how many cubes there are?" "What letter is this?" The little girl answered all of the questions correctly, and the teachers were very pleased with her readiness for kindergarten. When the child left the screening with her mother she said, "You know, Mommy, I don't think I want to come to this school anymore. The teachers here don't know anything!"

Many teachers feel that questioning children is a good way to find out what they know about various things. However, you can learn a wealth of information from children in a more relaxed and natural way by simply observing and listening to them, as well as by practicing other strategies mentioned in this chapter. Children more readily offer information when *they* are able to choose the topic—generally one that is important to them at that particular moment—than when they are "drilled" by adults on a subject that is not connected to what children are involved in at the time.

Think for a moment about the way you converse with other adults. Generally the questions you ask are sincere and are asked because you want information about a particular subject that you do not already possess ("What time should we meet you?" "How did your husband react when you gave him his birthday gift?" "What do you plan to do on your vacation?") Questions addressed to young children should be asked for the same reason— to gain more information about a subject or to find out more about what a child is thinking or doing. The next time you start to ask a child a question, consider whether or not you already know the answer. If you do, you may want to rethink your question and consider choosing a different interaction strategy. You might be surprised by how often you ask children unnecessary questions!

The idea of sharing control with children in work-time activities and conversations has been discussed at great length in this chapter. When you ask questions of children, whether open-ended or closed, it generally puts *you* rather than the children in control of the conversation. Take a look at the way the adults direct the conversation in the next two examples.

Child: (In the art area stringing dried, colored pasta to make a necklace.)

Adult: (Enters the art area and sits down by the child.)

Child: *I'm making a beautiful necklace to wear.*

Adult: *What colors are you putting on your necklace?*

Child: *Red and yellow and purple and pink.*

Adult: *How many pieces of pasta do you have on there so far?*

Child: (Counts the pasta.) *Seven.*

Adult: *What shape is the pasta you're using?*

Child: *Circles.*

Child: (Standing at the sand table, slowly adding a bucket of water to the sand. He mixes and squeezes it with his hands.)

Adult: (Pulls up a child-sized chair and sits next to the child. Puts her hands in the sand and mixes it as he is doing.)

Child: *I'm getting it wet and mixin' it all up.*

Adult: *This reminds me of the beach. Have you ever been to the beach before?*

Child: *Yeah. That's where my grandma and grandpa live.*

Adult: *What types of things do you see at the beach?*

Child: *Lots of shells, and sometimes we see guys catching fish.*

Adult: *Have you ever seen a crab on the sand?*

Child: *Nope.*

Adult: *What do you do at the beach?*

Child: *We . . . we build sand castles and play in the water on our Boogie boards.*

In the first example, the adult was very much in control of the conversation. She asked several closed questions, to which there was only one correct answer. In the second example, the adult asked questions that were more open-ended in order to gain information about the child's beach experience. These questions stimulated more conversation and gave the child more freedom to talk about his experiences than the questions in the first example, so they were more appropriate. However, the adult was still in control of the topic, and the child didn't have much opportunity to speak about what was really on his mind (which was certainly not the beach, as you'll see in a moment).

Rather than control conversations by asking children unnecessary and irrelevant questions, you can **acknowledge what children say** and **make contributions** or comments to the conversation. These strategies enable children to stay in control of the conversation and their activity, demonstrate that adults are sincerely interested in what children are saying, and encourage children to expand or extend the conversation. Let's take another look at the two scenarios described earlier, this time as they might have occurred if the adults had used acknowledgments, contributions, and comments as support strategies instead of asking a lot of questions.

Child: (In the art area stringing pasta to make a necklace.)

Adult: (Enters the art area and sits down by the child.)

Child: *I'm making a beautiful necklace to wear.*

Adult: *Oh, a necklace.*

Child: *Yep. I'm going to wear it to my party.*

Adult: *You're having a party?*

Child: *Yeah, my birthday party. I'm going bowling.*

Adult: *It's been a long time since I've gone bowling.*

Child: *My daddy goes bowling a lot. Sometimes he brings me with him and sometimes I have to stay home. When I go with him, he lets me roll his ball down the lane.*

Adult: *Those balls are pretty heavy!*

Child: *Yeah, but when I go for my party, I'll get one that's not so heavy.*

Adult: *Oh, I see.*

Child: (Standing at the sand table, slowly adding a bucket of water to the sand. Mixes and squeezes it with his hands.)

Adult: (Pulls up a child-sized chair and sits next to the child. Puts her hands in the sand and mixes it as he is doing.)

Child: *I'm getting it wet and mixin' it all up.*

Adult: *You're mixin' it all up with your hands.*

Child: *Yep, and when I'm finished mixin' it up, I'm going to make it all smooth.*

Adult: *Hmmm.*

Child: *Then I'm going to make a road.*

Adult: *Oh, a road.*

Child: *Yeah, and over here is where the trucks are going to dump the garbage.*

Adult: *The garbage? I bet that smells bad!*

Child: *Yeah. When my mom and I drive past the city dump we roll up our windows and hold our nose, like this!* (Pinches his nose.)

Adult: (Imitates his actions.) *I've driven past there, too, and I do the same thing!*

Child: *Yeah, 'cause it really stinks!*

Adult: *It sure does!*

Encourage children to problem-solve

When children have the opportunity to freely explore an interesting environment, they will naturally encounter problems and obstacles related to materials (physical problems) and to other children (social conflicts).

Physical problems

Physical problems occur as children experiment with and explore various materials: *How do I put this block on my building without making the rest of the blocks fall down? Hey, the color paint I want isn't here . . . how can I make some purple? I want to move this table over there, but it's really heavy.*

When an obstacle interrupts children's play, many adults either solve the problem for the children or simply ignore it. However, everyday problems are valuable opportunities for children to learn how things work, to see things from different viewpoints, to try new strategies, and to gain confidence in their ability to solve problems themselves. Rather than try to eliminate *all* problems from your classroom (which is neither desirable nor possible), encourage children to work through the obstacles they encounter, offering only as much of your support as they need.

As you observe and interact with children during work time, **watch for children who may be encountering problems.** Many of these children will be able to solve the problems on their own, but others may need some assistance—particularly those who tend to walk away from problem situations, abandon their intended plan because of an unexpected challenge, or appear frustrated by a difficulty. There are several strategies you can use to support these children and encourage them to problem-solve.

Pretend play often presents many opportunities for problem solving—like how to get those capes, hats, and masks to stay on!

It is often difficult for us as adults—who have had more experience with obstacles and who are more efficient at solving problems—to watch children in their sometimes clumsy attempts to work out the problems at hand. We tend to forget how beneficial it is for children to work at overcoming obstacles on their own. Rather than intervene immediately when you see children having difficulty, make a conscious effort to **give children some extra time to try solving the problem themselves.** When you do this, trusting children to succeed on their own, you will be amazed at the creative and inventive solutions children often come up with. In addition, children will learn that they can often find their own solutions rather than always have to rely on adults for assistance.

If you notice that children are becoming frustrated in their efforts to solve a particular problem, **acknowledge their feelings.** Commenting on their frustration and giving them a chance to express themselves may help them to continue to problem-solve rather than give up. Such comments as "It looks like you're having trouble unscrewing that lid, Jordan. It's making you upset" can encourage children to let go of their feelings and focus again on the problem.

You can also **offer children a simple suggestion** for solving their problem. Comments such as these often help point a child toward a possible solution: "I wonder what would happen if you turned that around." "Yesterday you used glue to hold your wood pieces together. I wonder if glue would hold that on your stick better than the tape." Your suggestions can help keep children from becoming so frustrated that they get discouraged and give up altogether.

Another effective strategy is to **refer one child to another for assistance.** Consider the following example.

Jevan: (Comes to the adult, who is with a child in the book area.) *Linda, the printer isn't working. Will you come help me with it?*

Linda: (Looks over at the computer area.) *It looks like Anna's over there. I remember she got the printer to work yesterday. Maybe she could help you.*

Jevan: (Returns to the computer area and approaches Anna.) *Anna, the printer isn't working. Can you fix it for me?*

Anna: (Stops playing at her computer.) *You have to fix it like this.* (Reaches over to the printer and presses a button. The printer realigns and begins printing Jevan's document.) *There. I fixed it.*

By referring children to their peers for help in solving problems, you help them to see that other children have strengths and talents and that they can be valuable resources when a problem arises.

Social conflicts

In addition to the physical problems children often face during work time, social conflicts also occur. Conflicts among children can arise for several reasons:

- **Children want to use the same object at the same time.** For example, two children want to play with the doll that has the pink dress, several children want to play with the new puppet their teacher introduced at greeting time, or two children want to use the microphone on the tape recorder.

- **Children want to use the same space at the same time.** For example, one child wants to build a race car track in the block area while another wants to "mow his lawn" in the same place, or one child wants to cover the art table with shaving cream while another wants to use the same table to look through toy catalogs and write her birthday list.

- **Children want a certain privilege.** For example, one child becomes upset when told it's another child's turn to choose the songs for the day; two children argue over who will be the first in line to go outside; or two children want to pass out the snack but only one is chosen.

- **Children have differing social needs and perceptions.** For example, a child is upset and feeling excluded because her best friend is playing with another child, or several children tell another child that he can't pretend to be the superhero because he is "too little."

Many adults view conflict as an unpleasant experience and would like to prevent it from ever occurring in their classrooms. While it is important to create an environment that eliminates *unnecessary* conflict situations (fighting over the paintbrushes because there are only two of them; pushing and shoving in the block area because it accommodates only three children at a time), differing viewpoints and opposing interests are a natural part of social interaction—even for adults—and offer children a valuable opportunity to engage in problem solving. Children who are able to deal with social conflicts by applying basic conflict resolution techniques will be better equipped to function successfully as adults.

When social conflicts occur, it's natural to consciously or unconsciously take sides with the children who seem to be the "victims" in the situation. This tendency may have its roots in our own conflict experiences as children, when the adults in our lives assessed the situation based on the evidence at hand and then punished or disciplined the guilty party. There is an alternative to dealing with conflict, however, and that is to use a **conflict resolution approach.** This approach consists of six steps that assist children in discussing and resolving social conflicts. These steps are briefly outlined here.*

First, **approach the conflict situation calmly.** As you move toward the children involved in a conflict situation, mentally prepare yourself for a positive outcome rather than think something like "Oh, no, here they go again. This arguing never ends!" Position yourself on the children's physical level and offer your calm, neutral presence. By staying neutral, you convey to children that you will respect all points of view and not judge or punish anyone.

Next, **acknowledge the children's feelings.** When children are emotionally caught up in a conflict situation, it is very important to validate their feelings by acknowledging that children are upset, angry, or sad. When you assure children that you understand and accept their feelings, children can let go of their emotions and begin to think clearly about solutions to the problem.

---

*For further information on the conflict resolution process, see *Educating Young Children: Active Learning Practices for Preschool and Child Care Programs,* by M. Hohmann and D. P. Weikart, 1995; *"You Can't Come to My Birthday Party!" Conflict Mediation With Young Children,* by Betsy Evans, in press; and *Supporting Children in Resolving Conflicts* (video), 1998. All are available from High/Scope Press.

A vital step in helping children resolve conflicts is acknowledging their feelings. Doing so enables them to let go of their feelings and concentrate on brainstorming possible solutions.

The next step is to **gather information** from the children involved in the conflict situation. Encourage children to describe the details of what happened, and listen carefully to each child without forming opinions or judging.

Next, **restate the problem.** This helps clarify the situation for everyone and communicates to children that you are indeed listening and that you understand what has been said. It may be necessary to ask questions to gain more specific information, and it is important to check with the children to make sure that your interpretation of the details are accurate and complete. In restating what children have said, rephrase any harsh language the children use. For example, if a child says "I hate him!" you might say, "You're really angry, Tim. You don't like what he did."

Once the problem is understood, the next step is to **ask for ideas for solutions** and to choose one together. This step involves getting children's input on what they think could be done to solve the problem. Your role is to listen to all of the children's ideas, however unrealistic they might seem, and to encourage children to think through each possible solution and choose one that they can all carry out.

Finally, make sure all children involved are satisfied with the chosen solution, and **be prepared to give follow-up support.** Occasionally, children will need assistance in carrying out their solution. They may not have fully understood the resolution or they may still be carrying some angry or hurt feelings, which could cause further conflicts. Following is an example of how one adult, Bryan, used these six steps to help two children in his classroom solve their problem.

Jenna is seated in the book area on the class's new bean bag chair, reading *The Runaway Bunny*. She gets up to get a different book, and while she is away Kaitlyn takes her place in the bean bag chair to give her "baby" a bottle. When Jenna returns with a new book, she tells Kaitlyn to move out of her chair. When Kaitlyn doesn't move, Jenna takes Kaitlyn's baby doll and throws it on the ground. Kaitlyn begins to cry, attracting Bryan's attention. He moves to the book area and kneels on the floor, positioning himself between the two girls.

Bryan: *Kaitlyn, you seem really upset right now.*

Kaitlyn: (Moves toward Bryan and buries her head in his chest, sobbing.)

Bryan: *You're really sad!*

Jenna: *She was sitting in my chair, and I wasn't done with it yet!*

Kaitlyn: (Still sobbing.) *I . . . I . . . I didn't know you were coming back.*

Bryan: *You two are both pretty upset, aren't you?* (Both girls nod their heads.) *Jenna, can you tell me what happened here?*

Jenna: *I was in the chair first. I went to get a new book and when I came back she was in my chair!*

Kaitlyn: (Stops crying and takes a deep breath.) *I . . . I needed to feed my baby her bottle. I didn't know she was coming back to the chair.*

Bryan: *So let me see if I understand what happened. Jenna, you were sitting in the chair, you went to get a new book, and when you came back, Kaitlyn was sitting in the chair—*

Kaitlyn: *'Cause I needed to feed my baby.*

Bryan: *—because she needed to feed her baby. But Kaitlyn, you didn't know that Jenna wanted to sit in the chair again. You thought she was finished. Is that right?*

Kaitlyn and Jenna: (Both nod.)

Bryan: *Okay, what do you think we should do to solve this problem?*

Jenna: *She should find somewhere else to feed her baby!*

Kaitlyn: *My baby is really hungry, and I need a good chair to feed her in.*

Bryan: (Remains quiet to let the girls think of some more ideas.)

Kaitlyn: (Quietly.) *My baby likes books. Maybe you can read to her an' I'll give her her bottle.*

Jenna: *Okay, but I want to sit in the chair.*

Kaitlyn: *Maybe . . . maybe we could both fit.*

Jenna: (Thinks this over.) *Okay.*

Bryan: *It sounds like you've come up with a solution. The two of you are going to sit in the chair together, and Jenna's going to read a story to Kaitlyn's baby while Kaitlyn feeds her. Is that okay with both of you?*

Kaitlyn and Jenna: (Both nod.)

Bryan leaves the book area but occasionally glances over to the two girls, making sure the solution they have chosen is working out for both of them.

As children gain more experience resolving conflicts with your support, they will become more skilled at the process. In time they will need less adult assistance and they may even offer to help other children resolve *their* conflicts!

Gather anecdotal notes and observations

As you observe and interact with children throughout work time, you will learn a great deal about the children in your care. Note how children solve problems and social conflicts, how they play, whether their play follows the plan they made at planning time, which children play together and which ones choose to play alone, and which types of activities seem to interest different children. An awareness of High/Scope's key experiences is useful for guiding your observations of

Keep materials handy for jotting down children's words and actions during work time.

children. Often, however, you may become so involved in the hustle and bustle of work time that you later forget the significant events you've observed.

Documenting children's activities and conversations is important for keeping an ongoing record of individual accomplishments and significant events. By recording essential observations, you can share important information with your team member at planning time and accurate anecdotes with parents. You can also use what you learn through documentation to plan activities based on children's interests and to make changes to the learning environment, such as adding materials that would support children's current play or eliminating materials that are no longer being used. Anecdotal notes are also important for completing assessment tools [for example, the High/Scope Child Observation Record (COR)] because they are based on accurate and factual accounts of children's achievements rather than vague recollections or assumptions.

You do not need to, nor could you, document everything every child does. Choose a few children each day to focus on. As you observe and participate with these children in their play, take down short, objective notes of important things they do and say. You can record what's happening in a variety of ways. One of the simplest ways is to jot down observations in a notebook or on file cards or self-stick notes. While you probably won't have time at the moment to write your observations in complete sentences, you can use abbreviations or symbols and several key words that will help you remember the specific event when you meet with your team member at the end of the day. During this time you can elaborate on the observation and rewrite it in sentence form. (See examples of abbreviated observations and complete anecdotal notes at left.)

Other ideas for documenting children's work include recording conversations or play episodes with a tape recorder or a video camera, taking photographs of children's creations, saving children's artwork

---

Sample Observations and Anecdotal Notes

Here are examples of "shorthand" notes jotted down by adults during work time, and the anecdotal notes written from them during team planning time. To save time when jotting down their observations, these adults have identified the children by their symbols.

3/7   WT. AA. □. Easel painting. "Drawed the storm we had last night."

3/7   At work time in the art area, Sam said (referring to his easel painting), "I drawed the storm we had last night."

10/22   WT. MMA. △ and ○. Cymbals & sticks. Sang Spider and Mary Lamb.

10/22   At work time in the music and movement area, Nydia and Diego used the cymbals and rhythm sticks and sang "The Itsy Bitsy Spider" and "Mary Had a Little Lamb."

11/1   WT. HA. ☼. Tutu/slippers. AA bag. Trick or treat. "When I say trick or treat, that means you have to give me something and I'll put it in my bag."

11/1   At work time in the house area, Carrie dressed up in the pink tutu and ballet slippers. She found a bag from the art area and went around the room saying "Trick or treat! When I say 'trick or treat' that means you have to give me something and I'll put it in my bag."

and writing samples, and (especially if children don't want to part with their work) making photocopies of their artwork or writing. (For more discussion on documenting your observations, see pp. 118–120.) Once you create a documentation system that is effective for your team, and you consistently take the time to record your observations of children during work time and the rest of the daily routine, you will see that the benefits are well worth the effort.

When Work Time Is Over: How to Support Children at Cleanup Time

As mentioned at the beginning of this chapter, a brief (10–15-minute) cleanup time immediately follows work time. This segment of the daily routine helps children make the transition from work time to recall time. Cleanup time should be a relaxed and enjoyable part of the daily routine; however, many of us view it as a chaotic and stressful time, often becoming upset over a messy classroom and uncooperative children. This section will offer several suggestions for making cleanup a little less harried and hectic. Keep in mind, however, that your attitude toward cleanup time is very important and will be sensed by the children. If you look at it as a fun and enjoyable part of the daily routine, so will the children. On the other hand, if you perceive cleanup time as a necessary, tiresome chore and become directive and authoritative with children rather than relaxed and supportive, the children will dislike it as well.

Give children advance warning that work time will be ending

Several minutes before it's time to clean up, signal the children that work time will be ending shortly. Alerting the children in this way gives them time to finish what they are doing and prepare for the upcoming transition to recall time. There are many ways to let children know that work time is almost over, including singing a song, ringing a bell or sounding another musical instrument, flipping the lights off and on, or simply telling the children that soon it will be time to clean up. Some adults choose a combination of the strategies mentioned. Consider the following example.

Laura and Nadine have been working with a group of preschoolers for several months. They have found that in order to prepare all of the children for the transition, it's necessary to give them several warnings that work time is almost over. At the beginning of the school year the teachers sang a song that repeated "Cleanup time is almost here," but they found that several of the children were so involved in their activities that they were not hearing or paying attention to the signal. After several instances in which these children were not ready to end their work-time activities, Laura and Nadine decided that they needed to do more to alert the children that cleanup time was approaching. They continued to sing their song but turned the lights off and on several times as well. Then they would give individual reminders to the children who needed them, telling them that they would have to stop playing very soon. While doing this, the adults talked to the children about which materials they would put away first or where they would put certain items when it was cleanup time. After a time of making this extra effort, Laura and Nadine found that the children were better able to make the transition into cleanup and recall.

Part of the reason for telling children ahead of time that it is almost time to clean up is to give them a chance to figure out when and how to continue their play that is not complete—whether in the next few minutes, later on in the day, when they go home, or the next day when they return to school. If they want to continue working on an activity the next day, for example, they must think of a way to keep the materials they were using together and in a safe place. You can encourage children to solve this type of problem, like the adult in the following example with 5-year-old Lacy.

Colleen: (Approaches Lacy, who is in the art area using craft sticks, glue, pieces of cardboard, yarn, and paint.) *Did you hear the cleanup song, Lacy?*

Lacy: *Yes, but I'm not finished making my Barbie house.*

Colleen: *Oh, you're not finished with it yet. What more do you have to do?*

Lacy: *I still have to put the yarn on it over here and here, and I haven't had time to paint it, either.*

Colleen: *So you still need to put yarn on it and paint it, too. If you put it away now, when do you think you could work on it again?*

Lacy: (Thinks for a moment.) *I could do it the next day when I come to school.*

Colleen: *I bet the glue that you put on it today will be dry by then.*

Lacy: (Thinks again, looking at her project.) *I don't want the kids that come to school after us to mess it up.*

Colleen: *What can we do so that the kids don't mess it up?*

Lacy: (Looks around the classroom.) *Put it on that shelf up there.* (Points to a high shelf that the adults use for storing materials, such as the first-aid kit, dishwashing detergent, etc.)

Colleen: *You think if we put your Barbie house up on that high shelf the children in the afternoon class won't be able to touch it?*

Lacy: *Yeah. Could you put this up there, too? There's not much left, and I need it.* (Shows the adult the yarn she was using.)

Colleen: *You want me to keep the yarn up there, too? Okay. I bet no one but teachers will be able to reach your Barbie house.* (Picks up Lacy's artwork and puts it on the shelf.) *Tomorrow when you want to work on it again, let me know and I'll get it down for you.*

Organize and label materials and containers to enable children to easily put items away

If there is no consistent, identifiable way materials are stored, children may simply guess where items go at cleanup time or throw them haphazardly on shelves or tables. To minimize confusion and mess, provide accessible storage areas and containers that are clearly labeled. Labels can be the object itself (a Duplo block, a dinosaur counter) or a tracing, drawing, catalog picture, box-top picture, or photograph of the item inside, perhaps accompanied by the word for the item. In the following example, note how teachers Pam and Juanita have made it easier for children to know where materials go, encouraging them to help clean up after work time.

> Danny and Roberto have been playing with Duplo blocks, Tinkertoys, and plastic dinosaur counters in the toy area. Pam and Juanita have just signaled the end of work time by flipping the lights off and on, and the boys start taking apart their "spaceship," tossing the pieces on the floor. They reach for three plastic containers, which are labeled with a picture of the Tinkertoys, a drawing of the Duplo blocks, and an actual dinosaur counter, and begin sorting the three types of toys and placing them in the appropriate bins.
>
> Jessie is in the house area, where she has been using the dishes, silverware, and pots and pans. She has just finished putting the dishes and silverware away and reaches for the first pot. Pam and Juanita have drawn outlines of the pots and pans in order of size on the back of a shelving unit to indicate where they belong. Jessie holds the medium-sized pot near the (first) small outline, realizes that it isn't the same size, and moves it to the medium outline. She picks up the large pan and places it on the large outline, then puts the small pan over the small outline.

Support children's problem-solving skills

As children bring their activities to an end, they may run into a variety of obstacles, from effectively using cleaning materials (a broom, dustpan, sponge) to wanting to put away the same toy another child does. Treat these difficulties as you would if they occurred at any other time of the day—by encouraging children to work through them. Take a look at the opportunities these children have to engage in problem solving in Pam and Juanita's classroom.

Shakira is at the art table, using a sponge to wipe off drops of paint from the table and floor. She wets the sponge at the nearby sink and carries it over to the table. Pam points out that the sponge is dripping water on the floor. Shakira looks at the floor, then at the sponge in her hand, and finally at Pam. Pam says, "I wonder what you could use to wipe up the water drops?" Shakira takes the sponge back to the sink and gets some paper towels to dry the floor. Then she squeezes out the sponge and successfully carries it over to the table without dripping any more water.

Vicki and Merritt have been working side by side at the bean table. When cleanup time comes, Juanita comments to the girls that there are a lot of beans all over the floor. They both run for the dustpan and broom to clean up the mess. When Merritt grabs them first, Vicki begins to cry, saying that she wanted to sweep up the beans. Merritt ignores her and attempts to use the broom and dustpan herself. Juanita remarks that it looks like Merritt is having trouble working the broom and dustpan alone and that it sounds like Vicki is upset about not being able to help. Merritt considers this and finally suggests that Vicki hold the dustpan while she sweeps, and then she'll hold the dustpan while Vicki sweeps. Vicki stops crying and asks "You're my friend, right?" Merritt gives her a hug and says yes.

Make cleanup time fun and enjoyable

While some children actually enjoy washing off the paintbrushes at the sink and watching the different colors of paint swirl down the drain, sorting the plastic kitty counters from the dinosaur counters, or meticulously arranging the stuffed animals along the couch in the book area, other children are not as enthusiastic about cleanup time. Some children want to continue what they have been doing; others have finished their activity and are anxious to move on to the next part of the day. Some children become rambunctious or hide under tables or in small corners when told it is time to clean up. One teacher voiced her frustration with a 3-year-old boy who, instead of putting materials away, would consistently begin exploring and playing with anything she gave him to put away.

One way to make cleanup time more enjoyable for everyone is to create put-away games or incorporate cleanup into children's ongoing play in a fun way. For example, a child who is pushing a wooden dump truck around the classroom instead of helping the other children clean up may be willing to drive the necklaces over to the house area to put them away. If a child is busy pretending to be a dog, say something like "Come here, doggy. I've got a scarf for you to put away in the movement area." The child might put the scarf around his neck and crawl over to the shelf where the scarf belongs. Another child might prefer to toss the beanbags in their storage basket rather than simply place them in it. Such strategies will make cleaning up seem like less of a chore and will encourage reluctant children to participate in a more productive way. (See the box at right for more ideas for cleanup games.)

Still, there may be some children who don't want to clean up no matter what kinds of games you introduce to make the task more enjoyable. Instead of becoming angry or frustrated when this happens, try to remain calm and optimistic about the situation. Using the problem-solving process (see pp. 100–101) with individual children or the group may help those who are having difficulty focusing at cleanup time. The following suggestion, joining children in the cleanup process, may also be helpful in this situation.

> ### Ready, Set . . . Clean Up!
>
> Here are some more ideas for making cleanup time fun and motivating for children. Use your imagination to come up with additional games!
>
> **Musical cleanup:** Play music (from a CD, tape, or record) while the children are cleaning up the classroom. When you stop the music, have the children move to a new interest area of their choice and clean up there. *Variation:* While you play the music, the children move however they choose from interest area to interest area. When you stop the music, have the children clean up the interest area they are in at that point.
>
> **Choose a picture:** Have picture cards available of the different materials in your classroom. Let children choose a card, and encourage them to find the item that matches the card and put it away. (See Chapter 7, p. 223, "Pictures.")
>
> **Magic wand:** Have children point a "magic wand" to indicate the area they would like to help clean.
>
> **What color are you?** Have children go to an interest area to clean based on the color they are wearing: "If you're wearing red, clean up in the art area today." Or use another personal characteristic, such as a letter in a child's name.
>
> **Sorting:** Ask children to put away all the blue things, big things, round things, etc.
>
> **Tool time:** Give children kitchen tongs and encourage them to pick up the toys and put them away using the tongs. Or, give children sand shovels to scoop up the toys.

Become a partner with children during cleanup

A large mess can seem overwhelming to children, and you can make the task of picking it up more manageable by assisting in the process. Cleaning up *with* the children, rather than simply telling them what to put away, will communicate to the children that you are their partner not only during their play but also at cleanup time. Consider the following example.

> Several children in one classroom have created a "garbage dump" in the block area. One child, Megan, is responsible for answering the telephone, taking orders from "garbage customers," writing the orders on a piece of paper, then giving the orders to the two boys "driving" the trucks. The "drivers" are responsible for following the orders given to them, "driving" large wooden trucks from the block area to different interest areas (specified on their orders) and bringing back "garbage," such as play food, scissors, manipulative toys, cotton balls, musical instruments, and dress-up clothes.
>
> The adult, Katrine, has been supporting the children in this play, and as the pile of classroom materials grow larger, she mentions several times that there will be many things to put away at cleanup time. She asks individual children which materials they will put away when it is time to clean up. Megan indicates that she will put away the instruments and the scissors, but the other children, Donovan and Kamil, are so involved in their play that they are not interested in planning for cleanup time. When work time ends, Katrine stays with the children in the block area to assist them in putting away the large pile of materials. Although Megan gets started immediately, Donovan simply walks around the pile, looking at it. Kamil walks away from the block area and begins playing with materials from the toy area. Katrine realizes that it might be easier for the children to manage the large pile if she helps them sort out the materials in it. She asks Donovan if he would like to put away the cotton balls or the beads, then goes to the toy area to ask Kamil if he wants to put away the food or the clothes. Once they make their choice Katrine asks them what they want *her* to pick up, and she starts putting away the specified materials from the pile.

Realize that there will be days when not all the materials will get put away

Keep in mind that even after being cleaned up, the interest areas may not look like they did before the children played in them. There may be smears left on the table, lids may be on the wrong markers, and some of the blocks may not have made it back to the appropriate shelves. Rather than follow children around at cleanup fixing what they've left undone, wait until after they depart for the day before you do a final cleanup of the interest areas.

On days when the children seem to be dragging their heels at cleanup time, avoid telling them that they cannot go outside or have large-group time (or whatever the next activity is) until they finish cleaning up. This makes cleanup seem like a chore or punishment and other activities like a reward. However, it may be appropriate to call children's attention to the fact that, for instance, the class is not able to start large-group time yet because the floor area where this takes place is still full of toys from work time. This may be enough of a motivation for them to finish cleaning up and move on.

If you notice that for some reason the children are taking an extremely long time to clean up, you may want to simply end cleanup and begin recall time. If the cleanup process takes too long, children will grow tired of putting things away, and you will probably become frustrated with the children and the situation. Rather than let this happen, allow yourself to bring cleanup time to a close even if some materials remain out of place. The remaining materials may even serve as valuable reminders to children at recall time for that day, and they can be put away later.

If children are routinely not cleaning up in a timely fashion, you have a perfect opportunity for some group problem solving. Use the message board to introduce the issue, and ask children for ideas on what to do about it. This may be particularly effective if children have had less time for outdoor time or large-group activities because cleanup time is taking longer than usual.

Ever have work times like this?! You can help children by partnering with them in the cleanup effort, sorting items, creating games—and keeping your sense of humor!

What About . . . ? Commonly Asked Questions About Work Time and Cleanup Time

Does each child have to go to each interest area?

Children are not required to go to each interest area in High/Scope classrooms and centers. In order to understand why, let's use an example that most adults can easily relate to. When shopping at a mall, very few people, if any, go into every store available to them. The reason for this is that not every store interests every person. For example, you might love spending time in a bookstore but have no desire to go to a clothing store. Another person might enjoy a sporting goods store but wouldn't have any interest in a store that sells craft items. Adults have different interests, and when they have a choice of stores, they will likely choose those that cater to their interests or needs. If you were told that you must go to a store that didn't interest you, you might look around to see what items were available, but after a short time you would probably become bored and want to leave.

This example can be applied to a preschooler during work time. Like adults, preschoolers have varying interests. One child might enjoy creating something in the art area but have little interest in the block area. Another child might be very interested in exploring the manipulatives in the toy area but have no inclination to spend time at the computer. If we make children go to interest areas that don't appeal to them, the children will probably look around to see what materials are available there, take some materials off the shelf and use them halfheartedly, then become bored and disinterested. Following are some additional reasons why children are not forced to go to each interest area in the classroom.

Plan-do-review is child-initiated rather than controlled by adults. By telling children which interest areas they must go to, or by making them spend time in all of the areas, you defeat the purpose of planning time. Remember, the plan-do-review sequence is a time in which children choose their own activities, follow through with their plans, and later reflect on their actions. If you direct the children where to go or what to do, *you* rather then children are in control of their actions.

Children's play is more purposeful when they are given choices. As discussed earlier, children's play is more purposeful and complex when they are able to carry out activities of their own choosing. The more experience children have in making plans and following through with them, the more they will stay involved in an activity and see it through until it is complete. If you direct children to play in an area that does not interest them, their play is likely to be simple and aimless rather than complex and purposeful.

You can introduce other materials and interest areas during other parts of the daily routine. For example, if you notice a child who never goes into the toy area and you feel that the child would benefit from and enjoy certain materials in that area, you could introduce the materials during a small-group-time activity.

Keep in mind that children's interests will gradually change over a period of time. Generally, children eventually notice and choose interest areas and materials that they previously never explored on their own.

Is there a time limit given to children in the interest areas?

During the 45–60-minute work-time period, children are able to move freely from one interest area to another without restrictions on how long they can or must play in each area. Again, let's use the example of adults shopping in a mall. Imagine yourself in your favorite clothing store. You've found some terrific bargains, and the clothes you've tried on fit perfectly. You've just exited the dressing room, ready to purchase your new clothes, when the store manager tells you your time is up. You must leave right away, and you don't have time to purchase the clothing you've chosen. Chances are you'd be annoyed that you weren't able to finish your shopping spree. You'd also probably feel frustrated that you didn't have any control over the situation and that you were told you had to leave a place and an activity you enjoyed.

Likewise, children can become upset and frustrated if you control the amount of time they spend in each interest area. Depending on their individual plans, children may stay in one interest area for the entire work time or may spend brief periods of time in several different areas. If a time limit is enforced, children may not be able to fully complete their intended plan, or they may have completed their plan and be ready to move to another area before their time is up. As with making children go to each interest area, setting time limits puts adults in control of children's activities.

Do you limit the number of children in the interest areas?

No. There are several reasons for *not* limiting the number of children who can play in each interest area.

Work time is about children carrying out their plans, not adults controlling traffic flow. If the interest areas in a classroom have limited available space, there is a possibility that after children have made their plans the area they planned to go to is "closed." Consider the following examples.

Planning experience: Children are given a piece of paper with the question "What's your plan for work time today?" written on it. Children are encouraged to draw a picture of what they want to do during work time, then the adult, Joy, writes down the words the children dictate.

Joy: *What's your plan for today, Nita?*

Nita: (Shows Joy her paper. She has drawn a very detailed picture of a building with animals and fences around it.) *I'm gonna go to the block area with Orlando. We're gonna make a farm with the blocks, and we're gonna make a barn and places for the animals to sleep with the fences. Every day the farmer has to go outside and take care of his animals, like feed them and make sure they got enough water and stuff. When it rains, he brings the animals into his barn so they don't get wet and dirty.* (She leaves the planning table, excited about her plan and ready to get started on building her farm. When she gets to the block area, all of the hooks where the children must hang their planning tags are full. She returns to the planning group to speak to Joy.) *No more room at the block area.*

Joy: *Oh, that area is full? Well, maybe you can build your farm another day. Where else would you like to play today?*

Planning experience: Patricia has drawn the interest area signs on small self-stick notes. A small train track has been set up in a figure-eight pattern at the planning table, and the sticky notes have been placed around the track. Children take turns pushing the train around the track and stopping it at the interest area sign where they plan to play.

Madison: (Moves the train around the track and stops next to the house area sign.) *I want to dress up in the clothes at the house area.*

Patricia: *There isn't any room at the house area anymore. Where else would you like to go?*

Madison: (Moves the train to the art area sign and looks at Patricia.)

Patricia: *It looks like that area is full, too.*

Madison: (Moves the train to the computer area sign.)

Patricia: *I think all of the computers are taken, but it looks like there's room for you to play in the book area.*

Madison: (Leaves the planning table and slowly moves toward the book area.)

In both of these examples, the children had a clear idea of what they wanted to do. Because the adults had limited the number of children who could play in each interest area, the children were not able to carry out what they had originally planned to do. The adults became focused on monitoring the interest areas and on managing the flow of children rather than on listening to, supporting, and helping extend the children's plans.

Limiting the number of children in an interest area affects children's planning and work-time behavior. When children realize that the interest areas they want to go to may be full by the time they get there, planning time essentially becomes a race to see who can plan the fastest in order to get to a desired area before it becomes full. Instead of thinking carefully about how they're going to carry out their plan and discussing this in a relaxed way with the group, children feel rushed and anxious about getting to the area where they want to play. Unnecessary conflicts can occur when, for example, two children arrive at an interest area to claim the last available spot, or when a child who wants to play with another child tries to save a place in the interest area for that friend.

Crowded interest areas provide an opportunity for children to problem-solve. If several children are crowded into an interest area, they may be very motivated to figure out a solution. They may decide to move the materials they wanted to use from that area into another area, or they might choose to come back when it's not so crowded. They may even decide to move some of the materials or furniture around to create more room. However children choose to solve the problem, working it out themselves enables them to stay in control of the situation. This is preferable to having an adult decide that "There's no more room for you. You'll have to go to another area." Children will generally be much more satisfied with a solution they choose themselves.

If the problem of overcrowding is ongoing and troublesome, take a look at your interest areas. Are they too small? too close together? Are there several that children rarely visit, leaving only a few popular and crowded areas? You may need to consider rearranging your learning environment in order to create larger and more spacious interest areas. If you have a small classroom, try limiting the number of interest areas to four basic areas, such as the house, block, art, and toy areas. This does not mean that you need to eliminate materials found in the book, writing, music, or other areas; simply incorporate those materials into one of the four basic areas. By decreasing the number of interest areas, you can create play spaces that accommodate larger groups of children safely and more comfortably. Be aware of which interest areas are most popular with your children, and make those areas the largest. Of course, as children's interests change throughout the school year, you can revise the layout of your classroom accordingly.*

If my role during work time is to move around the room and support children's play, when am I supposed to lead my art projects?

During work time all the activities are initiated by the children. Therefore, adult-led activities and projects are not appropriate. Instead, your role is to stock each interest area with a variety of interesting and appropriate materials that children can freely choose from to carry out their plans. Then during

*For more information regarding setting up the learning environment, see *Educating Young Children: Active Learning Practices for Preschool and Child Care Programs*, by M. Hohmann and D. P. Weikart, 1995; and *Getting Started: Materials and Equipment for Active Learning Preschools*, by N. Vogel, 1997. Both are available from High/Scope Press.

work time, you can follow children's leads, participate as a partner in their play, and introduce new ideas based on their chosen activities. If there are a variety of art materials readily and consistently available to children, they can use them to create their own artwork if they wish.

If there are specific materials or experiences you would like to offer children (for example, a new material or one they don't often play with at work time, or a key experience you have not observed children engaging in very often), there are opportunities to do so during other parts of the daily routine, such as small-group time and large-group time. Even during these times, however, it is important to provide open-ended materials and activities that will interest children and to allow them to use the materials as they wish rather than give them instructions for completing a particular project. For instance, instead of telling children that they are going to use collage materials to make a teddy bear like your model, set out the collage materials and say, "I wonder what you can do with these today." As the children use the materials you've provided in ways that are meaningful to them, you can support their individual choices by using a variety of support strategies, such as imitating what they are doing, commenting on their actions, and extending their play.

Each day during work time, conflicts occur at the easel. Only two children can use it at one time, but there are usually about five children who want to. Do you have any suggestions?

An obvious solution is to purchase another easel, but budget or space restrictions may make this impractical for you. There are many other possibilities for dealing with this situation. Try taping easel paper to an empty wall or placing it on a table for the children to paint on. They may not be as interested in the easel as they are the process of painting. You may also want to provide a variety of materials for the children to paint in addition to paper, such as boxes, cardboard tubes, or pieces of wood. You could introduce these materials during small-group time and then add them to the art area. You might be able to use the back of a storage cabinet or toy shelf as a second easel. Another possibility may be to move the easel you have outside and offer easel painting as a choice for outdoor time. There are easels that are designed to be hung from a fence, but if this does not fit your budget, pieces of flat cardboard can be attached to a fence with clothespins.

Like any other issue that might arise in your classroom, this one could present an opportunity for children to engage in problem solving. You might wish to discuss the problem as a large group before work time or on an individual basis whenever it comes up, allowing the children to offer possible solutions to the problem. Remember to stay open to children's ideas. They may come up with solutions that you never would have thought of, and they will benefit from working with one another to solve the problem.

I don't have time to play with children during work time. I'm too busy hanging up their easel paintings, filling the water table, turning on the computer, and getting materials out of my cupboard for them to use. Before I know it, work time is over. How do you find the time to be supportive and interact with the children?!

Work time does tend to be a busy time of the day in High/Scope classrooms and centers. However, if you find that your time is being spent on trivial tasks (such as those you mentioned) rather than on playing with and supporting children, observing them, helping resolve conflicts, and taking anecdotal notes, you need to make some changes. Here are some suggestions.

Prepare as much as possible before the children arrive. Daily chores, such as filling the water table, replenishing paint containers, and preparing snack and small-group or large-group materials, can usually be completed before the children arrive or after they have departed on the previous day. Tasks such as these usually don't take very long to complete and are much easier to do when you're not trying to support children in carrying out their plans. Perhaps you have parent volunteers or student helpers who would enjoy helping you prepare for the day before the children arrive.

Create a learning environment that promotes children's independence. Arranging the environment so that children can do things independently is another way to free yourself from time-consuming responsibilities during work time. Materials should be easily accessible to children. For example, place materials that children will use on low, open shelves in containers that

Set up your environment to enable children to be as independent as possible. For instance, have clips and a drying rack or pins and a low bulletin board for children to hang up their own drawings and paintings.

are clearly labeled rather than in closed cupboards or on high shelves, where only adults have access to them. Find a way for children to hang up their finished artwork themselves, perhaps on a low drying rack specifically designed for this purpose or clipped to a low clothesline with clothespins. Encourage the children to try doing these types of tasks on their own or to ask other children for assistance. Be prepared to offer support if they do need your help, however. By taking the time to show children how to complete these tasks and trusting that they will be capable of doing them, you will be free to focus on supporting children's activities during work time. Learning to do things on their own will also keep children from being dependent on you, and they will see themselves and one another as capable contributors to the classroom.

At work time, I'm spending so much time writing anecdotes that I don't feel I have enough time to play with the children anymore.

Keep in mind that you don't have to write long, elaborate notes, nor do you need to write something about each child each day. Your anecdotes should be short—a few sentences at most—and include only unique or significant information. For instance, if Tony ties both his shoelaces for the first time one day but is only able to tie one the next, record only the first accomplishment. Here are some more suggestions for making the task of taking notes more manageable.

Use shortcuts when writing anecdotes. To save time when taking notes on children's activities, abbreviate long words and names. For example, write *TA* for *toy area,* *AA* for *art area,* *WT* for *work time,* and *CUT* for *cleanup time.* If the children in your classroom have symbols they use to recognize their own and other children's names, you can use these symbols to indicate the children in your anecdotes rather than write out their names. For example, when writing anecdotes about Christopher, who has a rather long name, his teachers draw his symbol, a square.

Another anecdote timesaver is to write down just enough information to help you remember the incident until you can take the time to rewrite the anecdote in a little more detail during your daily team planning time. If you choose to do this, however, be sure to rewrite the anecdote as soon as possible, while the episode is still fresh in your memory; otherwise you may forget significant details.

Take photographs and videotapes of children. In addition to collecting written anecdotes during work time, consider taking photographs of children engaged in their activities or setting up a video camera to record the children at play. This is a particularly effective way to document detailed play that children are involved in, such as a dramatic play episode, or a complex project that can't be preserved, such as a block structure. After the children have gone for the day, take time to review the documentation you collected with your team members, and write some corresponding anecdotal notes.

Keep children's artwork and writing samples. Save some samples of children's artwork and writing that they have completed during work time. Add them to the children's portfolios to document their progress throughout the school year. These samples can be shared with parents when you meet with them to discuss their children's progress. If children don't want to part with their creations, make a photocopy of their work for yourself and let the children keep the original.

Take anecdotes during other parts of the daily routine. Because so many of the key experiences are evident during work time, many adults feel that this is the best time to collect anecdotal notes. While work time does offer a perfect opportunity to observe the children involved in a wide variety of important experiences, it is not the only time in which you can gain noteworthy information about the children. You can collect anecdotal notes at any time from children's arrival at school until their departure, including transition times, meal or snack time, small- and large-group time, and outside time.

Collect anecdotes steadily over an extended period of time. One reason for collecting anecdotal notes is to aid in child assessment, which usually occurs several times throughout the school year. Some adults delay observing children and collecting anecdotal notes until right before the scheduled time to complete the assessment tool. During those few weeks, an anecdotal-note-taking frenzy occurs as adults frantically try to collect all of the documentation needed to complete their assessment tool accurately. During this time they may find themselves too busy to interact with the children.

To prevent a situation like this from happening to you, begin writing anecdotal notes during the first week of school and continue to write a few each day after that. Spreading the note-taking process over a period of time, and frequently checking to make sure your notes cover all the areas you'll need for a complete assessment, will permit you to focus your attention at work time on supporting the children.

Make collecting anecdotes a team effort. The responsibility of observing children and taking anecdotal notes should not rest solely with one adult in the classroom. Have your teammate and any other adults who are familiar with or have frequent interactions with the children participate in the note-taking process if they understand it and are comfortable with it. These can include co-teachers, teacher assistants, parents, student teachers, therapists, social workers, and volunteers. Having all team members assist with collecting anecdotes will result in a greater number of notes and will ease the burden of writing from your shoulders. Another reason it is helpful to have more than one adult observing the children is that adults with different backgrounds and areas of expertise often focus their attention on the same play episode in different ways. For example, therapists may be tuned in to children's speech and language, movement, or self-help skills; social workers may focus on children's interactions with each other; and teachers and teacher assistants may be more aware of how children are engaging in the key experiences as they play. You will gain different insights into children's behavior by having different adults observe and take notes.

When conflicts among children come up during work time, I don't have time to do the problem-solving steps. They take too long, and the other children need me.

When you first introduce children to the conflict resolution process, you may spend a great deal of your time walking them through the problem-solving steps. As children become more familiar with the process, however, the amount of time you need to spend assisting the children will likely decrease. There may even be times when children problem-solve together without your assistance. Here are some suggestions for making the process go more smoothly.

Rely on other team members. In most early childhood classrooms there is usually more than one adult interacting with the children. Generally when one team member is involved in problem solving with some of the children, the other is able to support the remaining children while they play during work time. Often team members instinctively develop a communication system, such as a look, gesture, or signal, to let each other know when they need assistance or support. You and your team member may need to use such a communication system when one of you is engaged in a conflict situation. For instance, if you are involved in a lengthy conflict resolution process and notice out of the corner of your eye another child about to have a "total body experience" with the finger paint in the art area, you might catch the attention of your team member and gesture toward the child in the art area. Your team member would understand that she is needed to assist that child while you finish helping the other child problem-solve. If a communication system doesn't naturally occur between you and your teaching partner, you may want to develop one during your daily team planning time.

Refer children who need assistance to another child. If you are helping children solve a problem and another child needs your assistance with something, try referring him or her to another child for help. This support strategy was described previously and communicates to children that their peers can be useful resources when an adult is busy helping others solve a problem. As children come to view adults' involvement in conflict resolution as merely another part of work time, they may eventually learn to automatically seek one another's assistance when an adult is not available.

Remind yourself why problem solving is important. If you become frustrated with the amount of time you're spending supporting the children in resolving social conflicts, you may need to remind yourself that the time you're investing now will pay off in the long run. By supporting the children in the conflict resolution process, you're acknowledging their feelings, encouraging them to talk to one another rather than use physical force, helping them see things from different points of view, and teaching them to work together to come up with a solution to their problems and conflicts. Consistently supporting the children this way will not only benefit them now but will also give them a framework for dealing with conflict in socially acceptable and productive ways as they become older.

During work time, should each teacher focus only on the children in her planning and recall group?

No. Work time—as well as large-group time, outdoor time, and transition times—offers you an excellent opportunity to interact with all the children in your classroom rather than just those children in your planning and recall group. Children also benefit from spending time with all the adults in the classroom during work time, since this enables them to form relationships with adults other than those they meet with during planning and recall.

You do need to be aware of the activities the children in your planning and recall group are involved in during work time. During recall you will be discussing the children's work-time experiences, and you will be better able to support them if you participated in their play or were at least aware of the activities they were engaged in during work time.

The video we saw in training says work time should be 50 minutes, but the children in my classroom always want to play longer. How do I fit in all the other parts of the routine yet have a longer work time?

High/Scope recommends allotting 45–60 minutes for work time because this seems to be an appropriate amount of time for most preschoolers. Any greater amount of time may cause children to become bored, which could lead to chaotic or less purposeful play. If the children in your classroom are still *actively* involved in carrying out their plans after 50 minutes of work time, you could extend your work time to 55 or 60 minutes. (You may be able to make up the extra 5 or 10 minutes by eliminating unnecessary transitions or shaving a few minutes off a few other parts of your daily routine.) While some of the older children in your classroom may seem to be highly involved in their activities after 60 minutes, other children may not be ready for such a lengthy work time.

Also worth mentioning is the fact that the other components of the daily routine offer many opportunities for children to engage in active learning and the key experiences, and should not be cut short or eliminated for the sake of a longer work time. (Refer to Chapter 1 for more suggestions on allotting time for each component of the daily routine.) If after allowing 60 minutes for work time children still seem to want to continue their activities, spend some time during recall discussing how children can continue or extend their play when they return to school the next day.

I have girls who want to play in the block area at work time, but the boys take up all the room and use all the blocks. How can I provide both boys and girls with the kind of block play they seek?

This situation offers the perfect opportunity for children to discuss the problem and come up with a solution together. You can discuss this issue at a time when all of the children are together, such as during greeting time or large-group time. If your classroom uses a message board to highlight important issues or happenings, you may want to draw a message to stimulate a conversation about this situation. For instance, draw a picture of some smiling boys playing with blocks and some girls with no blocks and frowns or sad faces. Tell the children what you see occurring at work time. Support them as they talk about the situation and their feelings, and encourage them to offer solutions to the problem—much like the process you would use when problem-solving with individuals, as discussed previously in this chapter. Accept the children's solutions, regardless of how impractical they might seem, and help them choose one that is acceptable to everyone involved. Talk about the specifics of implementing their solution: "What would that look like? What happens if . . . ?" Be prepared to offer follow-up support in the block area if it's needed.

Nobody ever plays in the toy area at work time. What should I do?

The solution to this problem may be as simple as introducing or re-introducing the children to the toy-area materials during planning or small-group time, or it may require adding new materials that challenge children and support their current interests. Observation and discussion with your team members can help you brainstorm some solutions. Here are some suggestions that may be helpful.

Assess and modify your current toy area. As the school year progresses and children's interests and developmental abilities change, your toy area—as well as your other interest areas—will need to be modified. If the materials in your toy area stay the same day after day and they don't support the children's current interests or challenge the children, they are likely to lose interest and find other places to play.

Look closely at the toys and materials available to the children. Do they reflect the children's interests? Do they support various types of play (exploratory, constructive, pretend, games)? Are they appropriate for children's developmental levels? Make sure the materials are open-ended and that they reflect the experiences and cultures of the children in your program. Also check that materials are safe, clean and well maintained, and inviting.

Look also at the way the materials are stored. Children should be able to clearly see the materials available to them and reach them independently. This can be accomplished by placing the materials on low shelves in see-through containers, baskets, or other storage bins without lids. Be sure the storage containers and the shelves on which the materials are placed have a variety of labels—actual objects, photos, drawings, words—so that children can consistently find and put away the materials they use.

Consider moving the location of your toy area. Simply moving the location of your toy area may entice children to explore it. Consider putting your toy area near a popular interest area, such as the house area. This might encourage children to explore the materials in the toy area or perhaps use some of the toys in the house area. For example, children might bring over some acorns or seashells from the toy area to use for "food" and poker chips or teddy bear counters for "money."

A factor as simple as lighting may be why your toy area isn't as popular as the other interest areas in your classroom. Read the scenario above to see how one teaching team has made their toy area more inviting to the children in their program.

Why Isn't Anyone Playing in the Toy Area?

Team members Celeste and Ron have noticed a decrease in the number of children playing in the toy area during work time. After discussing their observations during a daily team planning time, they assess the area and make modifications to some of the materials. Realizing that the toy area contains mainly commercial toys, such as beads and puzzles, they add some natural and found materials, such as boxes of different sizes, buttons, egg cartons, and smooth stones. They also add a few labels to the containers that they have never taken the time to make before. Celeste and Ron continue to observe the toy area and the children's use of it during work time, and they notice that while several of the children are now choosing materials from the toy area, they are moving them to a sunny area near one of their sliding glass doors. The popular bean table is located near this area.

Celeste and Ron spend some more time in the toy area and realize that it is located in a dark and cold corner of the room—not a very inviting space. They decide to move the toys to the sunny area by the doors, move the teacher storage shelves to the former toy area, and put the bean table where the storage shelves were. When the children arrive at school the next day, Celeste and Ron inform them about the changes in their classroom by drawing a message on the message board. Over the course of the next few weeks, more and more children make plans to go to the toy area during work time. The bean table continues to be popular as well.

Children sometimes incorporate planning props into their work-time explorations, as these children have done with this long, narrow cardboard box.

Take tours of the classroom during planning time, or use materials from the toy area as planning props. If you've taken the time to assess and modify the materials and location of your toy area and you still don't notice the children making plans to spend time there, you may want to take a tour of the whole classroom with the children as a planning experience. When taking the tour, bring children's attention to the materials located in the toy area: "I see kitty cat counters, paper cups, and buttons in the toy area. What do you see?"

You can also try using the toy area materials as planning props. Small cars, teddy bear counters, pine cones, pegboards, beads, Duplo blocks or people, counting cubes, dollhouse figures, and even puzzles from your toy area can all be used in creative ways during planning. (See Chapter 7 for some ideas.) As often happens, children may enjoy the planning experience so much that they want to continue playing with the materials you used as props. You can then let the children know that these materials are available in the toy area if they want to use them at work time.

Plan a small-group activity in the toy area or with materials from that area. Offering materials from the toy area during small-group time, or holding small group in the toy area, may help to introduce children to those materials or rekindle their interest in them. Once the children have had the opportunity to play with the materials during small-group time, they may be more inclined to make plans to return to the toy area during work time.

The principal in our building thinks work time in our classroom is noisy and chaotic. What can we do to help her see that the children are actually being constructive and carrying out their plans?

When children are actively exploring and pursuing their own interests and goals, the classroom *will* seem noisy and chaotic because so many activities are taking place. However, there are several things you can do to help your principal (as well as other administrators, staff members, and parents) understand that constructive learning is occurring.

Invite your principal to observe the entire plan-do-review sequence. For your principal to understand what is really happening at work time, it would be helpful for her to have an opportunity to see planning, work, and recall time in action. When she observes the process from start to finish, she will see that the children are making plans and establishing goals during planning time, playing with purpose and engaging in active learning during work time, and reflecting on their work-time experiences during recall time. If possible, set up a time to meet with your principal after she has visited your classroom so that you can discuss what she saw and answer any questions she may have.

Share literature and videos that describe the plan-do-review sequence. Print and video resources would offer good follow-up information to your principal's visit. These resources describe in more detail the process and the rationale of the plan-do-review process. The book you are reading, as well as *Educating Young Children: Active Learning Practices for Preschool and Child Care Programs* (Hohmann and Weikart, 1995, High/Scope Press), may be particularly helpful in explaining planning, work, and recall time. The videotapes *How Adults Support Children at Planning Time, How Adults Support Children at Work Time,* and *How Adults Support Children at Recall Time* (all available from High/Scope) show children involved in the plan-do-review sequence and have accompanying dialogue explaining the rationale of each part of the sequence. After reading and viewing these materials, your principal should have a better understanding of the plan-do-review process. You may even find she has become a staunch supporter of it!

Invite your principal to parent meetings. If you plan to offer a parent meeting that describes the plan-do-review process, consider inviting your principal, too. Explain planning, work, and recall time simply and clearly, and be sure to include activities that make the concept of the plan-do-review sequence more concrete. (See Chapter 6 for more detailed suggestions on presenting information about plan-do-review to parents.) Your principal will probably appreciate the opportunity to learn more about your program and will enjoy spending time with the parents of the children in your program.

Doesn't having all of the areas open and all of the materials available to children at work time create an awful mess? What about children who just dump things? I'm afraid cleanup time will take forever!

As discussed earlier, children who have the opportunity to think through their intentions and share their plans with interested adults during planning time are generally more focused during work time. This helps to keep children from randomly moving from interest area to interest area, dumping materials along the way.

When children are first introduced to the interest areas and the materials in the classroom, they may be anxious to explore all the materials at once! To avoid overwhelming children with too many choices, you may want to reduce the number of materials available in each interest area until the children have had a chance to become familiar with their choices. Gradually add materials as you learn more about the children's interests and their developmental levels. Also, take a tour of the classroom during planning time, or plan small-group-time activities in the various interest areas to allow the children to explore the materials available to them. Being familiar with the materials will help them be able to make a plan for work time.

This is not to suggest that children who engage in planning never dump toys or make a mess in the interest areas. When this does occur, follow the suggestions previously given in this chapter for making cleanup time more manageable. These include encouraging children to put their materials away as they finish playing with them during work time, offering warnings to let the children know that cleanup time will be coming soon, making cleanup fun and enjoyable by playing games, and assisting and supporting children in the process of cleaning up.

Should we have children clean up their toys before moving to a new area?

Because each child and each circumstance is different, it is difficult to give a definite yes or no answer to this question. Consider the following work-time situations.

> Three-year-old Chad has been attending a preschool program for a week and a half. He usually heads right for the computer area during planning time instead of meeting in the art area with the rest of his planning group. The adults realize that Chad is anxious

to get started on work time, sense that the computer area must be a comfortable and safe place for him to get started, and understand that since he is young and relatively new to the program it will take some time for him to understand the plan-do-review process. After spending several minutes in the computer area, Chad usually moves around the classroom, randomly taking toys off the shelves, exploring them, and then moving on to a different place in the room.

When the adults in the classroom discuss Chad during a team planning session several days later, they agree that it is time to begin encouraging him to put some of the materials he has explored back on the shelves before moving to a new interest area. For the next couple of days, the adults support Chad in picking up the materials he took off the shelves by pointing out the labels on the containers and the shelves, helping him put the materials away, and following his lead when he makes up his own cleanup games.

Several days later, the adults notice that Chad has left several materials out that he had been playing with in the toy area and is now painting at the easel in the art area. He seems very involved in what he is doing there, and the adults observe him continue painting for the next 23 minutes. This is the first time Chad has stayed involved in an activity for more than a few minutes, and the adults feel that if they interrupt him to make him put away his materials, he will get distracted and not return to his work at the easel. The adults decide to pick up the materials Chad had been using in the toy area rather than make him clean them up. They do, however, show him how to hang up his painting when he is finished at the easel. They also help him wash out the paintbrushes and put the lids on the paint containers at the end of work time.

Four-year-old Cameron and 5-year-old Kyoko have just completed a 40-minute play episode in the block area. The two boys have built a house using large, hollow blocks, cardboard boxes, and blankets. They have brought several items to their house from the house area, such as dishes and silverware, telephones, food, and babies. When they are finished, they make a new plan to go to the toy area and work on some puzzles. When the adult, Bridget, notices this, she approaches the boys and encourages them to put away the materials they had been using from the block and house areas. Cameron and Kyoko are concerned that in the meantime someone might take the puzzle they want to use, and after problem-solving with the adult, they choose to bring the puzzle with them to the block area so they can watch it closely. Because there are so many materials in the block area to be put away, Bridget assists them with the task. When they are finished, Cameron and Kyoko return with their puzzle to the toy area.

Trent, 4, has worked for 20 minutes in the block area, placing unit blocks on the floor, positioning road signs in various places along the blocks, and driving several cars on his "road." His friend LeDre asks if he'd like to come to the art area with him, and Trent agrees. Before he leaves the block area, Trent asks Matthew, 3, if he'd like to play with his road. Matthew accepts this offer and continues to play with the blocks and cars for the rest of work time. When work time is over and Trent has put away his art area materials, the adult encourages him to go back to the block area and help Matthew put away the blocks, road signs, and cars.

In each of these examples, the adults considered the individual children and situations before deciding whether to have them put away materials they had been using. What was appropriate for Cameron and Kyoko may not have been appropriate for Chad, and what was appropriate for Chad may not have been appropriate for Trent. The decision of whether or not to make children clean up their materials before moving to other interest areas is ultimately left to your discretion.

The children in my program don't clean up at cleanup time. What should I do?

As with many situations in early childhood classrooms, if a part of the daily routine isn't moving smoothly, it's necessary to figure out what the reasons are and how to address them. There may be several reasons why the children in your program are not cleaning up when it's time, and you may need to modify your cleanup time by trying some of the following suggestions.

Organize your room to make cleanup easier. The learning environment should be designed to help children be as independent as possible. As explained earlier, provide a consistent place for all materials in the classroom and clearly label containers and shelves so children know where to put materials when they are finished using them. This not only makes cleanup time easier and more enjoyable for children but also makes it easier for children to find the items again later.

Provide children with warnings that cleanup time is approaching.
Remember that one of your roles during work time is to bring it to a close.
This includes giving children several warnings that work time will be ending
shortly, such as ringing a bell, singing a song, using a verbal reminder, or
using a combination of all three. Without a warning that work time is almost
over, children will almost always be reluctant to immediately stop what they
are doing and begin cleaning up their materials. They are likely to continue
playing during cleanup time, trying to finish their activity, rather than put
the items away.

Make the task of cleaning up manageable. Another reason children
may be reluctant to clean up is that they are overwhelmed by the task. There
are several ways to make cleanup more manageable. Try to encourage the
children to clean up after themselves throughout work time. If materials are
consistently put away as children finish with them, there won't be as much
to put away at cleanup time.

If the amount of toys to be put away accumulates (and there will be
times when it will, regardless of how much you encourage children to
clean up during work time), children may not know where to even begin
at cleanup time. Adults can generally look at a large mess and decide what
steps they're going to take to clean it up. For example, you might decide to
put all of the clothes away first, then all of the shoes, and finally the accessories (jewelry, sunglasses, and belts). Once those are put away, you might
decide to tackle the pots and pans, the dishes, then the silverware, and finally the food. You can help children tackle one part of their mess at a time by
suggesting ways to sort the materials: "How about if you find all of the necklaces and put them in this container. I'll find the sunglasses and put them in
here." "I'll put away all the blue beads. What color beads are you going to
put away?"

**Encourage cooperation among children and make cleanup time
fun.** As mentioned earlier, cleanup time will go much more quickly and will
seem less of a chore if you assist in the effort and encourage *all* the children,
not just the ones who used the materials, to help during this time. Finally,
creating games and encouraging the children to make up their own cleanup
games will make the task of cleaning up more enjoyable.

4

Looking Back:

Recall Time

Recall time ("review") is the last segment of the plan-do-review sequence and immediately follows the work-time/cleanup time portion of the day. This 10- to 15-minute period offers children the chance to reflect on their actions and experiences from work time and helps bring closure to the activities they were involved in.

While the purpose of recall time is different from planning time, there are similarities between the two segments. Like planning time, recall takes place in a small-group setting, with children and an adult meeting in a cozy and intimate place where conversations can be held in a relaxed and unhurried manner. Children meet with the same group and in the same location they do for planning. This way, participants are able to hear everyone's plans for work time and then later share their experiences and accomplishments together—including whether their original plans were carried out, modified, or abandoned. Another similarity between planning and recall time is that the games, props, and strategies adults use for one segment can generally be used or adapted for the other.

There is one important difference between planning time and recall time: although each child in the group is encouraged to *plan* every day no matter how large the group is, if there are more than five or six children in the group it may be advisable to *recall* with only half the group on any given day. Otherwise it becomes a challenge to keep the children interested in the entire recall process, because there is no work time for them to begin after they have each finished sharing, as there is after planning time. Additional strategies for keeping children interested and involved in the recall process will be discussed later in this chapter.

In the following pages you will learn what recall time is and why it is important for young children, as well as strategies to use for supporting children during recall. Finally, we will look at some questions frequently asked by teachers about the recall process.

What Is Recall Time All About?

Thinking back on work-time experiences

As planning time offers children a chance to imagine events that have not yet occurred, recall time allows them to think back on those events. Children form a mental image of what they did and draw some meaning from their experiences. Picturing and thinking through past events helps children learn that they have control over their actions and choices and helps them view themselves as capable doers. Because children are still acquiring this ability to reflect on the past, recall time should immediately follow work time and cleanup time so that children's experiences are still fresh in their minds (as well as in the minds of adults, who support children's recollections).

As these children mark their recall sheets to identify the interest areas they played in, the adult will encourage them to think about and share what they did in those areas and what they learned from their experiences.

Sharing experiences with other children and adults
Communicating personally meaningful experiences

As children reflect on their work-time experiences, they use language or some other means of communication to describe to others what they did or what materials they used. This is a new ability that preschoolers are developing, and practicing it on a daily basis during recall time helps children become more detailed and elaborate in their description of their work-time activities. By talking about their experiences, children are able to construct a better understanding of them. This use of language to convey their ideas about their own experiences is essential to their development as thinking adults.

During recall time, children are free to choose which work-time experiences to share with the group. Some children might choose to recall a lengthy and complex activity they had planned for and subsequently carried out; others might relate an activity they were involved in only briefly and rather by chance. Other children might choose to share the very last thing they did at work time, regardless of whether it was their most "significant" activity or not, simply because it is the most recent event and the easiest for them to remember. The emphasis is not on the children's recalling what *you* may feel is their most important experience from work time; rather, this is an opportunity for children to use language to share *personally meaningful* thoughts and experiences with others.

Recalling in a variety of ways

Chapter 2 discussed the wide range of ways children express their plans. Similarly, children's language at recall time may range from very simple one- or two-word accounts to extremely detailed and lengthy descriptions of what materials they used, who they played with, what obstacles occurred during their play and how they solved them, and any interesting things they learned from their experiences. Some children may not use any language at all; they may simply point or gesture to indicate what they did at work time. Take a look at the following recall time conversations, and note the various ways children describe their work-time experiences.

Jana: *Would you like to tell me about what you did during work time today, Allison?*

Allison: *There.* (She points to the woodworking bench.)

Jana: *You're pointing to the woodworking bench. Can you tell me what you did over there?*

Allison: *Paint.*

Jana: *I saw you using the paint during work time. Do you want to show the rest of the children in our group what you painted?*

Allison: *Yeah.* (Runs over to the shelf where the pieces of wood she painted are drying. She picks up one piece but realizes the paint is still wet. She puts the piece down, wipes her hand on her shirt, and returns to the group.) *It's wet.* (Shows her dirty hand to the adult.)

Jana: *The wood pieces are still wet, so you left them on the shelf to dry?*

Allison: *Yeah.*

Liam: *Maybe we can look at them when we get ready for outside time.*

Jana: *Sure. That way we can still see what Allison did, but we won't have to touch the wood.*

Recall: An Enjoyable Time for All

When children have had the opportunity to choose their own activities during work time and to decide which of these are most important to them, they become very enthusiastic about sharing their accomplishments and experiences with others at recall time. Recall becomes a social time, where children who played together during work time can talk about the fun they had, problems they solved, and ways they might change their activity the next time, and also hear about other children's experiences. This enthusiasm makes recall time more enjoyable and meaningful for all of the children involved. It also makes it more interesting for adults and offers them an opportunity to understand how children are thinking, socializing, and solving problems.

Cheyenne: *What do you want to tell me about your work time, Jamal?*

Jamal: *I played with the marble game.*

Cheyenne: *Oh, the marble game. How did you use it?*

Jamal: *I stacked all the things up and dropped the marble down.*

Cheyenne: *What happened when you dropped the marble down through the plastic tubes?*

Jamal: *It shooted out like a cannonball!*

Malik: (Laughing.) *Yeah . . . just like a cannonball!*

Cheyenne: *Did you take it apart at cleanup time, or is it still together?*

Jamal: (Now laughing with Malik.) *It's still together.*

Cheyenne: *Do you want to show the rest of the children how it works?*

Jamal and Malik: (Get the marble game from the toy area, bring it back to the recall group, and demonstrate how the marble shoots out when they drop it through the plastic tubes.)

Gina: *What did you do today at work time, Dakota?*

Dakota: *Well, first I goed to the book area with Quinn, and we looked at the book that he bringed from home. Then, we goed to the house area . . .*

Quinn: *Yeah, and we were doctors.*

Dakota: *Pet doctors, and we taked care of sick animals.*

Gina: *What was wrong with the animals that you treated?*

Dakota: *Well, first there was a cat that gotted sick, but we gave it some medicine and it feeled better.*

Quinn: *Yeah, and Karen brought us her turtle, and remember we wrapped him up with the Band-Aid?*

Gina: *I saw you using the bandages, but I didn't realize you were taking care of a turtle!* (Pauses for a moment to let the boys respond.) *Is there anything else you want to tell me about your work time?*

Dakota: *Well, after we played there, we goed to the art area, and that's when we maked those robots.* (Points to some structures on the art shelf made out of marshmallows and toothpicks.)

Gina: *Oh, you made robots, too. You were both pretty busy today, weren't you.*

Quinn: *Uh huh, and guess what else we did.*

Gina: *There's more?* (Pauses while both boys giggle.) *I wonder what else you could have done!*

Quinn: (Reaches into his pocket and pulls out a picture drawn with markers. A few recognizable letters are printed on the paper.) *This is for you. I drew it and Dakota wrote the words.*

Dakota: *Yeah. It says, "I love you, Gina. You are my bestest teacher."*

Gina: *Thank you! You really were busy today!*

Nia: (Puts several different materials that she saw children using during work time on the floor. Her recall group sits in a circle around them.) *Nicholas, can you show me what you played with today during work time?*

Nicholas: (Looks at several of the materials for a moment, then picks up the cassette tape. He holds it up so everyone can see.)

Nia: *You listened to music today, didn't you?*

Nicholas: (Nods his head.)

Nia: *Do you want to show us anything else you played with?*

Nicholas: (Leaves the group and returns with the tape recorder from the music area.)

Nia: *You brought back the tape recorder. I saw you in the music area today, listening to the tapes.*

Nicholas: (Puts the cassette tape in the tape recorder and pushes the "play" button.)

Nia: *You were listening to the monkey song. Maybe we should sing that today at large-group time.*

Nicholas: (Smiles and nods his head.)

All children, regardless of their cognitive or verbal skills, will benefit from listening to adults and other children reflect on their work-time experiences and from reflecting on their own experiences. All children can participate in recall time if you modify your approach, just as you would when interacting with children with special needs at any other time of the day. Specific ways to do this will be discussed later in this chapter.

Beginning to connect planning, work, and recall time

Children benefit most from their work-time explorations when they have an opportunity to use language to explain what they did and what they learned. By reflecting on their actions and the plans they made earlier, children begin to make the connection between making a plan and following through on it. Although it may take some time before children make this connection, it will happen eventually. When it does, it will lay the foundation for the children's ability as adults to set goals, stick to them until they have been achieved, and work through problems and obstacles that may arise.

Continuing to reflect on work-time experiences after recall

Discussion of work-time activities does not necessarily end with recall time; children often continue to talk about their experiences at snack, small-group time, outside time, or whatever segments of the daily routine are left. Children will also talk about meaningful work-time events at home with their parents and family, long after recall time has ended. When children return to school the following day, they may continue the play episode they were previously involved in or a similar one. They may reflect back on how they set up their activity, what materials they used, and what problems arose. They may then base their new activity on their experiences, choosing to modify or extend their play.

How to Support Children During Recall Time

As with planning time, adults take on a supportive role during recall, using various props, games, and strategies to encourage children to describe their work-time experiences. The examples given earlier demonstrate some of the ways you can support children during recall time, including repeating what children say, asking open-ended questions directly related to what they talk about, and interpreting their gestures. This section will describe in more detail several adult support strategies that will help make recall time more meaningful for both you and the children. Although the purposes of planning, work, and recall time are different, you will probably notice many similarities between the recall support strategies discussed here and the ones previously suggested for planning and work time.

Provide children with interesting props and games

Most children are very excited about having a chance to tell everyone in their group what they did at work time or to show something they made. Many children are also interested in listening to others describe what *they* have done, but depending on their developmental levels and their involvement in the work-time experience being discussed, children may or may not be able to wait through other children's descriptions.

One way to actively involve all children in recall time so that they do not get restless while sitting and listening to others is to provide interesting props and games (for example, having old phones for children to "call" you and discuss their experiences, or singing a chant in which one child at a time is named and gets to recall next). Such activities help hold children's interest while they wait their turn to recall, and recall then becomes a fun time that children look forward to.

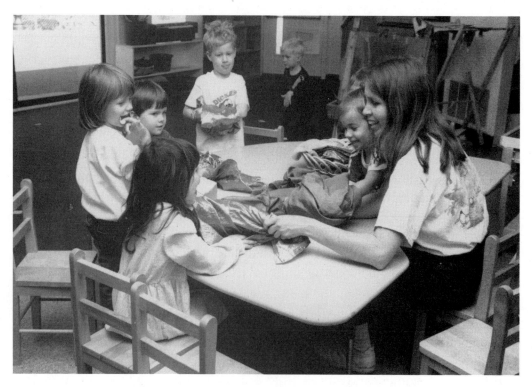

An element of mystery in this recall game helps keep children interested in the recall process. Each child retrieves an object from the bag and guesses who played with it at work time.

While it's important to keep recall time exciting and interesting with a variety of activities, occasionally the group may get carried away with the novelty of a prop or game and lose sight of the main purpose for recalling. For example, children may be more interested in playing with the provided props or in playing the recall game than in actually telling what they did at work time. Keeping in mind children's need to explore materials and objects that are new to them, consider introducing new props at other times of the daily routine so that children will not spend planning or recall time simply exploring the materials. Keeping the games simple and straightforward will also ensure that the focus remains on the purpose at hand.

Most planning games and experiences can also be used for recall, with only small modifications necessary. As we will discuss later, however, in general the planning and recall experiences on any particular day should be different. Ideas for planning and recall activities will be discussed in detail in Chapter 7.

Ask children open-ended questions

Begin recall discussions with a general, open-ended question, such as "What did you do during work time?" or "Would you like to tell me (us) what you did at work time today?" After a child has had a chance to respond, consider asking more specific questions about the experience the child has described. Questions should be asked sparingly and only to more fully understand the child's experience. For example, try to avoid questions that focus on trivial details ("What color dress did you have on?" "What shape were the blocks you used?") unless they are relevant to the conversation or the play experience. Instead, ask questions that encourage children to talk about the discoveries they made, how their work-time experiences related to their original plans, or how they solved a problem they encountered. Questions beginning with "How did you . . . ?" "What happened after . . . ?" or "Why, do you think, . . . ?" encourage children to use language in new ways to construct meaning. These types of questions will also elicit much more detailed and thoughtful responses from children. Such responses give you a better understanding of how children are thinking.

Using props and having children recall with a partner are ways to enable all children to participate actively in sharing their experiences.

Take a look at the following recall-time interactions, in which the adults ask questions to gain more information about the children's experiences at work time. Notice that, although the adults encourage the children to expand on their descriptions, the conversations are fairly brief.

Samantha: *Would you like to tell me what you did today at work time, Tomas?*

Tomas: *I played at the "take-apart table."*

Samantha: *Can you tell me what you did at the take-apart table?*

Tomas: *I took apart the telephone!*

Samantha: *Oh! How did you take apart the telephone?*

Tomas: *I used the screwdriver and those things over there.*

Samantha: *Can you show me "those things"?*

Tomas: (Goes to the shelf and returns with a pair of pliers.)

Samantha: *Oh, you used the pliers.* (Pauses to let Tomas speak, but he doesn't.) *Did you find anything interesting inside the telephone once you took it apart?*

Tomas: *Yeah. There were a bunch of wires and metal things and stuff like that.*

Samantha: *I wonder what all of that is for.*

Tomas: *So people can call each other up and talk and stuff!*

Kathy: *What did you do during work time, Suki?*

Suki: *I used the train.*

Kathy: *The one in the block area or toy area?*

Suki: *The block area, and I made a track for the train to go on and a train station, too.*

Kathy: *Oh, what did that look like?*

Suki: *Well, the track went like this* (uses her finger to draw an imaginary track in the air), *and the station went like this.* (Again, she uses her finger to "draw" a train station in the air. She makes what appear to be peaks on the rooftop.)

Kathy: *How did you make this part of the train station?* (Imitates the movement Suki made to indicate the peaks on the rooftop.)

Suki: *I put a long block on the top for the roof, then I put the triangle blocks on top of that to make this part.* (Again, she "draws" the top of the train station.)

Listen to children's responses

Too often when we ask children questions, we appear to be paying attention but our thoughts are actually elsewhere. Perhaps we're thinking of the next question we're going to ask in order to keep the recall conversation going; maybe we're silently planning ahead to the next activity; or we may be focused on the actions of other children in the recall group. Make a conscious effort to focus solely on what the children are saying, and resist the temptation to let your mind wander or become distracted. Not only does this show respect for the children, it also helps you respond appropriately to what has been said.

It's also important to understand that children are still mastering their recall skills and that it may take some time for them to respond to your initial question or statement about what they did. Because recall may take extra time with children who are new to the process, you may be tempted to bombard them with questions in order to trigger their memories of what happened at work time. Give children plenty of time to think back to their experience, form a mental image of what happened, and then express that image through words or actions.

Repeat or rephrase what children say

This strategy, mentioned in the previous chapter on work time, conveys the message that you are genuinely interested in what children are saying. Repeating or restating children's recall accounts also encourages children to expand or elaborate on their experiences in whatever way is important to them. Here are some examples of how this strategy might be used during recall time.

Anthony: *What did you do during work time, Mariah?*

Mariah: *I played the dinosaur game at the computer.*

Anthony: *Oh, the dinosaur game.*

Mariah: *Yeah. The one that makes the noises like the dinosaurs make.* (Growls loudly.)

Anthony: *Those dinosaurs make loud noises!* (Pauses for Mariah to respond.) *Is there anything else you want to tell me about your work time?*

Mariah: *I helped Melissa fix the printer, 'cause it didn't work.*

Anthony: *You fixed the printer.*

Mariah: *Yep. I pressed the button that fixed it.*

Anthony: *You knew what button to push.*

Mariah: *Yep, 'cause I fixed it before when it didn't work, too.*

Karina: *What can you tell me about your work time, Aziza?*

Aziza: *I went over there.* (Points to the book area.)

Karina: *You went to the book area.*

Aziza: *And I watched Goober* (the pet hamster).

Karina: *Oh, you watched Goober.*

Aziza: *Yeah. He was sleeping, but then he woked up.*

Karina: *He woke up, huh?*

Aziza: *Yeah, then he started drinking some water and eating his food.*

Karina: *He must have been hungry.*

Aziza: *Yeah, but he wanted to get out of his cage.*

Karina: *He wanted out?*

Aziza: *Yeah, 'cause he kept looking at the roof and standing up, like he wanted out.*

Karina: *It sounds like he really wanted out.*

Aziza: *I think he's lonely.*

Karina: *You think so?*

Aziza: *Yeah. I think you need to get another hamster to keep him company.*

Karina: *I see.*

Interpret nonverbal children's gestures and vocalizations

Children who are nonverbal or who have limited language may recall by pointing to places where they worked, gathering materials they used during work time, or using gestures to indicate what they did during work time. You can support nonverbal children's recalling in a number of ways. You might simply state what you see them pointing to or looking at and then ask specific questions to help elicit more details. Providing a collection of objects or representations of objects (such as photographs or drawings of toys or interest areas) for children to select from is another way of enabling them to indicate what they played with or which areas of the room they played in. You can also show photographs or a video clip of the children playing during work time and talk about what they are doing. Encourage the more verbal children in the group to join you in the discussion. Consider the following examples.

Erin: *Are you ready to tell me about your work time, Kiara?*

Kiara: *Da.* (Nods her head.)

Erin: *What did you do today?*

Kiara: *Da.* (Points across the room.)

Erin: (Looks in the direction Kiara is pointing.) *Are you pointing to the computer area?*

Kiara: *Da.* (Points again, but this time toward the water table.)

Erin: *Oh, I see. You played at the water table.*

Kiara: *Da.* (Nods her head again.)

Erin: *What toys did you play with while you were at the water table?*

Kiara: *Da.* (Gets up from the recall table and goes to the shelf near the water table. She returns with a baby doll, washcloth, and soap.)

Erin: *I see you've got a baby, a washcloth, and a bar of soap. How did you use them?*

Kiara: *Da.* (Rubs the baby with the washcloth.)

Erin: *You're rubbing the baby with the washcloth. You gave the baby a bath today.*

Kiara: *Da.* (Smiles and nods.)

Noelle: *Maxwell, today I saw you using the maraca.* (Pulls out a maraca from the recall bag and shakes it to get Maxwell's attention.)

Maxwell: (Turns his head toward the sound and makes eye contact with the adult.)

Noelle: *Can you show us what you did with this maraca?* (Places it in Maxwell's hand.)

Maxwell: (Grasps his fingers around the maraca and slowly begins shaking it.)

Make specific comments on what you saw children doing during work time

Although it is not always possible to play with *every* child during work time, knowing what the children in your group did during this time is helpful when it's time to recall. This is especially true with children who are not able to verbally describe their work-time experiences. Even if you are interacting with children who are in other recall groups, occasionally scan the classroom to see what the children in your own group are doing. You can then support their recall with statements like these: "I remember seeing you . . . " or "Weren't you using the . . . ?" You can also collect materials you saw children using and bring them to recall time. These strategies may help children remember details of what they did and, as mentioned, are particularly helpful for children who need assistance in communicating their work-time experiences. Consider the following examples.

Naoko: *What can you tell me about your work time, Austin?*

Austin: *I drawed letters.*

Naoko: *I remember seeing you in the writing area.*

Austin: *Uh-huh, and I maked a letter for Julie, and she was in the house area, and I took the letter to her.*

When children use gestures to describe what they did at work time, imitate the gestures and interpret them verbally, as this teacher does: "You colored a picture and went 'round and 'round."

Naoko: *I saw you give Julie an envelope.*

Austin: *That's what I put her letter in! I put it in a embelope, and I licked it and I took it to her in the house area.*

Abigail: *I collected some things you played with during work time today, Gilian.* (Puts a variety of materials on the table for Gilian to look at.)

Gilian: *Cookie.* (She picks up a ball of play dough and a cookie cutter.)

Abigail: *I made cookies with you today.*

Gilian: *Eat.* (She puts the play dough near Abigail's mouth.)

Abigail: *Yes. After we made the cookies, we ate them. Do you remember what else we did?*

Gilian: (Picks up a glass from the assortment of materials.) *Drink.*

Abigail: *You remembered that we drank juice with our cookies.*

Write down children's recall accounts

Several strategies discussed so far communicate to children that you value what they are saying. Another way to do this is to write down what the children say, perhaps on a drawing children have made of their work-time activities or as a note for them to share with their family. Children can also be encouraged to write down their own account in their own way, if they wish. Although it isn't necessary to always use this strategy, writing down children's recall accounts lets them see their own words and ideas transformed into print. In addition, you can use these recall accounts to write your formal anecdotal notes during daily team planning time. These anecdotal notes can then be shared with other team members as well as with parents, or they can be used to help your team complete required program assessment tools. Take a look at the following examples of how adults record what children say at recall time.

The children in Susan's recall group are on the floor, gathered around a large sheet of white butcher paper. They are using pencils, colored pencils, and crayons to trace around the objects they used during work time. When Susan introduced the recall activity, she encouraged those children who played together to sit next to each other, hoping this would trigger more conversation about their mutual work-time experiences.

Susan: (Positions herself on the floor next to Catrin and Tara.) *I see the two of you tracing materials from the movement area.*

Some children may want you to write down their recall accounts, while some will prefer to "write" their own.

Tara: *I'm drawing around the ribbon ring, 'cause that's what I danced with today.*

Susan: *I remember you had about ten ribbon rings in your hands while you were dancing.* (Pauses and waits for a response while Tara continues to trace around the ribbon ring.)

Catrin: *I played with them, too. But I also played with the scarves, and that's what I'm tracing.*

Susan: *I see you tracing around the pink scarf.* (Pauses.) *I noticed the two of you were dressed in the tutus while you were playing with the scarves and ribbon rings.*

Tara: *Yeah. 'Cause we were ballerinas, and we danced to the music.*

Susan: *Would you like me to write what you did at work time on the paper, next to what you've traced?*

Catrin: *Yeah. Put down, "Me and Tara were beautiful ballerinas, and we danced with ribbon rings and scarves."*

Susan: (Writes next to their drawings, "Catrin and Tara were beautiful ballerinas, and they danced with ribbon rings and scarves.")

Tara: *We danced just like those ballerinas did when my mommy and daddy took me to see* The Nutcracker.

Susan: *I didn't know you went to see* The Nutcracker! *Did you know that I used to dance in* The Nutcracker *before I was your teacher?* (Pauses while the girls giggle.) *I'll bring in some of my old pointe shoes and pictures for you to see tomorrow.* (Writes a note to herself so she remembers to bring those materials from home.)

Tara and Catrin: (Look at each other and smile.)

Susan: *Was there anything else you'd like me to write about your work time?*

When recall time is over, Susan encourages the children to cut out their tracings with scissors. Many of the children decide to take their drawings home with them, but Tara and Catrin hang their pictures, with the words they dictated, in the movement area.

Combining Support Strategies

It is often useful to apply a combination of support strategies to encourage children during recall time. Below is an example of how one teacher implemented many of the interaction strategies discussed so far—asking questions, listening to children's answers, repeating or rephrasing what children say, and making comments on what children did during work time.

Tanesha: *What did you do during work time today, Amad?*

Amad: *I built a mansion in the toy area.*

Tanesha: *A mansion! How did you build that?*

Amad: *I used the Lincoln Logs to build the mansion and the little building by the pool.*

Tanesha: *Your mansion had a pool, too?*

Amad: *Yeah. I used one of the big bowls from the house area to make the pool.*

Tanesha: *I heard you in the house area asking Samantha for a bowl. I didn't realize you were using it to make a pool for your mansion. What gave you the idea to build a mansion with a pool?*

Amad: *I saw it on a movie that I watched with my mom and dad.*

Tanesha: *Oh, you got the idea from a movie.*

Amad: *Yeah. The one in the movie was really big, and it had two really mean dogs in it, and every time someone came to the mansion the dogs would chase them away, but not the man that lived there—only strangers.*

Tanesha: *I see. Did your mansion have dogs, too?*

Amad: *Nope. I couldn't find any.*

Tanesha: *I'll try to find some in the storage closet later today so you could use them another time, if you'd like.*

Michael has prepared self-stick notes for his recall group, with each child's name and symbol printed on one of them. For a recall activity Michael encourages the children to find objects in the room they played with, put their sticky notes on them, bring them back to the group, and place them in a "recall bag." One by one he pulls the materials out of the bag and encourages the children to describe what they did with the materials during work time.

Michael: (Pulls a beanbag from the recall bag.) *Here's a beanbag, and it has Shane's name and symbol on it. Shane, do you want to tell me what you did with the beanbags today?*

Shane: *Me and Latasha played with 'em.*

Michael: *How did you play with the beanbags?*

Shane: *We threw 'em into the buckets in the block area.*

Michael: *Would you like me to write anything down on your sticky note about the game you and Latasha played?*

Shane: *Yeah. Write, "I beat Latasha, 'cause I made more baskets than her."*

Michael: (Writes this on the sticky note.) *Do you want to take your note home for your grandma to see what you did?*

Shane: *Yeah.*

Michael: *Why don't you put your note in your take-home folder.*

Use encouragement rather then praise

Chapter 2 explained several drawbacks to praising children's ideas when they state their plans for work time. Using praise during recall time can also negatively impact children.

First, rather than encourage children to extend or expand on their description of what they did during work time, words of praise tend to cut the children's descriptions short. Children sense your approval and satisfaction and often feel they do not need to add anything more to their recall account. While this may help speed up recall time, you usually miss out on a genuine understanding of what children are describing, and children do not get the full benefit of thinking through the details of what they did during work time.

Another disadvantage to using praise when listening to children's recall summaries is that once children hear other children being praised for something they did at work time, they often feel that they have to compete with the others in order to satisfy you. They begin to rely on your praise, and when they don't receive it they question whether what they did or said was good enough. Thus, they learn to depend on another person's evaluation of their efforts rather than on their own evaluation.

Many of us who work with young children have been trained to praise children and are unaware of the negative effects of doing so. As discussed in Chapter 2, encouraging children's recall conversations is a more effective alternative to using praise. The adult support strategies presented in this chapter—such as writing down children's accounts, restating what they say, commenting on what they did—are all effective ways to acknowledge children's work-time experiences and encourage them to elaborate on their recall descriptions.

Help children make the connection between their original plans, their work-time experiences, and their recall accounts

The more experience children have with the plan-do-review process, the more they will begin to understand the connection between making a plan, following through with it, and reflecting back on it at recall time. You can assist children in making this association by noting whether they carried out their plan during work time, then commenting on this at recall time. For example, you might say, "I remember you planned to. . . . " or "At planning time, you said you would. . . . Is that what you did?"

As discussed earlier, children don't always carry out their intended plans, and they should not be made to feel wrong if they did not. Even if children did carry out their original intentions, they may choose to recall a different activity they participated in, and this is fine. Regardless of which experiences the children choose to describe, support them as they share those experiences. While we do emphasize plan-do-review as a connected sequence, it's important to remember that children benefit from remembering and reflecting on their work-time activities even if those activities did not arise as a result of a plan.

Encourage children to carry over their activities to the following day

Although a 45–60-minute work time generally offers children enough time to carry out their intended plans for the day, children often enjoy repeating their activities or extending their play episodes into the following day. Sometimes, too, children become interested in an activity they hear someone else describing at recall time, and they decide they want to try it out themselves the next day. If children express a desire to participate in a particular activity on another day, or if they are disappointed with not being able to fully carry out their plans, you can use recall time to encourage them to make plans for the following day while the ideas are still fresh in their minds. You may even want to write down these plans as a reminder for the next day. Here are some examples of teachers helping children extend their activities to another day.

Marsha: *Kylie, can you tell me what you did during work time today?*

Kylie: *I went over there.* (Points to the woodworking table.)

Marsha: *You're pointing to the woodworking table.* (Looks at the other children in her recall group.) *Should we try to guess what Kylie did over there today?* (Pauses while the children become interested.) *Kylie, can you show us with your hands what you did in the woodworking area? Then we'll try to guess.*

Kylie: (Puts one hand on the table, pretending to hold something small between her thumb and index finger. Lifts her other hand in the air and makes a hammering motion. Several children guess that Kylie hammered with the hammer and nails.)

Marsha: *Kylie, is that what you were doing in the woodworking area today?*

Kylie: *Yeah, but I only did it a little while, then it was time to clean up. I was going to make a present for my daddy.*

Marsha: *Is that something you'd like to do tomorrow?*

Kylie: *Yeah, but I don't know how to make a boat by myself.*

Rajiv: *I know how to make a boat! I done that lots of times.*

Marsha: *Rajiv, would you like to help Kylie make a boat tomorrow?*

Rajiv: *Okay, but you don't need to use the hammer and nails. You only need wood and glue.*

Marsha: *Kylie, is that okay with you?*

Kylie: *Yeah, but do you know how to make a pink and yellow boat?*

Rajiv: *Sure I do.*

Marsha: *So, Kylie, you and Rajiv are going to work on making a pink and yellow boat for your daddy tomorrow?*

Kylie: *Yep!*

Mark: *Kameko, can you tell me about your work time today?*

Kameko: *I played with the shaving cream on the table.*

Mark: *You used something else with the shaving cream, too. Do you remember what those were?*

Kameko: *Yeah. I found the sponges and squished 'em in the shaving cream!*

David: (Laughs.) *I want to do that tomorrow!*

Mark: *You'd like to use the sponges and the shaving cream tomorrow, David?*

David: *Yeah.*

Mark: *Maybe I should write that down so you remember tomorrow at planning time.* (Takes a piece of paper from a nearby shelf and writes, "David wants to play with the shaving cream and sponges tomorrow.") *Where do you want to keep this until planning time tomorrow?*

David: *I'll put it in my cubby.*

Mark: *Okay. Kameko, was there anything else you wanted to tell me about your work time?*

The following day during planning time, David brings his sheet of paper with Mark's written reminder to the planning table. When it's his turn to share his plan, he shows Mark his paper and smiles. They read it together and discuss David's plan in more detail.

Janet: *Calla, do you want to tell us what you did at work time today?*

Calla: *I played the alphabet soup game at the computer.*

Janet: (Explains to the children in the recall group.) *The alphabet soup game is a new computer program that Calla's parents let us borrow for a few weeks.*

Jacob: *I want to play that game tomorrow. Can I, Calla?*

Calla: (Nods.)

Janet: *You'd like to make a plan to play the alphabet soup game tomorrow, Jacob.*

Jacob: *Yeah.*

Janet: (Writes a note to herself to remind her of Jacob's plan.)

The following morning during planning time, Jacob plans to play in the block area with his friend Daoud. Janet reminds him that he wanted to play the alphabet soup game at the computer like Calla did the day before. Jacob tells Janet that he has changed his mind and doesn't want to play that game; he'd rather play with Daoud.

Anticipate that children's ability to recall will change over time

When you first introduce recall time, children may not fully understand what they are supposed to do. Their ability to translate memories into words will need time to develop. You may feel frustrated with the lack of detail and complexity in children's initial recall descriptions, and your expectations of what recall time should look like may not be fulfilled. Understanding how children's ability to recall changes over time will help you feel less frustrated and better able to support children at their current level of expression.

Expect children's recall descriptions to be very simple at first. Children who are new to the recall process may share their work-time experiences by pointing or gesturing; using one- or two-word descriptions that include the name of an object, an area where they played, or a child they played with; or using very simple sentences. Of course, all children are different, and depending on their developmental level and their prior experience from home or other preschool programs, some children may use more detailed descriptions right from the beginning.

As children gain more experience with the whole plan-do-review process, you can expect to hear them describing their experiences in a more detailed and thorough manner. Gestures usually turn into words, and simple sentences into lengthy descriptions. As children understand the purpose of recall time, they become more enthusiastic about sharing their stories and accomplishments with their friends in their recall group. Being consistent in implementing recall time and using the adult support strategies that have been discussed in this section will help you support children in transforming their mental images into clear recall accounts.

When children are given a daily opportunity to freely express what they did at work time, and when they are encouraged by adults in a variety of ways, their ability to recall will naturally improve over time.

One way in which children's recall accounts change over time is that they reflect with their friends on what they did together at work time.

What About . . . ?
Commonly Asked Questions About Recall Time

Shouldn't all the children recall every day, just like they all plan every day?

Ideally, yes. If there were fewer than five or so children in your recall group, you would be able to listen to each child in a relaxed and unhurried way. With such a small, intimate group, the children would likely remain enthusiastic while listening to one another reflect on their actions from work time.

Connections Between Children's Play and Recalling

Children's ability to recall their activities often parallels the complexity of their play. Over time, with a stimulating environment to freely explore and with adult support and encouragement, children's play becomes more rich and complex. For instance, at the beginning of a school year, you may observe many children playing in very simple ways for very short periods of time. Likewise, children's initial recall accounts will tend to be rather short and vague. By the end of the school year, however, the same children are usually playing for longer periods of time and with greater detail and purpose, and their descriptions at recall time reflect this more complex play.

As each child draws a picture of his or her work-time experiences, the adult can ask a few children to share their experiences in more detail.

Realistically, however, very few adults have such a small number of children in their recall group. Many adults have eight to ten or even more. In these situations, it is unrealistic to expect to thoughtfully listen to each child share what he or she did at work time. It would be equally unrealistic to expect children to be active and enthusiastic participants during such a lengthy recall process. These are not issues at planning time, because children can get started with work time as soon as they are finished planning. At recall time, however, children usually must stay with the group until everyone is ready to move on to the next activity.

If you have a large number of children in your recall group, you can recall with half of the group one day and the other half the next. When you give yourself permission to do this, recall will become a relaxed time in which children can reflect on their work time and share their experiences with you and with their friends.

Regardless of whether all or only some of the children verbally share their experiences with the recall group, all children should have an opportunity to participate in some way during recall time. When choosing recall games or experiences, carefully select activities in which each child can

Recall Activities That Involve All Children

- Ask children to go to an interest area where they played and bring back a material they used during work time. Then have them trace around their object on a piece of paper. As the children are busy tracing, move from child to child, conversing with some of the children about what they did during work time.
- Place a large sheet of paper on the floor. Give each child a marker and encourage children to sit or lie around the paper. Ask the children to draw a picture of what they did during work time. As they are doing so, move around the group and listen to them reflect on their experiences.
- Pull a child's symbol or picture from a bag. Ask this child to give the group clues about (or to pantomime) what he or she did during work time. Encourage the other children to try to guess the activity the child was involved in.

actively take part. Consider the recall experiences in the box above, in which all of the children are encouraged to participate regardless of whether they verbally recall with the adult.

Another way to keep children actively involved while you listen to some of them recall is to encourage them to recall with a partner or two. This is particularly effective if the children who are recalling together also played together during work time. In the box at right are some examples of recall activities in which children are encouraged to share their work-time experiences with a partner.

When you choose to recall with half of your group one day and the other half the next day, you may want to keep track of which children had the opportunity to recall by making either a mental or written list. It is easy to inadvertently overlook children who are less verbal or less insistent about sharing their experiences, and keeping a list will help you remember to give all children a chance to recall. Even with a list, however, remain flexible about who recalls on any particular day.

I think everyone should be quiet at recall time and listen to each other.

Remember that active learning (discussed in the previous chapter) is at the core of the High/Scope Curriculum and occurs throughout every

Recall Experiences With a Partner

- During work time, use an instant camera to take pictures of the children in your recall group playing together. Then at recall time, encourage the children who played together during work time to sit together, and pass out the pictures you took for the pairs (or small groups) to discuss. As the children share with one another, move around the group, listening and making comments on their discussions. If a child chose to play alone during work time, encourage him or her to share the picture with other children or with you and explain what he or she was doing.
- Encourage children to sit with a partner, perhaps a child they played with during work time. Have them use puppets to share their work-time experiences with each other. As the children are doing this, move from child to child to participate in some of the recall conversations.

part of the daily routine, including recall time. One of the five ingredients of active learning is *language from children,* and adults should plan recall experiences that will support this and all of the other ingredients of active learning (*materials, manipulation, choice,* and *adult support*).

As adults, we sometimes prefer children to be quiet, because then we feel we have more control over the situation at hand. We may be comfortable allowing children to be noisy during work time but feel less comfortable with a noisy recall time. While it may seem that children benefit from being quiet and listening to one another, they actually gain more from freely conversing and sharing with other children and adults. Remember that one way children construct knowledge of the world around them and make sense of their experiences is through language. This is not to say that everyone talks at once and no one listens at recall time; several recall-time games and props that have been discussed do encourage children to take turns sharing their experiences. However, it is not appropriate or realistic to expect a group of preschoolers to sit quietly for 10–15 minutes and wait until it's their turn to speak.

Talking and sharing with other children about personally meaningful experiences is one of the most enjoyable and exciting aspects of recall time for preschoolers. Generally, when children are interested in what other children have to say and have something to hold their attention, they will listen to one another. However, limiting active involvement and expecting children to be quiet while they listen will most likely diminish their enthusiasm and excitement. Having only half the group at a time recall, encouraging children to recall in pairs, and actively involving each child in the process are a few ways to ensure that children *will* listen to one another and retain their enjoyment in the recall process.

Is snack or mealtime a good time to recall with children?

As discussed before, children recall their work-time experiences throughout the entire day. Since mealtime is a very social time, you may hear children discussing what they did during work time. However, snack or mealtime should not replace recall time.

At snack time a variety of distractions can keep you from fully attending to children's recall accounts. Likewise, the children often become distracted. They are busy passing juice to one another, serving themselves, talking about the food and whether or not they like it, telling the child who passed out the spoons that they didn't get one, or discussing the new design on their napkins. Spills may occur, children may argue over who gets the last carrot, and some may need help opening their individual package of string cheese, and you must be focused on helping the children solve these and a number of other problems that might arise. Children deserve to have your full attention when they are sharing their work-time experiences, and because of the typical dynamics of snack or meal-time, it is extremely difficult to make this time of the daily routine an effective recall opportunity.

Each day, the children in my preschool class plan by using a planning board and recall by "writing" or drawing in their journals. They just don't seem interested in the planning or recall process. Do you have any suggestions?

Try varying the planning and recall games and experiences you offer from day to day. Although it is important to keep the focus on the purpose of planning and recall time, it is also important to offer a variety of interesting props and experiences to keep children motivated.

Adults often choose to repeat planning and recall games and experiences for consistency in the daily routine or because doing so takes much less effort on their own part. However, if the same activities are used day after day, the routine becomes dull and both adults and children tend to grow bored and disinterested. With a little extra time and effort in designing and preparing new planning and recall games and experiences, these parts of the daily routine will stay fresh and exciting for you and the children in your classroom.

If I use the Hula-Hoop game (for example) for a planning experience, do I have to use it as a recall game, too?

No. In general, the planning and recall games and experiences you choose for a particular day should not be the same. Many planning experiences *can* be modified to become recall experiences, but having different planning and recall activities on the same day will offer some variety and keep those times of the day interesting and exciting for children.

On occasion the children might enjoy planning and recall activities that are closely tied together. This is particularly effective with children who understand the connection between planning, work, and recall, but less experienced planners/recallers also enjoy and benefit from these activities. Look at the examples in the box on p. 156 and consider how these experiences help children understand the plan-do-review sequence as a whole. Please note that although these activities encourage children to consider whether they followed through on their original plans, the intent is not to make them feel wrong or guilty if they did not. Remember that it is important to support children's recall accounts whether they did what they planned or not. Also, children should not be forced into recalling a particular experience that they had planned and carried out if they would rather discuss something else they did.

Ideas for Tying Together Planning and Recall Experiences

Planning experience: Children take turns talking into a microphone, recording their plans for work time on tape.

Follow-up recall experience: Have the group listen to each child's original plans on tape. After hearing each plan, discuss what that child actually did during work time and whether it was what he or she had planned to do. If you recall with only half your group each day, you could repeat this experience the following day with the children who did not recall the first day. Or, discuss half of the children's taped plans at recall time, then finish listening to the tape during snack time if children wish.

Planning experience: Ask children to clip a clothespin to a cardboard wheel with the interest areas pictured on it, indicating which area they will work in. They can then explain what they plan to do in that area. Leave the clothespins in place and put the wheel where it will not be disturbed during work time.

Follow-up recall experience: Display the wheel with the clothespins still attached. Discuss whether or not the children went to the interest areas they had previously indicated, and ask the children to talk about what they actually did during work time. In order for all children to have a turn, have them recall with a partner.

Planning experience: Ask children to draw a picture of what they plan to do during work time, and write down the children's explanation of their plans.

Follow-up recall experience: Return children's pictures to them and encourage them to think about whether they followed through on their original plan or not. If they choose to do so, children may draw another picture on the back of their paper showing what they did at work time. Move from child to child, discussing their work-time experiences and comparing what they had planned to do with what they actually did.

A child in my class spent 45 of the 50 minutes of work time building a very detailed and intricate block structure. For the last few minutes of work time, the same child went to the art area and explored the paint, glue, scissors, and markers. At recall time all he talked about was playing in the art area, with no mention of his efforts in the block area. Should I have asked him to talk about what he did with the blocks?

You might have mentioned that you saw him in the block area at work time and waited for his response. He might have chosen to elaborate on this part of his work time or to return to his retelling of the art activity. You could then have followed his lead and encouraged him to discuss whichever activity he wanted to. It may simply have been that he talked about his artwork because it was his last activity and therefore easier for him to remember!

It's important to allow children to decide for themselves which experiences from work time they want to share with the others in their recall group. Think back to the previous chapter on work time and the four types of play that were discussed (exploratory, constructive, pretend, and games). Each type of play is equally important and beneficial for children. Some adults, however, tend to perceive exploratory play as less important or meaningful than the other types of play, and they might expect that children will choose a constructive-play experience to recall instead of an exploratory experience. Regardless of which experiences *you* think are more meaningful for children to describe during recall, accept the children's choices about what is important to *them* and follow their leads, as you would at any other time of the day.

We recall at the end of the day so that children will remember to tell their parents what they did at school. Is this okay?

Scheduling recall time at the end of the day is fine as long as it immediately follows planning and work time. Many teachers plan their schedules so that the plan-do-review sequence follows large-group, small-group, snack, and outside time. As mentioned in Chapter 1, it doesn't matter where the plan-do-review sequence falls in the daily routine as long as the sequence is uninterrupted.

However, if recall time is scheduled at the end of the day but planning and work time occur at the beginning of the day (and there are other activities in between) then you should modify your daily routine. The plan-do-review sequence is most effective and beneficial for children if they are able to recall their activities immediately after they have taken place. Although preschoolers are increasingly able to remember and reflect on their recent experiences, they will have a more difficult time remembering the details of their work-time experiences if other activities occur between work time and recall time.

Parents often express concern that their children don't remember or are not able to tell them what they did at school, or that their children only talk about the ride home or what happened on the bus. Certainly we want parents to know what activities their children are involved in at school, but breaking up the plan-do-review sequence so that recall time occurs at the end of the day is not a satisfactory solution. You can involve parents and share information about their children's school experiences by showing them children's creations or writing samples, sending home representations of planning/recall experiences, and sharing anecdotal notes on a regular basis. These and other suggestions are discussed in detail in Chapter 6.

If we're having a busy day, is it okay to skip recall time?

Just about every classroom adult can relate to having a busy and chaotic day, when cleanup time lasts longer than expected, the schedule is altered due to special events, or the children are acting just plain nutty! There may be several reasons for wanting to eliminate recall time, but more often than not this is done for our own convenience rather than for the children's benefit, and is not recommended.

If plan-do-review falls near the end of the day, parents can recall with their children when they come to pick them up.

Remember that plan-do-review is a *sequence* and should not be disrupted. Children come to depend on the consistency of the plan-do-review sequence, and they tend to become confused and anxious when their routine is changed. Another reason not to eliminate recall time is that children benefit from and enjoy this time of the day. It offers them a unique chance to share exciting news and stories from work time and brings a sense of closure to their work-time experiences.

If the reason you're tempted to skip recall time is that you're running behind in your daily schedule, you could shave off a few minutes of recall time and whatever other segments of the daily routine you have left (small group, outside time, snack time, etc.). A few minutes taken from each segment could give you a significant amount of extra time.

If you need to compensate for a shortened day due to a special event (a field trip or an all-school picnic, for instance) and you know about it in advance, it would be better to eliminate a part of the day other than a segment of the plan-do-review sequence (for example, outside time or small-group time). Or, have a slightly shorter work time that day, leaving adequate time for recall. Be sure to alert the children and parents to any change in the routine a day or so in advance and on the actual day, perhaps during greeting time or large-group time.

If you sense that the children are not going to respond positively to recall time because they are extremely active that day or because they are excited about an upcoming event (it's Halloween, or a child in your class is having a birthday party that afternoon and everyone is invited), don't abandon recall time altogether. It is important that children be able to rely on a predictable routine and calm, supportive adults, particularly on stressful days. Try simplifying your recall experience; for example, if you had planned to take a tour of the classroom with children moving any way they chose from one area to another, instead have a rope that the children hold on to, pretending to be a quiet caterpillar as they move around the room.

If you feel that even a simplified version of your planned experience will be too overwhelming for your children, opt for a very simple experience that children are familiar with and respond well to. You should always have several planning and recall props or games handy for occasions such as these. Here are some experiences you can add to your repertoire of old standbys: telephones (p. 210), cameras (p. 210), grab bag (p. 215), mystery bag (p. 216), Hula-Hoop (p. 217), area cards (p. 219), and writing tools (p. 220).

I have a child in my recall group who always wants to go on and on about everything she did at work time, and often there isn't enough time for the other children to talk. What do I do about this?

It's okay to spend some extra time with children who want to elaborate on what they did. When you do this you can begin with the other children the next day. However, if you find that a particular child is dominating recall time on a regular basis, you may need to give that child some extra attention outside of recall time. For instance, encourage her to talk about what she did while you put away materials together during cleanup time. This should not *replace* the child's opportunity to share her experiences during recall time, though, because many distractions may occur during cleanup time that will make it difficult for both you and the child to concentrate on your recall conversation. In addition, she deserves and probably enjoys the opportunity to share her experiences with her peers, and the other children in the group will benefit from hearing a more verbal child's description of her activities.

Another strategy to try during recall time is to encourage children who played with the talkative child that day to share in the conversation. This enables her to still participate in the conversation while others have a chance to talk as well. Encouraging children to recall in pairs or small groups is another way to focus on some of the other children in your group while giving the more talkative child ample opportunity to share her work-time experiences with friends.

You can also encourage the very verbal child to recall using other means, such as drawing or building a representation of what she did. Perhaps she can do this while others are recalling verbally. As she describes her drawing or other representation to the group, other children may be drawn into the conversation.

5

Getting Started: Implementing the Plan-Do-Review Process in Your Program

Now that you know what High/Scope's plan-do-review process is all about, how do you put it into place in your own program? Reading this book and other information on the plan-do-review process without having the experience of using it in your program may make the process seem abstract and difficult to understand. But be assured that once you actually take the children in your program through the steps of planning, work, and recall for several weeks, you will better understand and appreciate how it all works.

This chapter is designed to give you some specific steps for introducing planning, work, and recall into your daily routine. As in the previous three chapters, this chapter ends with some questions that are frequently asked by teachers who are still unclear about using the plan-do-review process or who have encountered some obstacles in their effort to do so. The information presented here will give you a good start on your way to fully implementing plan-do-review in your classroom.

How Do You Begin?

Revise your daily routine

One of the first steps is to assess and make modifications to your daily routine or schedule in order to accommodate the plan-do-review sequence. If possible, any decisions about changing your daily routine should be done by the entire teaching team rather than by just one member. All members of your team will be affected by the changes, and working together will ensure an easier transition for everyone involved. Before you read on, you may want to review the information on the High/Scope daily routine that was presented in Chapter 1.

As you rearrange your daily schedule, be sure to allow enough time for all the components of the plan-do-review sequence. When the time comes to implement the whole sequence, you don't want yourself or the children to feel rushed. Remember that planning time generally lasts 10–15 minutes (less if you're just beginning the process or have a group of very young children), work time ranges from 45 to 60 minutes, cleanup time is approximately 10 minutes, and recall time usually takes 10–15 minutes (again, less when you are first introducing the sequence).

Most early childhood programs already incorporate some sort of work-time experience into their daily routine. This portion of the day is often referred to as *center time, play time, choice time, active learning time,* or *free play.* If your program is already implementing such a period of time and it lasts 45–60 minutes, that may work well as the work-time portion of your daily routine. If this existing segment of your daily routine is shorter or longer than the recommended 45–60 minutes, you may need to make some modifications.

The more you and the children go through the sequence of planning, doing, and reviewing, the more comfortable and enjoyable it will be for all of you.

Likewise, most programs already set aside time for cleanup after the children are finished playing in the various interest areas. Some programs specifically call this *cleanup time;* others simply include it as a part of their work time, center time, or play time. Generally, incorporating cleanup time doesn't require much modification to your daily routine.

Most programs usually don't already have planning time or recall time unless the adults have been introduced to High/Scope's curriculum, so finding time for these two portions of the plan-do-review sequence may be your most challenging task. Most programs don't have an extra 20–30 minutes in their daily routine that aren't being used, and you may be saying to yourself, "I barely have time to fit all of the current activities into our routine. How am I going to find 30 more minutes for planning and recall?!"

First, remember that at the beginning planning and recall may take only 10–20 minutes combined (5 to 10 minutes for each segment). Therefore, you may not need to find such a large chunk of time for these parts of the day at first. However, you and your teaching team will need to look seriously at what is happening throughout the rest of your daily routine. Carefully consider the flow of your day, especially the amount of time you spend in transitions. Simply moving some of your learning periods around and eliminating unnecessary transitions may free up time for planning and recall. You may also be able to find extra time by eliminating or shortening some of your existing learning periods.

In the following pages we'll look at how several different teaching teams revised their daily routines not only to include the plan-do-review sequence but also to address other issues they felt were not working in their current sequence of events. Included are schedules of the teams' original daily routines and their revised routines.

Example 1

Gabriella and her co-teacher, Paul, decided to eliminate their 20-minute show-and-tell for several reasons. First, they noticed that only a few children actually were benefiting from and truly interested in this time of the day. Except for those who had been chosen to share that day and those who were more verbal, few children were actually getting the opportunity to talk. Second, they were disturbed by the competitiveness they saw among the children. The children came from diverse socioeconomic backgrounds, and those whose parents had higher incomes were bringing very expensive and elaborate toys to share, while those children whose parents weren't as wealthy were not able to do so. Third, after learning about the five ingredients of active learning (materials, manipulation, choice, language from children, adult support), Gabriella and Paul decided that show-and-tell had very few of these ingredients. More and more it seemed an inappropriate activity to them.

Paul and Gabriella decided that replacing show-and-tell with the plan-do-review sequence would help solve these problems. They felt that recall time, especially, was a good replacement for show-and-tell because all the children would be engaged in active learning experiences during this time, each child would have a chance to share something of great personal importance, and competitiveness would be minimized as all the children had the same materials to choose from in their classroom.

Original daily routine, Example 1

8:30–8:45	Greeting time
8:45–9:05	Show-and-tell time
9:05–10:00	Work time/cleanup time
10:00–10:15	Snack time
10:15–10:35	Large-group time
10:35–10:55	Small-group time
10:55–11:30	Outside time

Revised daily routine, Example 1

8:30–8:45	Greeting time
8:45–9:00	Planning time
9:00–9:50	Work time/cleanup time
9:50–10:05	Recall time
10:05–10:20	Snack time
10:20–10:40	Large-group time
10:40–11:00	Small-group time
11:00–11:30	Outside time

Example 2

The first thing this teaching team, Rose and Shakira, noticed when reviewing their daily routine was that their center time was longer than the recommended time period of 45–60 minutes. They also realized that the children weren't able to spend enough time outdoors because all of the other segments of their routine were so long. They decided to take off 5–10 minutes from each learning period and make each one fit into the time frame that High/Scope recommends. They also changed the names of their learning periods so that each would designate a place or a process rather than a specific activity.

Original daily routine, Example 2

8:00–8:30	Arrival, calendar, weather, helpers
8:30–10:00	Center time
10:00–10:20	Snack time
10:20–10:45	Song and story time
10:45–11:10	Arts and crafts time
11:10–11:30	Outside time

Revised daily routine, Example 2

8:00–8:20	Greeting time
8:20–8:35	Planning time
8:35–9:30	Work time
9:30–9:40	Cleanup time
9:40–9:55	Recall time
9:55–10:15	Snack time
10:15–10:35	Large-group time
10:35–10:55	Small-group time
10:55–11:30	Outside time

Example 3

Upon reviewing their daily routine, Molly and Adrienne decided that it was very choppy and that the children spent more time transitioning from one activity to the next than they did engaged in the activities themselves. The team agreed that the children weren't able to really focus during their free-choice time because it was so short, and their play seemed aimless as a result.

Molly and Adrienne also felt that with their large and diverse group of children, it was difficult for many of the children to pay attention during story time. It was during this period (as well as during transitions) that the adults were spending a lot of time helping resolve social conflicts, because the children always seemed to "pick on" one another. They decided to eliminate story time, especially since the children were exposed to books in a much more intimate way during work time and other parts of the daily routine.

Next the teaching team looked at the arts and crafts, math, and science portion of their day. After realizing that they could make these types of activities more appropriate and exciting for children by providing open-ended materials during work time and small-group time, the team eliminated this portion of their day. They replaced it with a small-group time.

Original daily routine, Example 3

9:00	Arrival	11:40—11:55	Books on the rug
9:00—9:20	Breakfast	11:55—12:15	Lunch
9:20—9:40	Bathroom, brush teeth	12:15—12:35	Bathroom, brush teeth
9:40—9:55	Outside time	12:35—12:55	Free-choice time
9:55—10:10	Story time	12:55—1:00	Departure
10:10—10:40	Free-choice time	1:00—2:00	Work in classroom (adults)
10:40—11:00	Large-group time		
11:00—11:40	Arts and crafts, math, science		

Revised daily routine, Example 3

9:00—9:05	Arrival	11:15—11:35	Large-group time
9:05—9:20	Greeting time	11:35—11:55	Small-group time
9:20—9:40	Breakfast	11:55—12:15	Lunch
9:40—10:00	Bathroom, brush teeth, books on rug	12:15—12:35	Bathroom, brush teeth, books on rug
10:00—10:10	Planning time	12:35—1:00	Outside time
10:10—10:55	Work time	1:00	Departure
10:55—11:05	Cleanup time	1:00—2:00	Daily team planning time
11:05—11:15	Recall time		

Example 4

After being briefly introduced to High/Scope's daily routine in a staff workshop, Susan and Desiree had decided to put recall time as close to the end of the day as possible so that the children would remember to tell their parents what they did during work time. After attending a High/Scope 2-day workshop, where they learned more about the plan-do-review process and the daily routine, Susan and Desiree realized that the sequence of planning, work, and recall should not be interrupted. They changed their routine accordingly, as illustrated below.

Original daily routine, Example 4	
8:30–8:45	Greeting time
8:45–9:00	Planning time
9:00–9:20	Small-group time
9:20–10:10	Work time
10:10–10:20	Cleanup time
10:20–10:40	Large-group time
10:40–10:55	Snack time
10:55–11:10	Recall time
11:10–11:45	Outside time

Revised daily routine, Example 4	
8:30–8:45	Greeting time
8:45–9:05	Small-group time
9:05–9:25	Large-group time
9:25–9:40	Snack time
9:40–9:55	Planning time
9:55–10:45	Work time
10:45–10:55	Cleanup time
10:55–11:10	Recall time
11:10–11:45	Outside time

Example 5

The teaching team in a full-day program, Ryba and Megan, realized that they needed to make some revisions to their routine. First, they had noticed that some of the children were arriving already fed, while others were still eating their breakfast as they walked through the door or hadn't eaten at all. They decided to offer a simple breakfast of fresh fruit, cereal, and juice to those children who were hungry when they arrived. The teaching team also noticed that most children arrived by 8:30 every day, even though the program didn't officially begin until 9:00. They agreed that an outside time early in the morning (from 8:30–9:00) would be an effective transition into the day, and it would still offer parents the option of waiting until 9:00 to bring their children to school.

Ryba and Megan also felt that there was too much "free play" throughout the day, with children's activity during this time having very little focus or purpose. There wasn't enough time for large-group activities, such as music and movement, since large-group time was spent taking attendance and reviewing the calendar and weather. The children seemed disinterested during these activities and often began arguing with one another.

As they revised their routine, the teaching team decided to eliminate some of the free-play time and change the remaining free-play period to work time, with planning before and recall after. With these changes they expected to start seeing children play with greater purpose in the interest areas. They also decided to eliminate discussion of the calendar and weather and have a shorter greeting time, which included sharing the daily classroom news. This allowed more time later in the day for large-group activities, such as music and movement experiences, fingerplays, and group games.

Staggered departure times throughout the afternoon created a challenge for Ryba and Megan as they revised their routine, because they wanted to somehow include the parents in the plan-do-review segment of the day. They finally decided to schedule a second segment late in the afternoon so that parents would have the opportunity to recall with their children when they picked them up at the end of the day.

Original daily routine, Example 5

7:00–9:00	Arrival and free-play time	11:00–12:00	Lunch/bathroom/prepare for rest time	2:45–3:45	Outside time or multipurpose room
9:00–9:30	Calendar, weather, attendance, daily news	12:00–12:15	Story time	3:45–6:00	Free-play time and departure
		12:15–2:15	Rest time		
9:30–10:00	Small-group time	2:15–2:45	Put cots and blankets away/bathroom/snack		
10:00–10:20	Snack				
10:20–11:00	Free-play time				

Revised daily routine, Example 5

7:00–8:30	Arrival, breakfast, book and toy areas available to play in	10:55–11:10	Recall time	3:00–4:00	Outside time or multipurpose room
		11:10–11:30	Large-group time	4:00–4:20	Large-group time
8:30–9:00	Outside time or multipurpose room	11:30–12:30	Lunch/bathroom/prepare for rest time	4:20–4:40	Small-group time
		12:30–2:30	Rest time/daily team planning time	4:40–4:55	Planning time
9:00–9:15	Greeting time			4:55–6:00	Work time/cleanup/departure (children recall with their parents as they are picked up at the end of the day)
9:15–9:35	Small-group time	2:30–3:00	Put cots and blankets away/bathroom/snack		
9:35–9:50	Planning time				
9:50–10:40	Work time				
10:40–10:55	Cleanup time				

Introduce the plan-do-review process to your children

Once you understand how the planning, work, cleanup, and recall segments are carried out and you have modified your daily routine to accommodate the sequence, you should be ready to introduce it to your group of children. You may want to let both parents and children know about it several days before you plan to introduce it (or before the first day of school, if it is the beginning of the school year). For parents, this might include a letter explaining what plan-do-review is all about (see Appendix B for some sample parent letters). You could also discuss it with parents when they pick up or drop off their children, on a home visit, or in a parent meeting. Most parents will be curious and will appreciate the information you give them.

A message board comes in handy for introducing and explaining the process of plan-do-review. Pictorial representations will help children understand the process better.

Children will need the sequence explained to them in very concrete and visual terms. (You'll read about one creative way to do this in the following scenario.) Start the explanations a few days ahead of time if you are implementing the process in the middle of the school year. However, keep in mind that until children have actually experienced the plan-do-review sequence for a while, they will not fully understand it.

Following are three scenarios to help illustrate how to go about preparing children for planning, work, and recall and how to start using the process in your classroom. Each scenario addresses a particular circumstance: introducing the sequence in the middle of the school year, at the beginning of the school year with a returning group of children, and at the beginning of the school year with a new group of children.

In the middle of the school year

If you are introducing the plan-do-review process in the middle of the school year, it is very important to explain the change to children and parents a few days in advance. As discussed earlier, any change in children's routine can be confusing and disruptive. Preparing children ahead of time, as illustrated in the following scenario, can reduce some of the confusion about the plan-do-review process.

After learning about High/Scope's plan-do-review process and revising their daily routine, Peggy and Constance decided during their daily team planning that it was time to prepare the children for the changes that would be occurring. They were both very eager to begin implementing this part of the High/Scope Curriculum, but they also realized that there were several things to be addressed before it could happen. The first step was to decide on which day they wanted to introduce plan-do-review and then to create a timeline of tasks they would need to accomplish before that date. The day they met to create this timeline was a Friday, and they decided that they would need at least a week to complete all of their tasks. Although it seemed natural to start the sequence on a Monday, Constance and Peggy realized the children might forget about the upcoming changes over the weekend, and they decided the children would benefit from a reminder the day before. They thus chose Tuesday as their target date for starting plan-do-review.

The biggest challenge for the two adults was to explain the upcoming changes to children in a way that was easy for them to understand. They already had a work time and cleanup time as part of their routine, and the rest of the segments followed High/Scope's suggested learning periods and were referred to in High/Scope terms (with the exception of large-group time, which they called *circle time*). So, the main change to the children's routine would be the addition of planning and recall time.

Peggy and Constance realized that they had never really understood the importance of having a predictable and consistent daily routine. They thus decided to make a visual aid that would let children know what portion of the day would occur next. This would help the children understand the new routine and be able to visualize where the plan-do-review sequence fit into the routine.

Peggy and Constance used pieces of construction paper to represent the parts of their routine. At the top of each paper they printed the name of one segment, then they covered the paper in clear plastic laminate. They included sheets for planning and recall time. Next, they took photographs of the children in action during greeting time, work time, cleanup time, small-group time, circle time, and outside time. They mounted each photo on its respective piece of laminated construction paper. They then arranged the signs in the same order as their daily routine, placing the blank planning and recall signs on either side of the work-time sign.

The tasks of taking the photographs, having them developed, and preparing the visual routine took several days to complete. During Thursday's team planning session, Peggy and Constance hung their new daily routine signs on a low bulletin board where the children could easily see them throughout the day. They decided to explain the routine to the children on Friday during greeting time. They guessed that some of the children would probably notice the routine on the bulletin board when they arrived at school and figured this would be a good opening for a discussion of the upcoming changes.

Constance and Peggy also decided to include a note to the parents in their weekly newsletter explaining that several permanent changes were being made to their daily routine and would begin the following Tuesday. They included a copy of the new routine and explained briefly what the plan-do-review process was and why it was important. They had already spent much time and effort communicating to the parents the importance of work time and play, so they focused most of their attention on planning and recall time. They let the parents know that they had already explained the change to the children. They also asked parents to remind their children about it over the weekend.

Just as Peggy and Constance had anticipated, when the children arrived at school on Friday several noticed the new daily routine signs on the bulletin board. The children were particularly interested in the photographs of themselves. To Peggy and Constance's delight, the children not only identified one another in the photos but also said things like "Hey! That's you and me playin' at work time!" "That's us at snack time, and here we are at circle time." The children wanted to know why there were "two empty spots" in the routine, which gave Peggy and Constance a natural opportunity to explain planning and recall time after everyone arrived.

After all the children had had an opportunity to look at the pictures of themselves, Peggy and Constance began their greeting time. During their daily team planning on the previous day, they had agreed that the children wouldn't fully understand the new routine (especially planning and recall time) until they had actually experienced it several times, so they decided to keep their explanation as simple and easy to understand as possible. They referred to the new routine depicted on the bulletin board and talked about each "time" or event in the sequence. When they got to the blank planning-time segment they explained that next week there would be a new "time," called planning time, that would come before work time. When they got to the blank recall-time segment after talking about the pictures of work time and cleanup time, Peggy and Constance explained that there would be another new "time," called recall time, that would happen after cleanup. Later, during their team planning, the two adults discussed how the explanation had gone. They agreed that having the signs and photos had been very helpful, and being able to point to the "times" when they were discussing them made the concept of a sequence of events less abstract and easier for the children to understand.

When the children arrived for greeting time on the following Monday, they found that Peggy and Constance had drawn several pictures on the message board. The first picture was of a moon shining next to a sleeping stick-figure child; the second showed a child standing and stretching next to his bed, with the sun shining nearby. The children were familiar with this message, which indicated "tomorrow" or "the next day." Once the group determined that they were talking about "the next school day," Peggy and Constance referred the children to the visual daily routine on the bulletin board and reminded them that they would be adding a planning time and recall time to their day. They asked the children if they could remember from the previous conversation when planning time would happen, then they asked when recall time would happen. Before going on to the next activity, Constance and Peggy explained once more that when the children came to school the following day, they would have planning and recall time.

During their daily team planning session on Monday, Peggy and Constance planned their activities for the following day. They discussed which types of planning and recall games and experiences to use to introduce these two new portions of the day. They agreed that they needed to begin with simple, concrete games and experiences rather than complicated and abstract ones.

Peggy decided that she would have her planning group (the same group of children that met with her for snack and small-group time) meet together at their table, and she would ask the children to think about what they wanted to do at work time that day. Next, she would give the children a basket and ask them to go get an object they wanted to use at work time. After they brought the objects back to the group and briefly talked about them, they would begin their work time.

Constance decided to give each of the children in her group a pair of "binoculars" (made from cardboard tubes) and then take a walk with them through the various interest areas of the classroom. She would ask the children to decide where they would like to play and to use their binoculars to look for something they might like to play with in that interest area. After the children decided on a material to play with they would briefly talk about it, then begin their work time.

Peggy thought that Constance's planning-time activity would be an effective way of recalling with her own group of children, so she decided to use the binoculars for the children's first recall experience. She would take the children on a tour of the classroom and encourage them to look through their binoculars for materials they had played with during work time.

For her recall time, Constance decided to have all the children hold onto a Hula-Hoop and move it through their hands. As they did this Constance would chant "What did you do at work time, work time? What did you do at work time today?" When she stopped chanting the children would stop moving the Hula-Hoop, and whoever was holding the part of the hoop that had been marked with a piece of tape would briefly tell what he or she did during work time. Constance and Peggy agreed that if any of the children were not able to verbalize what they had done, Constance would encourage them to go to an interest area and bring back something they had played with.

When the children arrived at greeting time on Tuesday, they noticed that Peggy and Constance had put a laminated paper star at the top of the greeting-time part of the visual routine. The two explained to the children that the star was there because it was greeting time right now. They asked the children where they thought the star would move to after greeting time was over, and all the children predicted that it would move to small-group time, which was the next "time" depicted on the routine. Peggy and Constance explained that during the day, they would move the star (or have a child move it) to the "time" that would come next.

The other topic discussed at greeting time was where the children would go for planning and recall time. Constance and Peggy explained that the children would meet at the same place and with the same teacher as they did for snack and small-group time. To help children remember where to go, they wrote the names and symbols of children in Peggy's group under her name and symbol and did the same for Constance's group. They then put the lists on the planning and recall parts of the visual routine. As the day went on, each time they moved the star they reminded the children which part of the day would be happening next.

Later that week, as Peggy and Constance were discussing how the children seemed to be adjusting to the changes in their routine, they agreed that keeping the day consistent and predictable was a big improvement over their old routine. Even as early as Wednesday of that week, the children seemed to understand that the "times" of the day happened in a specific order, and they were able to predict what was going to happen next with the aid of the visual routine. At first Constance and Peggy were a little disappointed with how the children had reacted to planning and recall time. Several seemed confused, not understanding why they had to talk about what they wanted to do rather than just being allowed to get started immediately. However, as the week progressed, they saw the children becoming more excited about telling others what they were planning to do and then sharing what they had done during recall time.

As the weeks progressed, Peggy and Constance took pictures of the children actively involved during planning and recall time. They added these to the visual routine. They were confident about their decision to add planning and recall time to their day, and they felt that following the daily routine consistently seemed to have a calming effect on the children as well as themselves.

At the beginning of the school year with a returning group of children

Children who are used to a particular way of doing things one school year expect it to stay the same when they return the next. Implementing the plan-do-review sequence at the beginning of a school year may cause some anxiety or confusion for returning children. You can prevent some of this by letting the children know ahead of time, during either a home visit or a classroom visit, that they can expect some changes. Keep in mind, however, that it's not necessary to provide a *detailed* explanation ahead of time of what plan-do-review involves.

Children who are returning for a second year may also need to be reintroduced to the classroom materials and interest areas if you have made substantial changes. However, they probably won't need too much time to become re-acclimated to their surroundings. Following is an example of how a teaching team introduced the plan-do-review process to a group of returning children and their parents at the beginning of the school year.

> Teachers Joe and Sharonda worked in a program that had recently hired a new director. Their previous director had supported a curriculum that focused on academic and adult-directed activities, and the daily schedule the teachers were instructed to follow put little emphasis on play. The new program director, however, was trained in and believed strongly in the High/Scope Curriculum, including the philosophy of active learning. When she began her position as director, she immediately set up extensive training workshops for all the teaching teams in the program. After their training was complete, the director met with each team individually to set up a plan for implementing the new curriculum and sharing the new philosophy with parents.
>
> Joe and Sharonda were very enthusiastic about what they had learned in training, but they were nervous about the parents' reactions to the new curriculum. The first task they wanted to complete was to set up their learning environment and daily routine according to what they had learned. Next, they sent invitations and made phone calls to invite the parents of the children in their class to a special parent meeting. This meeting would introduce and explain active learning and High/Scope's plan-do-review process as well as the other components of the daily routine. Joe and Sharonda invited their new director to the parent meeting so that the parents could meet her and so that she could support Joe and Sharonda in answering any questions and concerns the parents might have.
>
> After the meeting, Joe and Sharonda made a list of the parents who were not able to attend and mailed them some information explaining what was discussed at the meeting. These parents also received a copy of the new daily routine, including the plan-do-review sequence, and were invited to contact either Joe or Sharonda if they had questions or wanted to meet regarding the curriculum changes.

The next step was to schedule brief classroom visits with the parents and their children. Even though most of the children had attended their program last year, Joe and Sharonda felt that since so many changes had been made to their learning environment the children would profit from a visit prior to the first day of school. Being familiar with the new learning environment and the materials in the interest areas would also benefit the children later during planning and recall.

Because many of the children had been in their classroom the previous year, Joe and Sharonda knew which children enjoyed spending time with one another. This made it fairly simple for them to create small groups for planning, recall, snack, and small-group time. They prepared a list of names of the children in each small group so that when the children came to visit, they could find out which teacher and children would be in their group.

At the parent meeting, many parents had scheduled a time to visit Joe and Sharonda's room with their children. Being sensitive to the fact that several parents worked during the day and would only be able to visit during the evening, Joe and Sharonda arranged their own schedules to enable them to stay until early evening on several occasions. They divided the responsibility of calling and scheduling classroom visits with parents who had not come to the meeting.

When the parents and children arrived for their visit, each child was encouraged to explore the interest areas and materials. Joe spent time playing with the children who would be in his small group while Sharonda talked with their parents. When the children visiting were scheduled to be in Sharonda's small group, she played with them while Joe talked to the parents.

During the visits Joe and Sharonda showed the children the visual daily routine (similar to the one explained in the previous example), which they had made by drawing stick figures and symbols to represent the various times of the new routine. They knew that the stick figures would seem abstract to the children and would not completely convey the concept of the new sequence of events, but they figured that once the children participated in the sequence a couple of times they would understand the visual daily routine more clearly.

These classroom visits were not solely for the benefit of the children. While the children played in the classroom, their parents were given more information about active learning and were encouraged to ask questions about the program's new philosophy and curriculum. The parents were also encouraged to move around the classroom to see how the learning environment had been set up.

After the classroom visits, Joe and Sharonda had a few more classroom and program responsibilities left, including developing their plan for the first day of school. Joe remembered that many of the children in his planning and recall group had used the steering wheel a great deal toward the end of the previous school year. He decided to use the steering wheel as a prop for his planning-time game. He would give each child a turn to be the "bus driver" and let the other children (the "passengers") follow behind as the driver took them to the area where he or she wanted to work. There Joe would encourage the child to find a material to play with, describe his or her plan for using the material, then choose another child to be the next "bus driver."

Sharonda decided to gather several materials from each interest area and show them to the children in her planning group. She would encourage the children to guess where she had taken the materials from, and then she would ask if there were any children who wanted to play in that area. If there were, she would ask them for a brief description of their plan. However, she and Joe both agreed that it might be too soon to expect a verbal description from some of the children, so they decided that Sharonda would not pressure them. Instead, she would simply let them go to their chosen interest area and talk to them about what they were doing once planning time was over and they had begun playing.

Joe and Sharonda planned to move from interest area to interest area during work time, spending time observing and interacting with the children. They wanted to begin taking anecdotal notes as soon as possible, not only to document what the children were doing and saying but also to assist in team planning for the following day.

When planning his recall-time experience for the first day, Joe wanted an activity that would be easy for the children to understand as well as something that would really interest them. He decided to take instant (Polaroid) photographs of the children during work time, then show the pictures to them at recall time. If he took one picture of every child in his group, each child would have a picture to take home and share with parents at the end of the first day of school. Joe felt that sharing the pictures with their peers and family members would be an exciting way for children to reflect on their work-time experiences and would be a concrete reminder of what they had done.

For her recall-time experience, Sharonda chose to collect some materials that the children had played with during work time. She would put all of the materials in a bag, let each child pull out an item, and ask who had worked with that material at work time. Since every child would have a turn and there was an element of mystery to the game, Sharonda felt that it would keep the children interested and excited. She remembered what she had learned about having each child be actively involved during recall time, so she decided to collect materials that two or more children had played with and encourage them to share their experiences together. Sharonda and Joe felt that this recall-time experience would, like Joe's, be a very concrete reminder of what the children had done during work time.

The last task Joe and Sharonda needed to do before school started was to clean out a shelf in their storage cabinet for planning and recall games and props. They had already begun collecting materials to make the games and had also found several props to use. Their director suggested that they use clear plastic laminate to preserve as many of their newly made games as possible since they would be using them throughout the school year and possibly longer. After they cleared off the shelf in the cabinet, Joe and Sharonda put all their props and materials on it so that they would be easily accessible when preparing for planning and recall times.

At the beginning of the school year with a new group of children

Although it can be challenging to begin each year with a new group of children, there are some advantages to having a "fresh start." For example, new children will not be confused by any changes you have made in the environment or the routine. Certainly there will be many aspects for them to get used to, but new children usually adapt very well after a couple of days of consistently following the daily routine, knowing that they can predict and anticipate what will happen next.

Following is an example of a teaching team that was hired and trained in the High/Scope Curriculum over the summer for a new preschool center opening in the fall and how they implemented plan-do-review. Because it was a new program, none of the children or adults had prior experience with the program or with one another.

Just as in the example above, these teachers, Becky and Felicia, invited the parents and the children to their classroom before school started so they could meet the teachers and become familiar with their new environment. A great deal of information regarding the program, its philosophy, and the daily routine had been sent to the parents over the summer. Because of the wealth of information they had sent and the opportunity parents would have to visit, Becky and Felicia decided that it was not necessary to ask the parents to attend a parent meeting right away. They decided they would wait about a month and then schedule a parent meeting with the assistance of their program's parent coordinator.

During the classroom visits, one adult stayed with the parents, answering any questions they had and taking care of enrollment paperwork. The other adult spent time with the children, introducing them to the names of the interest areas and encouraging them to explore the materials in each area. Becky and Felicia agreed that if the children were familiar and comfortable with the learning environment when they arrived on their first day of school, they would have a clearer idea during planning time of what they would like to do.

For the first couple of days of school, both Becky and Felicia took the children on tours of the classroom during planning time. They wanted the children to see the materials available and to make them aware of the names of each interest area. On their tours, Becky and Felicia played games like *I spy,* in which they would say something such as "We're in the house area now. I see plates, cups, silverware, play dough, and clothes to dress up in. What do you see?" They would then encourage the children to contribute to the game as much as they felt comfortable doing. To make their tours more interesting they used various props, such as rope (to hold on to while following the leader around the room) sunglasses (to look around the interest areas), and steering wheels (to "drive" to the areas).

During the first week Felicia and Becky spent work time moving from interest area to interest area, playing with and observing the children. Because they had no prior experiences with any of the children (with the exception of a couple of contacts before the fall), they especially wanted to observe the types of play children were engaged in; the way they solved problems, both with materials and with other children in the classroom; and which children spent time playing with one another.

Recall experiences for the first few days were very simple and concrete. The adults planned activities in which the children were able to touch the objects that they had played with, go to the interest areas they had played in, or show the adults and the other children who they had played with. Since Felicia and Becky were observing and interacting with the children at work time, they were able to help children reflect on their activities with statements like "I remember we. . . ." "I saw you doing. . . ." or "Weren't you playing with . . . ?"

Another way Becky and Felicia made the children more familiar with the classroom materials was holding small-group time in various interest areas rather in their designated area. For example, Becky would meet with her group at the table where they always had small-group time, then they would move to an interest area and explore the materials there. This idea was especially effective in introducing new interest areas to a couple of children in Becky's group who so far had made plans only to go to the computer area and then stayed there for the entire 50-minute work time.

In addition to all of the ideas they used to introduce the plan-do-review sequence to the children, Becky and Felicia made a visual daily routine for the children to refer to.

These three examples of introducing plan-do-review under different circumstances should give you plenty of concrete ideas for implementing the process in your own program. Incorporate your own ideas, too, ones that you have developed over the course of many years of experience working with young children and their families. You know your children, program, and teaching style better than anyone, so trust yourself and your creative instincts, and do what's best in your particular situation.

After You Get Going: Maintaining the Plan-Do-Review Process

Keep in mind that it will take some time for the children in your program to understand the process of plan-do-review. Likewise, it will take several trials of carrying out the sequence for you and your team members to feel confident about your role during planning, work, and recall time. In particular, if you are new to the ideas of sharing control with children, playing as a partner, and the other support strategies mentioned in this book, it may take you a while to feel comfortable interacting with children in a new manner. The remainder of this chapter will focus on ideas that will help you continue the successful implementation of the plan-do-review process in your program.

Meet with your teaching team

Make time for daily team planning

If you are not already doing so, set aside a period of time each day to meet with the other adults who work in your classroom or center. Most often, teaching teams schedule their planning time at the end of the day, after the children have gone home; others meet during nap time, for example, due to the structure and schedule of their program. In order to make this time most effective, meet at the same time and place each day and let others know that you are in a meeting and should not be disturbed unless necessary. It's also helpful to have all the materials you will need for your planning sessions located nearby.

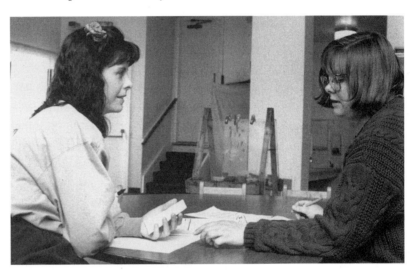

During team planning time, share the anecdotal records and observations of the children that you and your team members have accumulated throughout the day. Record these observations, which you will later use to complete assessment tools and share with parents. Use this time and your observations to also plan activities for the following day; to modify interest areas or materials; or to discuss upcoming activities, such as classroom visitors, field trips, and other special events.

During team planning, discuss anecdotal notes you took during plan-do-review (as well as at other times of the day), and talk about how the children seem to be adjusting to the new routine.

Team planning time is also a perfect opportunity to discuss how the plan-do-review process is working in your program and to share experiences and feelings about how the day went. Your team members are familiar with the children in your planning and recall group and may be able to offer helpful suggestions if you're experiencing some challenges (you may be able to assist them in this respect, as well). Along with sharing your frustrations, celebrate your successes!

Share anecdotal notes and observations of children

The observations you and your team members record throughout the day can give you a great deal of information about the children as well as about your program. Discussing and assessing these observations can assure your teaching team that the strategies you are implementing are working successfully. It may also uncover areas where you need to make some modifications. Take a look at the following observations made by team members during the plan-do-review sequence. Consider what the adults learned about their children, their teaching strategies, and their program after discussing the anecdotal notes together.

Anecdotal Note #1

10/3 While playing a planning game in which children gave verbal clues about what they each would do during work time, Stephanie left the group and went to the house area. She returned with a baby doll and told Christine, "Feed baby."

After discussing this observation with her team member, Christine concluded that this planning game was too abstract for Stephanie. The language required to play the clue game was much more advanced than what Stephanie was capable of producing, and Christine realized that many of the other children in her planning group had had difficulty with the game as well. After discussing this with her team member, they determined that Stephanie and the other children would benefit from more concrete planning games. They agreed to continue observing the children and to possibly try the game later in the school year if they felt the children were ready.

Anecdotal Note #2

9/15 When asked what her plan was for the day, Alyssa shrugged her shoulders and said, "I don't know." When asked which area she wanted to go to, she stood up on her chair and looked over the art area shelving unit. She pointed to the block area and said, "I want to play with the train over there."

As Alyssa's teachers discussed this observation, they wondered if the reason Alyssa stood on her chair to make her plan was that she needed to see over the shelving unit. They moved to where Alyssa had been sitting and realized that the unit was taller than the other furniture in the learning environment and did indeed obstruct children's view of the rest of the classroom. Because it was the beginning of the school year and Alyssa was not yet familiar with all the materials in the interest areas, it was difficult for her to make a plan without seeing the choices that were available to her.

Crystal and her co-teacher rearranged several pieces of furniture in the classroom to create an open view for all the children during planning and recall time.

Anecdotal Note #3

1/20 At planning time, Lorenzo made a plan to use the new sponges and paint in the art area with Hunter.

1/20 At work time, Lorenzo dipped the sponges in the paint and patted them on a piece of paper, then moved to the toy area. He pulled a bucket of plastic frogs off the shelf, dumped them on the floor, and went to the house area. There he took the empty food boxes, plates, and glasses and let them fall on the floor.

Lorenzo's teachers, Larissa and Tim, had noticed him doing this before, and they agreed that it was probably because Lorenzo was a new child in the program and also very young. By the second week, Larissa and Tim felt that they had given Lorenzo plenty of time to explore the learning environment. They wondered if perhaps he would become more involved in his play if an adult stayed near him, incorporating some of the adult-child interaction strategies they had learned at a recent High/Scope workshop (such as playing in parallel and commenting on what Lorenzo was doing). The two adults planned for Tim to spend at least the first part of work time with Lorenzo the following day, practicing several of these strategies.

Anecdotal Note #4

3/21 At work time in the house area, Jacob told Lakeisha, "I'm gonna make butterscotch cookies. You want some?" He went to the art area and brought the play dough back to the house area. He rolled the play dough into balls and flattened them with his hand, then put them on a plate and into the "oven." He called Lakeisha over when they were finished and said, "The cookies are ready. Come eat."

Natalie, the adult who wrote this anecdote, shared it with her team member, Chantra, during their daily team planning time. Chantra mentioned that the day before, she had observed two other children taking the play dough from the art area to the house area to make "cookies" and "pizza." Since it seemed to make sense to the children to use the play dough in the house area when pretending to bake, the two adults decided that they would put some of the play dough in the house area the following day. They also agreed to watch how the children played with it and to add materials to support their "baking" play if it continued. Natalie also suggested visiting the neighborhood bakery with the class.

Anecdotal Note #5

  8/27 At cleanup time, Erica was asked to put all of the shoes back where they belonged. Erica took the shoes from Amy and put them in the toy refrigerator in the house area.

  Amy, Liz, and Faith had labeled the shelves and containers for the materials in the toy area and the block area when they initially set up their classroom, but they hadn't felt it necessary to label *all* the materials in every interest area. After they read this observation and similar ones they had accumulated, it was apparent that the children weren't sure where to put some of the materials at cleanup time. This also meant that they didn't know where to find the materials they needed to carry out their plans during work time. The teaching team decided to spend some time labeling the rest of the materials in their classroom.

Anecdotal Note #6

  12/14 At recall time Miguel said to Kiara, "Is it almost time for snack? I'm tired of playing this game."

  At first Kiara was disturbed by Miguel's statement, but after talking with her team member about it she realized that he wasn't being rude or disrespectful. He was simply telling her in his own way that recall time was becoming too long. At the beginning of the school year, Kiara and her team member had scheduled a 15-minute recall time into their daily routine. Since then, however, the recall games and activities were lasting much longer, sometimes as long as 25 minutes. Kiara decided to try keeping the time to 10–15 minutes.

Refer to High/Scope resources for assistance

If you have read Chapters 2, 3, and 4, you should have a good understanding of why planning, work, and recall are important for young children to participate in. Understanding that children who have the opportunity to make plans, carry them out, and reflect on their actions with a supportive adult will profit from doing so is the first step toward implementing the plan-do-review process in your own program. If after a period of doing so, you and your teaching team have questions or simply need reassurance that you're on the right track, refer back to the strategies and suggestions presented in this book. You may find that some sections are more helpful after you've had a chance to try the process than they were the first time you read them.

Perhaps you and your team have tried introducing the plan-do-review process in your classroom and have run into some obstacles. You meet regularly to discuss solutions and have reread parts of this book for answers, but things are still not going smoothly. High/Scope has many other resources available that may help you make this time of the day more beneficial and satisfying for children and adults alike. For instance, High/Scope's preschool curriculum manual, *Educating Young Children: Active Learning Practices for Preschool and Child Care Programs* (Hohmann & Weikart, 1995) and the books *Supporting Young Learners 1* (Brickman & Taylor, 1991) and *Supporting Young Learners 2* (Brickman, 1996) offer additional information and practical suggestions for implementing planning, work, and recall time.*

To see these parts of the daily routine in action, take a look at a series of videos filmed at High/Scope's Demonstration Preschool in Ypsilanti, Michigan: *How Adults Support Children at Planning Time, How Adults Support Children at Work Time,* and *How Adults Support Children at Recall Time.** Viewing these videos may make the process more concrete for you and give you more confidence in carrying out the plan-do-review process.

If you would like to receive training in the plan-do-review process, consider participating in High/Scope's 2-day workshop on this subject.** This workshop is taught by knowledgeable consultants who have extensive training in the entire High/Scope Preschool Curriculum. Much of the information covered in the workshop has been addressed and explained in detail in this book, but attending the workshop will give you an opportunity to discuss the information with other adults who are interested in implementing plan-do-review. Those who attend this workshop generally vary in their knowledge of and experience with the process and may ask questions during the workshop that range from very basic and general to very specific. Attending a High/Scope workshop—whether on plan-do-review or any of the many

---

*For information on ordering any of these products, please see pp. 252–254.
**For information on this or any other High/Scope training, please call 734-485-2000, ext. 218, or e-mail *training@highscope.org*.

other aspects of the curriculum—also enables you to speak individually with a consultant, who can offer clarification when you are confused, suggestions when you've run out of ideas, and support when you need encouragement.

The materials mentioned are also helpful for explaining the plan-do-review process and other aspects of the High/Scope Curriculum to parents, administrators, and other teachers. It is beneficial to have the understanding and support of these individuals as you seek to implement planning, work, and recall time in your classroom, and you should share the rationale and benefits of the process with them. Keep in mind, however, that although their support is valuable, it is not strictly necessary for the successful implementation of the process.

As mentioned throughout this chapter, implementing the plan-do-review process in your program will be exciting and probably somewhat intimidating at the same time. It will take some time before you, your co-teachers, and your children become familiar and comfortable with the process. Continue to keep the lines of communication open between team members, take advantage of the many resources High/Scope offers, and be assured that you and your children will become more accustomed to plan-do-review each day.

What About . . . ? Commonly Asked Questions About Implementing the Plan-Do-Review Process

We've been doing our daily team planning while the children are playing during work time. We're so busy getting prepared for the children's arrival before school and cleaning up after school that we just don't have any other time to meet with each other. Do you have any suggestions?

Many teachers struggle with trying to find time during their day to meet for half an hour or so with their teaching team. However, work time is not an appropriate time to meet. Remember from Chapter 3 that your role during work time is to be actively involved with the children, supporting and extending their play and learning. It's impossible to do this if you are focusing your attention on team planning.

With support from your administrator and a determination to make daily team planning time a priority, you will probably be able to develop some creative solutions to your difficulty. For some teaching teams, finding time to plan is simply a matter of time management. When teams make it a priority to meet consistently for half an hour each day, they are often surprised at how much they are able to accomplish in that time period. For other teaching teams, however, the solution is not as simple. The following suggestions have worked successfully for many teachers. They may be helpful for you, too, depending on your particular type of program.

- Meet during the children's afternoon nap time. If you need someone to be with the children during this time, perhaps you can have parent volunteers or older student helpers to stay with the children while you plan, or hire high-school or college students.

- Ask for parent volunteers or older student helpers to help prepare snack, fill the water table, or prepare easel paints before the children arrive. This may free up enough time for you and your colleagues to plan before school begins.

- Likewise, ask for parent volunteers or older student helpers to help straighten up your interest areas, clean paintbrushes, empty the water table, sweep the floor, or clean off the tables after the children depart for the day. Again, not having this responsibility may give you enough time to plan after the children leave.

- Ask for parent volunteers or older student helpers to supervise your group of children while they are eating their lunch. Find a spot to plan (for instance, on the other side of the room) where you are far enough away to avoid distractions yet close enough if you are needed in an emergency.

The parents in our program think the plan-do-review sequence is a waste of time. They would rather see us "teaching" their children academics, such as reading, writing, math, and science concepts. Is it okay to pull children aside during work time in order to work on "learning activities" with them, such as writing their names, recognizing letters, and counting?

First, children should not be pulled away from their intended plans during work time for any reason. Work time is a child-initiated time of the day, in which children are free to follow through on the plans they have made and adults support them as they do so. The purpose of child planning is defeated if adults interrupt children in order to initiate specific, task-oriented activities.

Second, remember that **children *are* learning important concepts as they participate in the plan-do-review process and other parts of the daily routine.** During planning time, for instance, they are learning how to anticipate actions and set goals for themselves. As they act upon the wide variety of materials available at work time, they are actively engaged not only in reading, writing, math, and science experiences but also in music, movement, creative representation, initiative, and social relations experiences. By providing and supporting enjoyable experiences that are based on children's interests and developmental levels—instead of "teaching" academic concepts—you enable children to participate in meaningful learning activities and to construct their own understanding of the world around them.

Taking notes on what children are doing as they play, and then sharing these with parents, will help parents better understand what their children are learning at work time.

Explain to parents the importance of an active learning educational approach. Parents want a high-quality early childhood education for their children, regardless of whether it is through a private preschool, a federally or state-funded program, an early intervention program, or a child care setting. They want to provide their children with the best opportunities in order to prepare them to succeed later in school. Many parents believe that the best way to prepare children is to enroll them in preschool programs that offer an academically oriented curriculum.

We know, however, from many years of research and child observation that young children learn best in a materials-rich environment where they can initiate active, hands-on explorations, reflect on their actions, and be observed and supported appropriately by adults. (Recall the finding discussed in Chapter 1 that having access to a variety of materials and having planning/recall opportunities are vital for children's development.) Research has also shown that a directive teaching approach in preschool does *not* give children an academic advantage in later school years over children who are allowed to initiate their own activities, and in fact a directive approach is associated with more personal and social problems as children get older (Schweinhart & Weikart, 1997). It is our responsibility as early childhood educators to share what we know about the way young children learn and to teach parents about practices that are developmentally sound. You need to help parents understand that the plan-do-review process—indeed the entire active learning approach—is *not* a "waste of time." Invite parents to visit the classroom or center, host parent workshops, and send home curriculum information. (Refer to Chapter 6 for more specific ideas on sharing information

An active learning, child-centered environment is filled with opportunities for children to learn about and explore concepts in math, literacy, science, and other areas.

with parents.) Point out to parents how engaging in active learning experiences and learning how to make choices and decisions help children become confident and ready to learn academics once they get to elementary school. This also prepares them for *life.* As parents begin to absorb this information, they will come to realize that *play really is children's work.*

We've just started using the High/Scope approach, including the plan-do-review process, in our program. The kindergarten teachers in our building are concerned that our children will not be ready for kindergarten because we are not teaching them the alphabet and other preacademics. What can we do to assure them that the children will be ready to move into their program?

The first and probably most important step you can take is to establish a partnership and open communication with these teachers, just as you would with concerned parents. Let them know that you share the same goals—that you want to do what's best for the children now, and that you want them to be successful later in school. Here are some practical ways to establish a trusting relationship and help these teachers see that the High/Scope Curriculum does indeed prepare children to be successful in kindergarten.

Explain how your program establishes the foundation for academic skills. Explain to the kindergarten teachers that in an active learning setting, adults provide a number of play and discovery experiences that lay the foundation for academic learning in years to come. For instance, High/Scope teachers understand the importance of establishing an environment rich in print, so they furnish the classroom with materials that offer children the opportunity to **recognize and read symbols and letters,** such as books, magazines, labels, phone books, alphabet cookie cutters, blocks with letters, and menus. In addition, adults read books, signs, notes, and other meaningful information to children. They build on children's natural interest in learning to recognize and copy letters, symbols, and other forms of written language.

Explain that children in your program also have opportunities to **experiment with print and develop the fine motor skills** they will need for writing by using a wide variety of materials, such as pencils, markers, paper, blank books, envelopes, note pads, stamps, and ink pads. As children see adults write down their plans and recall experiences and adults' own observations and notes to parents, children come to understand that thoughts and ideas can be written down and communicated to others.

Describe how adults also create a learning environment in which **logic and mathematics concepts** are built in and occur naturally. Children are engaged in *classification, seriation, number, space,* and *time key experiences* as they use different sizes and shapes of blocks to create a spaceship; play a game in which they move fast and slow; match small, medium, and large pots with their respective outlines on the shelf; and count the number of children needing a napkin at snack time. As children engage in these types of experiences, adults support and extend individual children's thinking and reasoning, without drilling them on rote concepts.

Spend time learning about one another's programs. Involve the kindergarten teachers in your program as much as possible so they become more comfortable with the preschool curriculum. Try to establish routine meetings—on a weekly, bi-weekly, or monthly basis—in which you can share information about your program and learn about the kindergarten curriculum.

Observing at planning and recall time will help other teachers understand these parts of the daily routine better.

During these meetings, explain the different components of the High/Scope Preschool Curriculum, including active learning, the key experiences, the daily routine, the learning environment, adult-child interaction strategies, and assessment techniques. If you're not already doing so, attend staff meetings with the kindergarten and other elementary teachers. Learn as much as you can about the school experiences your children will be participating in when they leave your program.

In addition to explaining your curriculum to the other teachers, invite them to visit your classroom when the children are involved in the plan-do-review sequence. This will enable them to see the benefits of having children make plans and set goals during planning time; follow through on their intentions, solve problems, and engage in a variety of play and learning experiences during work time; and use complex language to reflect on their actions during recall time.

Invite the kindergarten teachers to also browse through your literature or videotapes about the High/Scope Curriculum. Share with them newsletters and other notes sent home to parents. When appropriate, share photographs, writing samples, artwork, and anecdotal notes that illustrate children's active learning experiences. You may also want to include these teachers in your parent meetings and social activities, particularly during the latter part of the year. This not only helps share information about your program but also gives parents and kindergarten teachers an opportunity to establish a relationship with one another before children enter kindergarten.

Develop transition strategies together. If you are unable to have regular meetings throughout the year with the kindergarten teachers, plan to meet several times in the spring or summer (depending on your school calendar) before the children in your program make the transition into kindergarten. During these meetings, develop strategies that will help prepare the children for this move. Consider some of the following transition strategies that have been used by preschool and kindergarten teachers.

- Have your preschoolers visit the kindergarten room while the kindergarten children are present. Plan ahead with the kindergarten teacher for all the children to participate together in an appropriate activity. Or, schedule the visit to occur during the kindergarten work time (or play time) and let your children participate.

- Plan an ice cream social (or other social event) for your preschoolers and their families to participate in. Encourage the kindergarten teachers to attend, and show the children and parents the kindergarten room where the children will be going.

- If your preschoolers will be attending a full-day kindergarten program, invite them to have lunch at the school one day. Let them order a hot lunch or bring a lunch from home, and invite parents to attend, too.

- Have the kindergarten children write a story describing what they like about kindergarten, and ask the kindergarten children or teachers to read the story to the preschoolers. Laminate the book and place it in the book area in your classroom.

- Take pictures of the kindergarten classrooms, the playground equipment, lunchroom, gymnasium, and any other areas of the building where the kindergarten children go. Display the photographs in your classroom on a bulletin board or in a photo album.

- Encourage the teachers to learn more about High/Scope through books, videos, and training. If there is interest, share information about setting up an appropriate learning environment and implementing the plan-do-review process in their own daily routine.

I have several parents who consistently bring their children to school late. We begin our day with planning time, and some of the children who come in late miss the entire planning experience. Others come in during planning and disrupt the groups. I'm thinking about eliminating planning time altogether because it's so chaotic.

Eliminating planning time is not the best way to solve this problem. The heart of the problem lies with the parents' lateness, and that is the issue you need to address. There are many factors that may be contributing to parents' habitual lateness; see the box on the facing page for common reasons chil-

When Parents Are Chronically Late

Parents may have difficulty bringing their children to school on time for any number of reasons. Here are some common obstacles parents face on school days, along with some suggestions for dealing with each situation.

Other children to get off to school. If parents are late because they need to first get their older children off to school, perhaps a neighbor or family member can help get those children to the bus or drive them to school. If the problem is that the parents have little ones to wake and get dressed for the ride, perhaps the neighbor or relative can drive the preschooler or watch the baby.

No reliable transportation. This is a common reason for children's being late to school. If possible, help the parents arrange a car pool with other parents in your program or take advantage of busing or public transportation.

Children have a hard time getting going in the morning. Mornings are often difficult for many families. Encourage parents to get children to bed early so they awaken more easily, and point out the importance of having a consistent routine in the morning. Since nagging children to hurry is often counterproductive, encourage parents to give children choices so they feel some control over the situation: "Which of these shirts do you want to wear today?" "Do you want cereal or toast and peanut butter for breakfast?" Parents can also use a problem-solving approach, as outlined in Chapter 3, to help resolve morning-routine issues.

Parent work schedules. Parents who work late nights or night shifts may not be able to get their children to school early in the morning. If your program has two sessions, perhaps the child could attend the later session instead. Or, perhaps a family member or neighbor could bring the child to school.

Child doesn't want to come to school. Occasionally parents will say their child is reluctant to come to school for some reason. Perhaps the child is fearful of some situation there or is having a hard time separating from Mom or Dad. In these cases, it's important to work with the family to address the child's hesitation and make both child and parent feel comfortable coming to school.

dren come to school late and some ways to address these situations. Remind parents of the time their children are to be at school when you see them at drop-off or pick-up times. If necessary, reinforce this through personal notes, phone calls, weekly newsletters, parent meetings, or home visits. Emphasize to parents the importance of bringing their children to school on time. Help them understand that many children need time to transition into the classroom each day and that this is not possible when they arrive in the middle of an activity. They benefit from being there as the routine begins, particularly if—as in your case—the first part of the day is planning time. Explain to parents that plan-do-review is a *sequence* and that the benefit of the whole process is diminished when children miss their opportunity to plan with the group. Also point out that it is disruptive to the rest of the class when a child comes in late, as you have to leave the planning group or the children you had started to interact with at work time to greet the latecomers. Remind parents that this is not a responsibility that will go away; they will be responsible for getting their children to school on time (whether they ride a bus, walk, or are driven to school) for several more years to come. They can begin developing good habits now, while their children are in preschool.

Chances are this problem will not be solved overnight. This, of course, means that your planning time may continue to be chaotic until your children begin arriving on time. Continue to start your planning time consistently at the same time each day, and reinforce to the parents the importance of getting their children to school on time to participate in this experience. If you start planning time later or eliminate it altogether, you'll only be sending the message that it's okay to be late. Give the children who arrive after planning time a few minutes to make the transition into school, then spend some time discussing what they plan to do during work time.

If the problem continues and is still very disruptive to the rest of the group, perhaps you can have a parent volunteer (one who *is* consistently on time) stand near the door to welcome latecomers. They might guide children to their planning group or plan with them if work time has already begun. Have the planning groups meet away from the entrance to minimize noise and interruption.

Another suggestion is to consider starting your day with greeting time or a quiet reading time (where children can look at books on their own or with an adult) instead of planning time. This would enable children to enter late without causing as much of a disturbance. It would also delay the starting time for planning, allowing most children to arrive in time to participate. This alternative is preferable to continued disruption of the planning process; however, you'll still need to follow up with parents and explain the importance of bringing their children to school on time.

I have several children who receive pull-out speech and language therapy and physical therapy services twice a week. Their therapy sessions always occur during plan-do-review, interrupting the plans children have made for work time. Do you have any suggestions?

Perhaps the therapists could work with those children in your classroom during plan-do-review instead of taking them out. Encourage them to work in the various interest areas the children have chosen and incorporate the therapy or exercises into the children's play. Of course, this may be difficult to accomplish depending on the particular therapy children need and also because such therapy by nature is adult-directed.

An alternative is to adjust your daily routine so that your support staff is in the room during small- or large-group time. The therapists may be willing to develop an activity with you that incorporates children's therapy and that is appropriate for the other children to participate in as well. If possible, develop these activities with support staff during your daily team planning time to be sure the activities include the five ingredients of active learning and are appropriate for your group of children.

If none of these suggestions will work in your particular circumstance, try to give the children *some* control over the situation. For instance, it might be possible to have children decide at planning time whether they want to work with the therapist first or play for a little while first. Perhaps therapists can plan with the children and decide together what they are going to do. If there are certain exercises or tasks that *must* be done, the therapists can ask children which one they want to do first, next, and so on.

The success of these suggestions depends greatly on individual program policies, administrative support, children's individual education plans, and whether or not your support staff are willing to try a different approach to therapy. Rather than suggest drastic changes all at once, slowly incorporate some of these suggestions over an extended period of time.

We take our children to the school library every Monday at 9:00. On Tuesdays and Thursdays we go the gym at 10:00. On Wednesdays our children go to the computer lab at 9:15, and every other Friday the music teacher comes to our classroom at 11:00. Some days we have to skip some of the segments of the plan-do-review sequence or other parts of the day because we just don't have the time. Our children are confused by this schedule and often have no idea which event comes next. What can we do?

As you probably realize, you need to create a consistent and appropriate daily routine for your children. Here are some suggestions for handling all these "specials."

Evaluate whether your children really need to participate in these activities. Often, activities such as library visits, trips to computer labs, or gym time do not include all of the ingredients of active learning and are directed or controlled by adults. These activities, often geared toward older children, may not be appropriate for young children.

Your learning environment and daily routine (specifically the plan-do-review sequence) may already offer the children in your classroom some of the same experiences as these outside specials but in more appropriate ways. For example, children often have opportunities during work time or transitions (such as greeting time) to explore books by themselves or with other children or adults. Perhaps you also read a book to introduce small-group activities. You might have a lending library available to children and families wanting to take books home with them. Likewise, many classrooms have computers that children can use during work time if they choose to do so. Children also have opportunities at various times of the day (work time, large-group time, outside time) to engage in music, movement, or gross-motor activities.

Have the specialists come into your classroom. Instead of interrupting the flow of your daily routine to take children out of the classroom, invite your school librarian or computer, music, or physical education teacher to come to your classroom. Encourage them to interact with children individually during work time, assist you or your co-teacher during a small-group time, or plan a small- or large-group activity for your children to participate in. Invite them to participate in your team planning session before they come to your classroom. Discussing the ingredients of active learning and appropriate adult interaction strategies will help these specialists plan activities that are appropriate for your group of children.

If your program requires your classroom to participate in specials, try to schedule them at a consistent time in your daily routine. For example, if your children are usually involved in small-group activities at 9:00, schedule a Monday visit to the library and a Wednesday visit to the computer lab at this time. Likewise, schedule physical education during your regular outside time. Regardless of how your day is planned, you should always let children know which activities are going to occur each day when they arrive at school (a perfect opportunity to use a message board).

6

Involving Parents in the Plan-Do-Review Process

n high-quality early childhood programs, educators strive to establish an effective partnership with parents to promote children's growth and development. When parents feel accepted and valued, and when they have an understanding of your program's curriculum and its benefits to their children, they will be more likely to support the program in meaningful ways. Moreover, they will play a more active role in their children's education both at home and in the preschool setting.

This chapter presents ideas for sharing information about the plan-do-review process with parents as well as ways to actually involve them in it. These strategies will help parents understand the value of planning, work, and recall time for their children's development and will also encourage them to use the process at home. Although the ideas and examples given in this chapter focus on plan-do-review, you can use them to share other aspects of your curriculum or various topics that are important and relevant to the parents you're working with.

Share the Importance of the Plan-Do-Review Process With Parents

When you explain the sequence of planning, working, and recalling to parents and help them understand the importance of the process, they are able to perceive the process as meaningful to their children's long-term development. They gain a better understanding of how planning time gives their children the opportunity to make choices and helps them become confident decision makers and goal setters. Likewise, they begin to view children's play during work time as purposeful and worthwhile rather than aimless and impulsive. Parents can also appreciate the benefits of having children evaluate and reflect on their experiences at recall time and helping them understand the connection between their plans and their actions.

There are several ways to share information about plan-do-review with parents, including discussing the topic at parent meetings, writing about it in classroom newsletters, or providing relevant materials in your lending library. These methods are discussed below.

Parent meetings

Parent meetings offer a unique opportunity to inform parents about various aspects of your program. When discussing the plan-do-review process, it's helpful to demonstrate to parents that adults participate in this process on a daily basis and that parents can easily use it with their children at home.

Appendix A contains an outline for a parent meeting on the plan-do-review process. This sample meeting briefly introduces the other components of the daily routine as well. Because the daily routine is such a core part of

Parent meetings are an effective vehicle for explaining and demonstrating various aspects of your curriculum. Be sure to offer parents opportunities to participate in the meeting.

the High/Scope Curriculum, this topic is most effective when presented to pkarents at the beginning of the school year. Adapt the outline in Appendix A to the needs of your particular group of parents.*

Newsletters

If you send home a weekly or monthly newsletter for parents, consider giving a simple explanation of the plan-do-review process in one issue. To make the process easier to understand and more interesting, include some examples of children's planning statements or recall summaries and anecdotal accounts of their work-time experiences. If you decide to share anecdotal notes in your newsletter, be sure to remove names or to use fictitious names for the children. Delete or alter any other identifying information in the anecdotes. If parents have not already signed release forms, get their permission to use their child's anecdotes. Reassure them of the steps you have taken to preserve confidentiality. Be sure to keep the notes brief and easy to understand so that busy parents have time to read them. Appendix B contains two examples of notes that teachers have sent home to explain and illustrate the plan-do-review process. Use these as guides to help you develop your own newsletter articles or parent notes.**

A lending library

Many early childhood programs have lending libraries for the families of the children they serve. These libraries are stocked with books and other materials of interest to both parents and children. The materials you include in your

---

*For additional ideas for parent workshops and meetings, see *The Essential Parent Workshop Resource: The Teacher's Idea Book 4,* by Michelle Graves, 2000, High/Scope Press.

**High/Scope is currently developing a series of information sheets for parents explaining the components of the High/Scope Preschool Curriculum, including the plan-do-review process, as well as a series of parent newsletters on topics related to the key experiences. These will be available in early 2001.

library will depend on available space and funding. Small lending libraries, for instance, may have room for only a limited number of books. Lending libraries that have ample space may include toys, puzzles, and picture books/tapes for children as well as resource books and videotapes for parents to check out. Still other programs may not have lending libraries but may offer parents the teachers' personal resource books if they are interested.

Whether you have a well-stocked library or a small collection of books, consider adding High/Scope literature and videotapes, particularly those that explain the plan-do-review process. The materials discussed in Chapter 5 (p. 185) would be valuable in helping parents understand plan-do-review and other aspects of the curriculum. Communicate to parents your willingness to answer any questions they may have regarding information in the literature or videotapes.

Encourage Parents to Participate in Planning, Work, or Recall Time

Although reading about the plan-do-review process will give parents some idea of what it's all about, they will have a much better understanding if they are able to see it happen and actually participate in part or all of the process. If possible, encourage parents to spend some time in the classroom during the plan-do-review part of the daily routine.

From the very beginning of your partnership let parents know that they are always welcome to spend time in your classroom. If parents have never observed the plan-do-review process, you may want to let them know ahead of time what to expect. Parents may feel perfectly comfortable actively participating with a number of children during planning, work, and recall time, or they may prefer to spend the time with their own child. Other parents may be more comfortable taking a passive role, simply watching the activities from a distance. Whatever their comfort level, it's important to support their presence in the classroom and their efforts to become more involved in their children's education.

While it may be fairly easy for nonworking parents to spend time in your classroom, it is usually a challenge for parents who work during the day. Most working parents would like to be more involved in their children's preschool experience if even for a few minutes of the day, and you may be able to arrange your daily routine so that they can participate in some part of the plan-do-review sequence. Following are a few ways various programs have accomplished this.

Encourage parents to stay for planning time when dropping children off

One of the advantages of High/Scope's daily routine is that it's flexible and can be arranged to fit the needs of individual programs. Remember, however, that the plan-do-review sequence should not be interrupted; planning time should always be followed by work time, cleanup time, and then recall time. You may wish to schedule the sequence at the beginning of the day so that parents can participate in planning time when they drop their children off at school. Of course this will not work if your children travel to and from school on a bus, but if parents bring their children to school it may be a possibility. Note how the program in the following example uses this strategy effectively.

Luisa and Mary are co-teachers at a small, private preschool that has been incorporating the High/Scope Curriculum for several years. This year they decided to encourage more parent involvement in their program. One challenge they faced, however, was the high number of working parents, who were generally not available to spend the day volunteering in their children's classroom.

Luisa and Mary took into consideration several factors when deciding how to rearrange their daily routine to accommodate busy parents. First, most children were brought to school by their parents. (There were a couple of exceptions, in which grandparents or baby sitters brought the children to school.) Second, the program began at 8:00, and parents were consistently on time. Third, most parents usually spent about 15 minutes in the classroom when they arrived, assisting their children with hanging up their coats, helping them get settled into the classroom, reading books with them, and visiting with other parents.

Mary and Luisa realized that although this "settling in" period was enjoyable for families, they might be able to use this time to involve parents in plan-do-review. They rearranged their daily routine so that the plan-do-review sequence occurred first, and they encouraged the parents to stay for planning time. Many parents were receptive to the idea, and they quite often stayed not only for planning time but also for the beginning of work time. One parent commented, "I used to ask my son questions like 'How was your day?' or 'What did you do today?' and he could never tell me what he did. Now, because I hear his plan every day, I at least have something to refer to when we talk about his day, even if he doesn't carry out his initial plan."

Encourage parents to recall with their children when picking them up at the end of the day

Just as arranging the plan-do-review sequence at the beginning of the day offers parents the opportunity to participate in planning time, arranging the sequence at the end of the day offers them a chance to recall with their children. This may be an option for some programs but not for others. Consider how this approach worked for the child care center in the following example.

As a teacher in a full-day setting, Ramón's biggest challenge was that children arrived and departed at different times throughout the morning and afternoon. To accommodate these staggered schedules, Ramón arranged his daily routine so that parents would be able to recall with their children when they picked them up at the end of the day. His morning routine included all of the components of High/Scope's daily routine, including the plan-do-review sequence. His afternoon routine included a 2-hour rest time followed by a leisurely outside time. When the children returned from outside, they participated in a second planning time. Within a half an hour to an hour and a half after the children began their work time, parents arrived to pick them up. Ramón encouraged the parents to help their children conclude their work-time activities, put away the materials they had used, and complete a "recall sheet" together.

This parent uses a hoop as a prop to recall with her son at the end of the day, something the child's recall group has done before.

Although Ramón's afternoon recall was different than a "traditional" review time, in which all of the children end their work-time activities at the same time and recall together in small groups, it was a modification that worked well for his program. Most of the parents appreciated the opportunity to spend some time with their children before rushing home to their hectic evening routines.

Ask parents to make planning and recall games

As much as they'd like to, in many cases parents are not able to spend time in your classroom to see plan-do-review in action. They may be working and have no extra time to stay in the mornings or afternoons, they may not have transportation to your site, or there may be younger siblings to care for. Those parents may still appreciate the opportunity to be involved in the plan-do-review process in some way. Consider asking these parents (and others who may be interested) to assist you in making planning and recall games and props.

As you read Chapter 7, which gives ideas for planning and recall time games and experiences, you may be overwhelmed with the thought of taking the time to gather materials and props and prepare games. Parents can help with these tasks, as many of the needed materials are easily found and the games are simple to make. Asking parents to assist you serves a dual purpose: you save time by having someone help you make the games or props, and parents have an opportunity to be involved in their children's program. The children will be very proud when you use a game or prop that was made by their mom or dad especially for their classroom!

Share Children's Plans, Work-Time Experiences, and Recall Accounts With Parents

If parents are unable to spend time in the classroom or help prepare games and props, you can still involve them by sharing their children's planning, work, and recall experiences with them. Some suggestions for doing this are below.

Send home representations of children's planning and recall experiences

Many of the planning and recall games and activities you will use in your classroom encourage the children to use gestures, pantomime, or language to choose their activities or to reflect on what they have done. There are many ways to document the children's actions or statements to share with parents. For instance, if children draw a picture of what they plan to do or they trace around an object they played with at work time, encourage them to take their drawings home to show their parents. (Or, you could make a photocopy of their drawings to share with parents at a later time.) Have children "write" down their plans or work-time experiences or dictate them to you, and share these with parents. Yet another idea is to type the children's statements about their intentions or experiences on the computer, print them out, and encourage them to draw pictures illustrating their statements. They can then show these to their parents. Planning and recall sheets and journals, which are described in more detail in Chapter 7, can also be sent home for parents to read.

Videotape or photograph children during the plan-do-review sequence

Children aren't the only ones who enjoy watching themselves participating in plan-do-review on videotape. For parents who aren't able to spend time in the classroom, a videotape may be the next best thing to being there. When you use these videos as a recall experience for children, it's best to show short clips of the children participating in work time. However, when you're using the videotapes to show parents the plan-do-review process in action, tape longer segments showing the children making plans during planning time, following through on them at work time, and reflecting on their experiences at recall time. You can send copies of the videos home for parents to view at their convenience, or perhaps you can watch them together during a home visit.

Taking photographs of children during work time is also an effective way to show parents what goes on during plan-do-review. This is particularly helpful in documenting children's creations or nonpermanent activities, such as structures made from blocks or building materials, dramatic play episodes, or creations in the sand table. Instant cameras are convenient to use in these situations because the photographs can be sent home the same day as the play episodes occur, enabling parents and children to recall together while the activities are still fresh in the children's minds. Photographs can also be posted in the entry area of the classroom or center so parents and children can recall and discuss the activities of recent days. Seeing the photographs may also trigger additional ideas for play as children get ready to plan for work time.

Display children's creations or writing samples

Too often, parents empty children's book bags or backpacks without really looking at the enclosed artwork, writing samples, or other creations. To encourage parents to take notice of their children's accomplishments, try displaying some of the creations on a shelf or wall in the classroom or center, or save them in a portfolio or box to share with parents. You might even turn your classroom into an "art gallery" and host an art show, complete with refreshments and literature on encouraging and supporting children's creativity. Attaching anecdotal notes to the children's art will make the creations even more interesting and meaningful to parents.

Share anecdotal notes and child observations informally at pickup and drop-off times or more formally at parent-teacher conferences.

Share anecdotal notes with parents on a regular basis

When you document children's planning, work, and recall statements and activities, you create vivid and detailed descriptions of children's active learning experiences. Sharing these anecdotes with parents gives them a glimpse into their children's preschool experiences. Specific, objective descriptions ("Laszlo dressed up like a clown and held a 'magic show' in the house area for several other children") are much more valuable than vague statements such as "Laszlo had fun at work time today." Detailed anecdotes also help parents ask their children more specific questions or make meaningful comments about their planning, work, or recall experiences. This, in turn, encourages children to discuss their activities in more detail.

Plan-do-review anecdotes can be shared with parents at various times, such as when they pick their children up from school or drop them off in the morning. Anecdotes can also be shared during parent-teacher conferences, in progress reports, or during home visits. Calling parents on the phone, sending home personal notes, or e-mailing anecdotes can help establish positive communication between parents and teachers as well as share important information about children's learning and development. To get a glimpse of children's home experiences, encourage parents to try taking anecdotal notes at home and share them with you.

Encourage Parents to Use the Plan-Do-Review Process at Home

It was mentioned at the beginning of this book that adults use the plan-do-review process in their everyday routines. It is fairly simple to implement into *children's* routines outside of school as well. Once parents have been introduced to the plan-do-review process and have observed their children at school thinking through and planning their goals and actions, staying focused longer and solving problems when involved in an activity, and thoughtfully reflecting on their accomplishments, they may be open to implementing the approach at home. You might send home a note encouraging parents to do so. Appendix C contains a sample note, offering concrete ideas for parents to try at home, that was given to parents of preschoolers at one center. Share this with your parents who may be interested, or use it as a guide in writing your own letter.

Spending the time and energy to inform and involve parents in the plan-do-review process will certainly be worth your effort. In addition to the ideas presented in this chapter, be creative and come up with some of your own. You will find that most parents appreciate the opportunity to learn more about their children's school experiences, and they will feel more comfortable taking the initial step to become involved in the plan-do-review process both at school and at home.

7

Planning and Recall

Games and Experiences

T hroughout this book we have presented numerous examples of planning and recall games and experiences, intended to make the plan-do-review process more meaningful and concrete for you. These examples have been compiled into this chapter, along with many others that have been developed and used by early childhood consultants and teachers implementing the plan-do-review process.

Use this chapter as a quick and easy reference guide when you and your team members are developing and preparing planning and recall experiences. As you choose from among the ideas presented here, adapt them to meet the unique interests and needs of your children. Planning and recall will be more meaningful and interesting for children if you have taken the time to observe them, are aware of their individual interests, and develop your planning and recall games and experiences accordingly.

Do not limit yourself to the experiences suggested here. Observe your children throughout the daily routine, noting the materials and activities they are especially interested in, and think of creative ways in which those materials or activities could be incorporated into a planning or recall experience.* Consider the following example of how one teacher developed a planning game using simple props from her own home that reflected the children's current interests.

> Tamika noticed several children dressing up in the clothes, hats, and gloves in the house area. She remembered that she had several pairs of long, satin and lace gloves in her storage room at home, purchased at a garage sale years ago. She also had a couple of pairs of old leather work gloves. Tamika decided to bring the gloves to school the next day to use as planning props. The children could put on a glove, point to an area where they wanted to work, then talk about what they planned to do in that area.

The games and experiences in this chapter are divided into four categories: props and partnerships, visibility games and tours, group games, and representations. A brief explanation of each category is also given. Although each activity is indicated as either a planning or recall experience, most of the activities can be used for both by making a few simple adjustments.

While planning and recall games and experiences help keep these times of the day interesting and exciting for children, it's important to remember to focus on listening to and supporting children's ideas for and summaries of work time. Keep the games and activities short, simple, and appropriate for the children's ages and developmental levels.

---

*For ideas on using small-group materials and activities as sources for planning/recall props and games, see *100 Small-Group Experiences,* by Michelle Graves, 1997, Ypsilanti, MI: High/Scope Press.

Finally, remember that the games and experiences in this chapter go hand in hand with the interaction strategies explained in previous chapters. The activities described here explain only how to use the suggested game or prop, not how to extend the children's plans or recall descriptions. For example, one planning game involves having children find an object they would like to use during work time and bring it back to the planning table, but it does not mention how to then encourage children to give details of their plans. Once you and your team members have decided which games or experiences to use, you may also want to discuss how you will support children as they share their intentions and experiences. Refer to Chapters 2 and 4 for specific support strategies, most of which can be used with any prop or game. For example, after the children have brought back to the planning table the items they plan to use during work time, you could have them demonstrate how they plan to use the items. You might decide to ask questions to find out more about the children's intentions, and you might also repeat or rephrase part of what the children say.

Props and Partnerships

Using a variety of props and encouraging partnerships are simple ways of making planning and recall time more interesting for children. **Props** are toys or materials that many teachers already have in their classrooms or that can be easily made, and often they are materials children have played with before and are comfortable using. Props are used to assist children in pointing to their intended work place or to indicate whose turn it is to share their intentions or experiences. Occasionally, children will choose to incorporate the planning props into their work-time experiences.

As mentioned previously, you can encourage children—particularly those who are older or more experienced—to plan or recall in pairs or small groups. In these **partnerships,** one child describes his or her plan or recall story while the other listens. Children then switch roles. Many of the props mentioned below can be used between partners.

Pointing or touching (nonverbal)

- Encourage nonverbal children to point to an area they wish to go to or touch an object they want to play with during work time. Model planning language for them by describing the area they are pointing to.

Large and small objects

- Children bring something they played with during work time to the recall group. Have large and small sheets of paper or large and small boxes nearby. After the children describe what they did with their object, encourage them to decide if their object would fit better on the large or small sheet of paper (or in the large or small box).

Telephones

- "Call up" children one at a time on an old telephone to talk about their plans for work time. If there are enough phones for everyone, children can converse with one another while they wait to plan with you.

Walkie-talkies

- Using a walkie-talkie, children discuss with you or with one another what they did during work time. The walkie-talkie can be real or made from a unit block or a small box and a straw taped on for an antenna.

Cameras

- Children use old cameras (without film) to "take a picture" of what they did during work time by pointing the camera at an interest area or object they played with.

- After children have shared their experiences with the recall group, they "take a picture" of the child they want to recall next.

- With a working instant camera, take pictures of the children playing during work time, then give them to children to discuss at recall time.

This child "takes a picture" of the area she wants to work in.

Binoculars or spyglasses

- Children look through binoculars (real or pretend) at an interest area they'd like to go to or materials they would like to use at work time. Pretend binoculars or spyglasses can be made from cardboard tubes or paper cups with the bottoms cut out.

Puppets

- Children tell a puppet (or a stuffed animal or baby doll) what they did during work time.

Steering wheels

- Individual children "drive" to an interest area where they wish to play during work time. When they drive back to the planning group, they are encouraged to tell everyone what they will do in that interest area. Or, they bring back an item they wish to play with and show it to the group.

- The child with the steering wheel "drives" the rest of the group to the interest area where he or she will play. After describing his or her plan, the driver gives the wheel to another child and begins work time in that area. The group repeats this until all children have left for an interest area.

Magic wands

- Children point a "magic wand" at an area they played in or a material they used. Wands can be purchased or made with materials such as a cardboard tube or dowel and streamers, glitter, or paint.

Old computer keyboards

- Children "type" their plans as they discuss them with the group.

Old computer mouse

- Provide pictures or signs designating each interest area. Children click the mouse on the picture of the interest area where they played.

- Children take the mouse to an interest area where they played during work time and click it on a material they used there.

Hats

- Offer a variety of hats for children to choose from. Children put on a "planning hat" to describe their plan.

This adult asks the children in her recall group to click the mouse on the card showing the interest area they worked in.

Flashlights

- Children shine a flashlight on an area where they worked or on an object they used during work time.

- Children take turns spotlighting one another to indicate who will recall next. If it's not distracting to the other recall group, try this with the lights off.

Video camera

- Using an old, donated video camera, children point to the area where they want to work and describe what they will do during work time. If you don't have access to an old camera, use a block or cardboard box for a pretend one. Children might also be interested in making a "video camera" during work time that the group can use during planning time.

- If you have a working video camera, record short clips of the children playing during work time. At recall time let children watch themselves on video and discuss what they were doing.

Feelie box or bag

- Place objects the children used during work time in a box or bag. At recall time, the children take turns touching an object in the bag, describing what it feels like, and trying to guess what it is. When the child pulls it out, whoever used that object during work time describes what he or she did with it.

Tape measure

- As you hold one end of a tape measure, the children take turns pulling the other end to the area where they are going to work. Children may want to read the numbers on the tape and pretend to measure how far they will have to go to reach their area.

- Make a pointer out of the tape measure by extending it several inches and pushing the button to keep it extended. Children use this prop to point to the materials they want to use or to an area where they want to play during work time.

String or yarn

- As you hold one end of a long piece of string or yarn, the children take turns stretching the other end to an area they played in during work time.

Boxes

- Set out boxes of various sizes on the planning table. The children go to find a material they want to play with during work time. When they return with the item, they talk about what they will do during work time, then take turns deciding which box their object would best fit in.

Tape or sticky notes

- Children bring to the recall table an object they played with during work time. They put a piece of tape or a sticky note on the object (with their name and/or symbol on the tape or note). When you pick up a child's object, the child tells how he or she used it at work time.

- Children place a piece of tape or a sticky note on a map of the classroom or a planning/recall board (see p. 221) to indicate where they will go during work time.

You're on! These children take turns explaining their plans to the group while on "television."

Tape recorder

- Children record their conversations about their plans for work time. You may wish to replay the tape during recall time and discuss whether the children followed through with their original plan or if they made new plans during the course of work time.

Television set

- Create a "television set" out of a medium-sized cardboard box by cutting out a large square and adding knobs for the volume, channels, etc. The children hold the box over their heads and talk through the square (as if they are on television), telling what they did at work time. To keep the "audience" interested, supply a "remote control" for the children who are listening to use.

Visibility Games and Tours

Visibility games and tours are concrete ways to show planners the interest areas and materials available to them, enabling them to choose a work-time activity. For recall, the complex task of reconstructing events from work time is made easier when children are able to return to the interest areas where they played, manipulate the objects they used, and/or show their classmates the actual structures or artwork they created. Because visibility games and tours offer such a concrete experience, they are very useful for younger children or children who are new to the planning and recall process. Many teachers use these strategies at the beginning of the school year and gradually move to more abstract games and experiences as children become more familiar with the learning environment and the plan-do-review process. Props such as those mentioned in the previous section are often used to enhance visibility games and tours.

Train, caterpillar, or snake

- Children form a line and move through the interest areas of the classroom to see the materials available. Once they decide where they will play, children may talk about their plan or simply get started with it.

Planning safari

- Children walk around the classroom, using binoculars (real or pretend, as described on p. 211) to spy an interest area to work in or a material to play with during work time.

Riding toy

- Children take turns riding a wheeled toy to the interest area they want to work in.

Musical instrument

- One child (the "bandleader") marches around the room playing a drum or other musical instrument while the other children follow. When the leader gets to the interest area where he or she played during work time that day, the child tells what he or she did and gives the instrument to someone else to be the leader.

Displays

- Collect and set out at your planning spot a variety of materials from the interest areas. Children discuss and manipulate the materials, decide which ones they would like to use during work time, then get started on their plans.

Grab bag

- Give each child a bag, basket, or box to collect an item they played with at work time. When they return to the recall group, they show the material and share what they did in more detail.

Visits to structures

- Encourage children to save the structures they made during work time (for example, a fort made from hollow blocks, a racetrack made with unit blocks, or a Lego school). During recall time, children lead the rest of the group to look at their structure, then discuss how they made it.

Gallery visits

- During recall time, children who worked in the art area lead the rest of the group to the bulletin board, drying rack, or art table to show and discuss their creations.

Group Games

The main purpose of **group games** is to determine whose turn it will be to plan or recall next. Because group games are fun, they help keep children interested in the activity while they wait their turn to plan or recall.

Once again, the emphasis during planning and recall time should be on encouraging children to share their intentions or experiences. If you find that more of your time is being spent playing games than listening to and supporting the children who are planning or recalling, consider whether the games you're using are too complex. Below are some examples of quick, simple group games that have been used successfully in many High/Scope classrooms.

Card match

- Make two piles of matching playing cards or pictures from a memory game. Each child chooses a card from one pile. From the other pile, turn over a card. The child with the matching card shares his or her plan.

Musical beanbags

- While a musical tape or CD is playing, the children sit in a circle and pass around a beanbag. When you stop the music, the child who is holding the beanbag recalls.
- Sit in a circle with the children. Toss the beanbag to the first child, who then recalls. That child then tosses it to another child to recall.

Mystery bag

- Put each child's symbol or photograph in a bag and have the children take turns pulling one out. The child whose card is drawn shares his or her plan with the group.

Hula-Hoop

- Children sit in a circle around a Hula-Hoop that has been marked in one place with paint or a piece of tape. Lead the children in a simple chant or song, and have them pass the hoop through their hands. When the chant is finished, the child whose hand is on or closest to the mark shares his or her work-time experience. Example of a chant to use: "What did you do at work time, work time? What did you do at work time today?"

Board game

- Make a circle out of tagboard or cardboard and partition it like a pie or pizza. Put a child's name and symbol or picture in each one of the sections. Then attach a plastic spinner to the center of the circle. Children take turns spinning the spinner, and when it lands on a child's symbol or picture, that child shares his or her plan.

Spin the bottle

- Children sit in a circle around a bottle or a cylindrically shaped block and take turns spinning it. When it stops, the child it is pointing to recalls next.

Ball

- Children sit in a circle facing one another. Roll a ball to a child and ask for that child's plan. He or she then rolls the ball to another child, who plans next.

Rhymes

- Make up a rhyme, such as "Clapping, clapping, clapping Cannah. It's your turn to recall if your name is Hannah." After that child has shared his or her work-time experience, repeat the rhyme and choose a new child to recall.

Musical chairs or carpet squares

- Put several chairs or carpet squares (one for each person in the group) in a circle, and distinguish one as a "planning seat." The planning seat could be a different color or size than the other chairs, or the carpet square might have a special picture taped to it. Play music as the children move however they choose (hop, crawl, skip, swim) around the circle. When the music stops, the children sit down on a chair or carpet square. The child who sits in or on the planning seat discusses his or her plan.

Colors and other attributes

- Choose a child to recall by saying something like "Whoever is wearing green, [red, purple] on their shirt can tell us about work time."
- Choose another attribute, such as shirt buttons, Velcro on shoes, belts on pants, etc.

String a bead

- Each child chooses a bead. When it's their turn to plan, the children string their bead onto a string held by you.
- Combine this game with the previous one. For instance, say something like "Whoever has a blue bead [square bead, small bead] can plan next."

Puzzle

- Choose (or let a child choose) a familiar classroom puzzle with the same number of pieces as there are children in the group. Each child takes a puzzle piece and fits it into the puzzle when it is his or her turn to recall.

Pegboard

- When it's their turn to plan, children place a peg in a hole in the pegboard or stack it on top of another child's peg.

Alarm clock

- Children put their heads down on the planning table or lie down on the floor and pretend they are sleeping. As you ring the clock to "wake up" each child, the child tells what he or she plans to do during work time.

Simon Says

- Play the game "Simon Says" to choose a child to plan next. For example, say "Simon says if you worked in the art area [block area, woodworking area] today, tell me about your work time."

Shell game

- Hide a small ball under one of several shells. Move the shells around and have the children take turns guessing which shell the ball is under. The child who finds the ball discusses his or her plan.

Song or chant

- Chant or sing a planning song. For example, sing this to the tune of

"Ninety-Nine Bottles of Beer on the Wall":
What's your plan for school today?
What's your plan today?
Look around and make a choice.
Elizabeth, what d'ya say?

Balance beam

- Children take turns walking across a balance beam (or around or through another obstacle). As they get to the end of the beam, they recall their work-time experience.

Rope

- Make a circle with a rope and use it in a way similar to the Hula-Hoop game described on p. 217.

- Form a circle with the rope and place it on the floor (a Hula-Hoop can also be used). Say something like "If you're planning to work in the house area today, step in the circle." Children in the circle describe what they will do during work time. After those children leave for the house area, repeat the game for another interest area.

Representations

Representation activities involve making or using symbols, photographs, pantomime, drawing, or writing along with spoken language. These types of games encourage children to visualize, describe, or represent their intentions and experiences more fully and are usually most successful with experienced planners and recallers.

Area cards

- Using drawings, magazine pictures, or photographs, create cards that represent all the interest areas in the classroom. Children use the cards as they talk about where they worked during work time, or they may arrange the cards in the sequence of where they worked first, second, and so on. *These cards can be used to enhance several other planning and recall games and experiences. You may want to make several sets of the cards in various sizes and cover them with plastic laminate for extended use.*

- Put the cards face down on the table or floor, or put them in a bag or box. Then turn over one of the cards or pull a card from the bag (you can have a child do this instead). Those children who worked in the interest area depicted on the card discuss what they did there.

- Place the area cards face up on the table or floor. When it's their turn to recall, children place a small plastic or wooden person, teddy bear counter, or poker chip on the area card where they worked.

Balance beam

- Tape small area cards to a balance beam. Each child takes a turn walking on the balance beam to the sign showing the area he or she plans to work in. If a balance beam is not available, stick a long piece of thick tape on the floor or line up large, hollow wooden blocks.

Beanbag toss

- Line up several buckets or baskets with small interest area cards taped to them. One at a time, the children toss a beanbag into the bucket or basket showing the area where they want to play. They tell the group what their plans are, then choose the next child to toss the beanbag.

Writing tools

- Choosing from a variety of drawing or writing tools, children trace an object they played with, draw a picture of what they did during work time, or attempt to write letters or words that describe their work-time experience. Or, they may dictate their experiences to you to write down. This activity works well with children with a wide range of developmental abilities. It also keeps children involved while you converse with some of them individually.
- Give the children a simple planning or recall "form" to fill out. (See Appendix D for sample forms.) Children may also draw a picture on the form of what they did or what they plan to do.

Planning pockets

- Attach several envelopes to a large sheet of tagboard. Draw or glue an interest area sign on each envelope. The children put their photographs or symbols in an envelope to indicate where they'd like to play during work time.

Clue game

- Give clues about what you saw a certain child doing during work time, and have the children try to guess who you are describing. For example, say "Today I saw someone in the movement area. They were holding the scarves in their hands and moving their feet like this" (slide your feet on the floor like an ice skater).
- Children give clues about what they did during work time. The rest of the group tries to guess what the clue-giver did.

Path or sidewalk

- Draw large squares on a long roll of paper, or use the squares of a sidewalk outside. In each square draw a symbol (with markers, paint, or sidewalk chalk) that represents an interest area in the classroom. The children take turns walking down the path or sidewalk and stopping on the square with the name and drawing of the interest area where they'd like to go. If you use paper for this activity, cover it with plastic laminate so you can roll it back up and use it again.

- When children have stopped on a square in the above activity, they wait on their square to see who else is planning to go to that area. They discuss what they plan to do there, and they could also count how many children are going to each area.

Chalkboard or wipe-off marker board

- Children draw or write about what they did during work time on a large or individual chalkboard or wipe-off marker board.

Planning board

- Make a large poster with all of the interest areas represented on it with drawings, photographs, or magazine pictures. One at a time, the children touch, write their name next to, place their symbol or photograph next to, or clip a clothespin onto the interest area where they plan to work.

Classroom map

- Draw a simple map of the classroom, indicating important items such as the interest areas, bathroom, doors, and so on. Children "walk" a small plastic person or animal to the interest area on the map where they want to play.

Children's planning/recall journals enable you to document the growth in their ability to express their intentions and experiences.

- Use small plastic or wooden cars instead of people. Children "drive" them to the interest area on the map where they plan to work.
- Create a "runway" on a long sheet of paper (or use wooden blocks), and give the children small airplanes to use. They "take off" from the runway and land on the interest area of their choice indicated on the classroom map.

Dollhouse figures

- Draw the interest area symbols on self-stick notes and place each note in a room in your dollhouse. Children place a dollhouse figure in the room representing the interest area they want to play in.

Recall train

- Set up a train track and place small area cards at various places near the track. One at a time, the children drive the train around the track, stopping at the interest area where they worked and describing what they did there.

Hammer a nail

- Sketch a simple planning board (described on p. 221) on a piece of wood or a piece of Styrofoam. The children take turns hammering a nail into the wood or a golf tee into the Styrofoam to indicate the interest area in which they would like to play.

Go fishing

- Draw the interest area symbols on pieces of paper that have been cut into fish shapes. Attach a paper clip to each fish. Give the children a "fishing pole" made out of a dowel, a piece of string, and a magnet tied to the end of the string. Children "go fishing" for the interest area where they played during work time that day.

Computer

- Type children's plans on the computer as they dictate them to you, then print them out for the children to keep. Children may also draw a picture on their printouts indicating what they will do during work time.

Graph

- Make a picture graph showing which areas the children played in during work time. After all the children recall, compare the number of children in each interest area and discuss which areas had the most children and which had the least children.

Pantomime

- The children take turns pantomiming what they plan to do during work time. The rest of the group tries to guess what their classmate is going to do.

Pictures

- Put together a collection of photos, drawings, or catalog pictures of all the materials in your classroom. Cover them with plastic laminate and sort them into boxes by interest areas. During recall time, encourage the children to find the pictures of the different materials they used. Older children may enjoy placing the pictures in the sequence in which they played with the materials. *Variation:* Have each child choose a teddy bear counter (or other small object) and place it on the picture of the material he or she played with.

Planning and recall books or journals

- Create these by placing several blank pieces of paper between two pieces of construction paper or wallpaper from discontinued sample books. Bind the pages together with fasteners, staples, or yarn. Children can create their own covers for their books if they wish. Encourage the children to "write" what they plan to do during work time in their journal, or have them draw a picture of their plans while you write down what they dictate to you. This is an effective way of documenting children's development as they become more experienced in planning and recalling.

Appendix A

Sample Parent Meeting

and Overheads

What Is Plan-Do-Review?

Goals

- To make parents aware of the purpose and importance of planning, work, and recall time
- To offer parents ideas for using the plan-do-review process at home

Materials

- A copy of your program's daily routine (either written on a handout or displayed on a piece of chart paper)
- Chart paper
- Markers
- Overheads A, B, and C: Summaries of planning time, work time, and recall time (pp. 228–230)
- Brief video clips of your classroom recorded during planning, work, and recall time

Introduction

1. Show parents a copy of your program's daily routine. Briefly and simply explain the components of the day—greeting, small-group, large-group, snack, outside time, and plan-do-review. Give examples of the types of activities that typically occur during these times of the day. Explain that during this meeting you will focus on the plan-do-review process, which includes planning time, work time, and recall time.

Opening Activity

2. Have parents divide into several small groups. Give each group a different activity or event to plan, such as a birthday party, a dinner party, a family vacation, a weekend getaway, or a building project. Encourage parents to spend about 10 minutes planning their activity. When they're finished, ask volunteers from each group to share their ideas with the rest of the parents. Afterward, encourage the groups to list several ways they would relate their experiences from their assigned event to friends or family who had not taken part. When they're finished ask them to share their ideas with the whole group, and record these on chart paper. Responses may include telling stories and showing photographs, videotapes, journals, or souvenirs.

Transition Statement

3. Relate the "Opening Activity" to your main topic of discussion by saying something such as the following: "In our classroom, planning time is similar to the plans that you made just now and to the plans that you make in everyday life. Work time is similar to the actual activity or event—the dinner party, the vacation, the project—while recall time is a chance for children to share their experiences with others, much as you would share *your* experiences of the event you planned."

Central Ideas

4. Show overheads A, B, and C. Discuss each with the group, relating points to the opening activity when appropriate. Encourage parents to ask questions and share comments.

5. Show a brief videotape of the children involved in the plan-work-recall sequence. For example, show 5 minutes of clips from planning time, 10 minutes from work time, and 5 minutes from recall time. Tie in points from the overhead when appropriate. Again, encourage questions and comments.

Reflections and Ideas for Application

6. Encourage parents to return to their small groups and discuss when and how they might use the plan-do-review process with their children at home. If they have older children, they might consider ways to use it with them as well. After they have had a chance to discuss their ideas with their fellow group members, encourage them to share them with the rest of the parents.

Follow-up Plans

7. In the weeks following the meeting, chat with parents about whether they've incorporated the plan-do-review process at home. If they have, encourage them to describe how, then with their permission share their experiences in your newsletter.

Overhead A

Planning: A Summary

What It Is
- Establishing a problem or goal
- Imagining and anticipating actions
- Expressing personal intentions and interests
- Shaping intentions into purposes
- Deliberating
- Making ongoing modifications

Why It Is Important
- Encourages children to articulate their ideas, choices, and decisions
- Promotes children's self-confidence and sense of control
- Leads to involvement and concentration on play
- Supports the development of increasingly complex play

Where to Plan
- In a place where intimate conversations can occur
- In a stable pair or group
- Where people and materials are visible

What Children Do as They Plan
- Develop the capacity to express their intentions
- Indicate their intentions through gestures, actions, and words
- Make vague, routine, and detailed plans
- Make perfunctory and real plans
- Make a variety of plans over time
- Engage in the planning process at home

Overhead B

Work Time: A Summary

What It Is
- Carrying out intentions
- Playing with purpose
- Participating in a social setting
- Solving problems

Why It Is Important
- Encourages children's playfulness
- Enables children to construct knowledge as they engage in the High/Scope key experiences
- Enables adults to observe, learn from, and support children's play

Where Children Work
- In the interest areas
- In cozy and open spaces

What Children Do at Work Time
- Initiate, work on, modify, complete, and change their plans
- Play in a variety of social contexts
- Engage in different types of play
- Carry on conversations

Overhead C

Recalling: A Summary

What It Is

- Remembering and reflecting on actions and experiences
- Associating plans, actions, and outcomes
- Talking with others about personally meaningful experiences

Why It Is Important

- Exercises children's capacities to form and talk about mental images
- Expands children's consciousness beyond the present

Where to Recall

- In intimate groups and places
- With those who shared the experiences children are recalling

What Children Do as They Recall

- Grow in their capacity to recount past events
- Select experiences to recall
- Construct their own understanding of what they have just done
- Recall experiences in a variety of ways

Appendix B

Sample Parent Notes Explaining Plan-Do-Review

Note 1

Dear Parents,

This year our program will be implementing the High/Scope Curriculum. Throughout the year, we will be sending notes like this home with your child to explain various parts of the curriculum. An important element of the High/Scope approach is a part of our daily routine called *plan-do-review*. This note will explain each part of this sequence: planning time, work time, cleanup time, and recall time.

Planning Time

During this time of the day, the children meet in small groups to make decisions about what they intend to do during the 50-minute work time that follows. They then share their plans with their classmates and teachers. Children can choose to play with materials from any of the various interest areas in our classroom. They are encouraged to think not only about what they will do during work time but also about what materials they might need to carry out their plans, who they will play with, and what they might do if a problem occurs while carrying out their plans.

When children first begin to plan, they may simply point to the area they want to play in or touch the materials they want to use. Later, they may describe their plans in simple statements. Over time, their plans become more detailed and may be described using words, drawings, or actions.

Following are some examples of how children express the plans they've made:

- When asked what he wants to do during work time, Alonzo points to the woodworking area.
- When Lauren's teacher asks her what her plan is for the day, she walks to the book area and holds up a book for the teacher to see.
- During planning time, Ruth's teacher asks what she'd like to do during work time that day. She answers "Sand."

Other, more detailed plans may include

- "I'm gonna paint a picture at the easel."
- "I want to play on the computers."
- "I'm gonna be the momma in the house area, and I'm gonna feed my baby, but first I have to make her supper."
- "I want to dress up in the costumes in the music and movement area, and put on a show for you to come see."

Work Time

After planning comes work time, when the children are able to play in the different interest areas of the classroom. Many of the children will carry out the plans they made during planning time while others will be anxious to make new plans and explore many different toys and activities. Children are not required to carry out their original plans, although we may discuss their new plans with them if we see them doing something different during work time.

During work time, children may be stacking blocks, gluing Styrofoam pieces onto cardboard, rolling out play dough, dancing to music, reading books, putting puzzles together, or dressing up and pretending to go to a wedding. The teachers play with the children during this time, helping them solve problems and encouraging them to try new ideas. While the children are busy playing, they are developing their intellectual, social, emotional, physical, and language skills.

Cleanup Time

After a 50-minute work time, the children and teachers spend about 10 minutes cleaning up the classroom. When you visit our classroom, you will notice that all of the containers and shelves where materials are stored have labels indicating where the materials belong. We have a variety of labels—some are drawings of the objects, some are photographs, and some consist of the actual objects themselves. This labeling system makes it easier and more enjoyable for the children to put the toys back in their place, and it guarantees that the materials they want to use the next day will be there for them. Learning to match a label with an object is also the beginning of learning how to read. It is the same type of connection children make when they begin to understand that letters match sounds and that written words stand for objects and actions.

Recall Time

Recall time is the "review" part of plan-do-review. During this 15-minute period, the children tell one another what they did at work time. It also becomes a time for children to show their classmates projects they may have worked on, such as a "princess house" made out of Legos, a "race car" made in the woodworking area, or a painting. In retelling what they did, children begin to think about how they carried out their activities and how they might do things differently next time. They also get lots of good ideas when they hear other children describing what *they* did! As with planning, children begin recalling with simple words or gestures. Later on, they describe what they have done in more detail. Reflecting on their earlier experiences and sharing stories with their friends during recall time is an enjoyable way to bring the plan-do-review sequence to a close.

One Final Thought

Thank you for taking the time to read this important information about the High/Scope Curriculum we are using in our program. If you have any questions about the plan-do-review process, or any other part of our curriculum, please don't hesitate to contact us. We'll be happy to discuss anything with you. Remember, you're always welcome to visit our classroom to see plan-do-review in action!

Note 2

Dear Parents,

Please take some time to read the following notes that we recorded in our classroom this week during plan-do-review. Since our last parent meeting covered the plan-do-review process, we thought you might enjoy this little glimpse into our classroom. (Parents of the children mentioned in the notes have given us permission to use their children's names.) Next month's newsletter will feature more classroom notes!

10/20

At planning time, Christopher and Tong said they were going to work together in the art area. When asked what they were planning to do there, Christopher stated that they were going to use the scissors and cut the "instruction paper" (construction paper).

10/20

At work time in the art area, Tong used the scissors to cut strips of construction paper while Christopher stapled the ends of the pieces together. After connecting several strips together, Tong said, "This is the longest snake I ever saw!" Christopher suggested they make it "as long as the classroom!" He used a black marker to draw at one end of the "snake" what appeared to be two eyes, a nose, and a mouth with a tongue sticking out. This play continued the entire 50-minute work time.

10/20

At recall time, Christopher and Tong took the teacher and the rest of the group to where they had placed their "snake." Tong showed the group how he had used the scissors to cut, and Christopher demonstrated how he had stapled the strips together.

10/21

At planning time, Tong and Christopher decided to go back to the art area and work some more on their snake. Tong said, "Today it's my turn to staple, and Chris is going to cut." Christopher replied, "Yeah. I'm gonna cut." Tyrone and Katie said they'd like to help make the snake, too.

10/21

At work time Christopher and Tyrone used scissors to cut strips of construction paper while Tong and Katie used the staplers to connect the pieces together. When they stretched the "snake" as long as it could go, it went from the block area (at the far end of the classroom), out the door, and into the hallway. As they stretched it they all giggled, and Christopher said, "This snake is the longest in the whole world!"

Several more children have since taken part in the "longest-snake-in-the-whole-world" project. They are still adding to their snake, but now they wait until outside time to stretch it out to see how long it is. Please stop by our classroom sometime to see this ongoing project. You'll be amazed at how long the "snake" really is!

Appendix C

Sample Parent Note Encouraging Plan-Do-Review at Home

Dear Parents,

By now you're aware that your children are involved in the plan-do-review process during part of the day at school. Most of you have taken part in some of the many opportunities to learn more about our program and have had a chance to visit your children at school. Your participation has been greatly appreciated!

Many of you have commented that you wish your children played or worked with as much purpose at home as they do at school. Much of this purpose and focus comes from the daily opportunity to set their own goals, carry out their plans, and reflect back on what they did—all part of the plan-do-review process. Here are some suggestions for using this process at home.

- Let your child see *you* make plans, follow through with them, then think back on what you did. For instance, let your child know what you're planning to do while he or she is at school, then share your experiences after school.

- When appropriate, let your child make plans with you for

    —Dinner

    —A Saturday outing

    —A family vacation

    —A birthday party or other celebration

    —A home improvement project

- After your preschooler gets home from school and has had some "down" time, encourage him or her to make a plan for the rest of the day or evening. Spend time with your child as he or she plays and carries out this plan, and when your child is finished be sure to talk about what he or she did. It might be a nice family tradition to recall or discuss everyone's day at dinner time or before bedtime.

- Use the plan-do-review approach with your school-aged children, too. It is especially helpful for planning their chores around the house and completing their homework.

These are just some ideas to get you started. You may have others! If you do decide to try plan-do-review at home, let us know how it works!

Appendix D

Sample Planning and Recall Sheets

Have children mark the area(s) where they plan to work or where they did work.

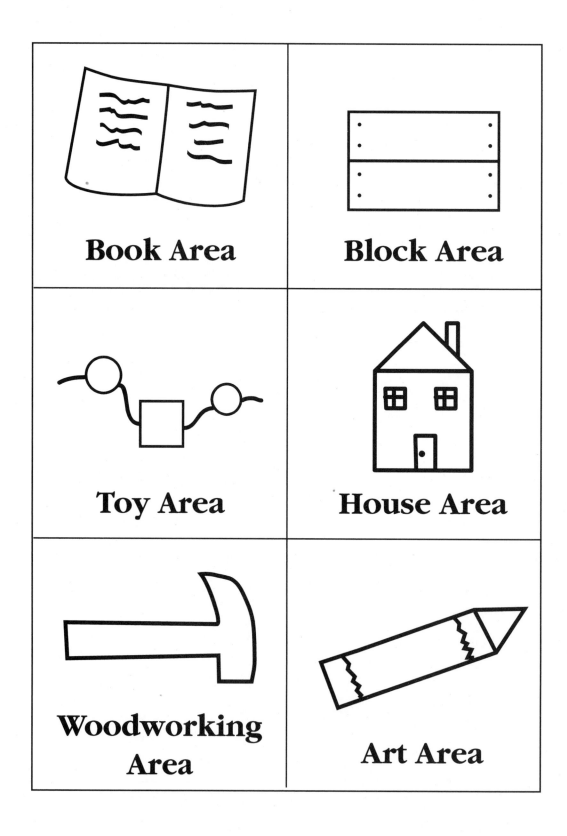

Book Area

Block Area

Toy Area

House Area

Woodworking Area

Art Area

Today I will work in...

1. _____

2. _____

Today I worked in...

1. _____

2. _____

Have children draw a picture of what they plan to do or what they did do during work time.

Bibliography

References

Epstein, A. S. 1993. *Training for Quality: Improving Early Childhood Programs Through Systematic Inservice Training* (Monographs of the High/Scope Educational Research Foundation, 9). Ypsilanti, MI: High/Scope Press.

Hohmann, M., and Weikart, D. P. 1995. *Educating Young Children: Active Learning Practices for Preschool and Child Care Programs.* Ypsilanti, MI: High/Scope Press.

Schweinhart, L. J., and Weikart, D. P. 1997. *Lasting Differences: The High/Scope Preschool Curriculum Comparison Study Through Age 23* (Monographs of the High/Scope Educational Research Foundation, 12). Ypsilanti, MI: High/Scope Press.

Related Reading

Brickman, N. A. (Ed.) 1996. *Supporting Young Learners 2: Ideas for Child Care Providers and Teachers.* Ypsilanti, MI: High/Scope Press.

Brickman, N. A., and Taylor, L. S. (Eds.) 1991. *Supporting Young Learners 1: Ideas for Preschool and Day Care Providers.* Ypsilanti, MI: High/Scope Press.

Evans, B. (in press). *"You Can't Come to My Birthday Party!" Conflict Mediation With Young Children.* Ypsilanti, MI: High/Scope Press.

Graves, M. 2000. *The Essential Parent Workshop Book: The Teacher's Idea Book 4.* Ypsilanti, MI: High/Scope Press.

Vogel, N. 1997. *Getting Started: Materials and Equipment for Active Learning Preschools.* Ypsilanti, MI: High/Scope Press.

Related Videotapes

How Adults Support Children at Planning Time. 1997. Ypsilanti, MI: High/Scope Press.

How Adults Support Children at Recall Time. 1997. Ypsilanti, MI: High/Scope Press.

How Adults Support Children at Work Time. 1997. Ypsilanti, MI: High/Scope Press.

Child Assessment Tool

High/Scope Child Observation Record (COR) for Ages 2½–6. 1992. Ypsilanti, MI: High/Scope Press.

Index

A

Academics, and plan-do-review.
See Plan-do-review
Active learning, 80, 153–54
  developing motor skills, 190
  importance of, 188
  ingredients of, 4, 66
  and logic and mathematical
    concepts, 190
  a mental process, 65–66
  a physical activity, 65–66
Adult-child interaction, 4
Adult interaction strategies
  cleanup time, 105–111
  planning time, 19–34
  recall time, 137–51
  work time, 80–103
Adults, monitoring role of, 65
Alarm clock, 218
Anecdotes
  collecting, 119–20
  in newsletter, 199
  sharing, 181–82, 206
  using shortcuts in, 118
Area cards, 219
Assessment, 4. *See also* High/Scope Child
  Observation Record

B

Balance beam, 218, 220
Ball, 217
Beanbag toss, 220
Binoculars, 211
Board game, 217
Boxes, 213
Brickman, N. A., 185

C

Cameras, 210
Card match, 216
Carpet squares, 217
Caterpillar, 215
Center time, 162
Chalkboard, 221
Challenging thinking, 92
Child language, 80
Children's activities, documenting, 104
Children's conversations,
  documenting, 104
Children's creations, using, 204
Children's initiative, 4, 14–15
Children's physical level. *See* Joining
  children on physical level
Choice, 66, 80
  and plan-do-review, 14
Choice time, 162

Classroom map, 221
Cleanup games
  choose a picture, 109
  magic wand, 109
  musical cleanup, 109
  sorting, 109
  tool time, 109
  "What color are you?", 109
Cleanup time, 7, 62, 105, 162, 233
  advance warning of, 105–7, 129
  closure, 111
  cooperation during, 129
  games, 109
  making manageable, 129
  organization, 128
  problem-solving skills in, 108
Clue game, 220
Colors and other attributes, 218
Commenting on what children
  do, 26–27
Communication
  and limited verbal skills, 50
  methods of, 51
Computer, 222
Computer keyboards (old), 211
Computer mouse (old), 211
Conflict
  and problem solving, 46–47
  unnecessary, 100
Conflict resolution, 100–101
  importance of, 121
Constructive play, 74–77
Containers, labeling, 107
Conversations, documenting, 104

D

Daily routine
  components of, 5, 7–9
  and plan-do-review, 7, 9
  revising, 162, 164
Describing, children's actions, 83, 85
Detailed plans, 16
Developmental abilities, range of, 55–59
Developmental level, 82–83. *See also*
  Mixed-age groups
Displays, 215
Dollhouse figures, 222

E

*Educating Young Children: Active
  Learning Practices for Preschool and
  Child Care Programs* (Hohmann &
  Weikart), 4, 125, 185
Encouragement, 32–33, 147
Entering a child's play, 86–87
Epstein, A. S., 3

Exploratory play, 72–74
and age, 74
Extending children's play, 90–92

F
Feelie box or bag, 213
Flashlights, 212
Following children's leads, 87–89
Following through, on plans, 55, 148
Free play, 162
Frustration, dealing with, 98–99

G
Gallery visits, 216
Games, 78–79
Go fishing, 222
Goals, ability to identify, 15
Grab bag, 215
Graph, 222
Group games, 216–19

H
Hammer a nail, 222
Hats, 211
High/Scope Child Observation
Record, 104
High/Scope Curriculum, 80
and daily routine, 199
High/Scope Demonstration
Preschool, 185
High/Scope Preschool Curriculum,
4–5, 185
and kindergarten curriculum, 191
High/Scope Preschool "Wheel of
Learning," 4, 5
High/Scope 2-day workshop, 185
Hohmann, Mary, 4, 125, 185
*How Adults Support Children at Planning
Time* (videotape), 125, 185
*How Adults Support Children at Recall
Time* (videotape), 125, 185
*How Adults Support Children at Work
Time* (videotape), 125, 185
Hula-Hoop, 217

I
Initiative. *See* Children's initiative
Interest area
number of children in, 47, 113–15
time limit for, 113

J
Joining children at developmental
level, 82–83
Joining children on physical level, 82

K
Key experiences, 4, 65, 103
categories, 68, 69, 70

creative representation, 69, 70
engaging in, 68
initiative and social relations, 68, 69
language and literacy, 69, 70
movement, 69, 70
music, 69
number, 69
seriation, 69, 70
space, 69, 70
time, 69

L
Labeling
children's actions, 83, 85
materials, 107
Language, from children, 66–67
Language skills, and planning, 50
Large and small objects, 209
Large-group time, 8, 121
Lateness problems, 193–94
Learning environment, 4
arranging, 46, 117–18
Lending library, 199–200

M
Magic wands, 211
Manipulation, 66, 80
Marker board, 221
Materials, 46, 66, 80
introducing, 53
preparing, 117
Mixed-age groups, planning with, 55–59
Musical beanbags, 216
Musical chairs, 217
Musical instrument, 215
Mystery bag, 216

N
Newsletters, 199
Nonverbal children
interpreting communication of, 141–42
planning with, 26–27, 50–51

O
Observing children, 82
sharing observations, 181–82
Outdoor time, 121
Outside time, 8

P
Pantomime, 223
Parallel play, 82
Parent meetings, 198–200, 226–27
and plan-do-review, 125–26
Parent newsletters, 199, 232–36, 238
Parents
anecdotal notes and, 206
in classroom, 200–2
making planning games, 203

Partnerships, 209
Path or sidewalk, 221
Pegboard, 218
Photographs, 118, 204
Physical problems, solving, 98–99
Pictures, 223
Plan-do-review, 148, 157, 158
    and academics, 187–88, 190
    adult participation in, 198
    after school, 10–12
    anecdotes, 206
    child-initiated, 112
    and choices, 14
    and daily routine, 7, 9
    and documented plans, 33
    effect of, 3
    as foundation for academic skills, 190
    goal of, 12
    at home, 206
    introducing, 169–80
    order in, 9
    and parent meetings, 125–26
    parent participation in, 200
    and preschoolers, 54
    presenting, 125–26
    recall time in, 132
    and special schedules, 157–58, 194–95
    on videotape, 204
    work time in, 64
Planning
    and changes in ability, 33–34
    complexity in, 53
    conventional way, 54
    and daily routine, 44
    details in, 30–31
    lack of interest in, 25
    and language skills, 50
    location for, 19, 21
    materials and space, discussing, 29–30
    with mixed-age groups, 55–59
    nonverbal, 26–27
    order of plans, 31
    in pairs, 45
    and previous activities, 31–32
    routine, 43–44
    time, 21, 53
Planning board, 221
Planning experiences, representations of, 203–4
Planning games, 14, 19, 21–22, 45, 138. See also individual games
    and children's ages, 208
    introducing, 53
    making, 203
Planning groups, 19
    changing, 20
    place for, 19–20
    size of, 44
Planning journals, 223

Planning language, modeling, 209
Planning pockets, 220
Planning safari, 215
Planning time, 2–3, 7, 16, 162, 232
    and daily routine, 19
    as language experience, 17
    purpose of, 14, 25
    a summary, 228
Plans
    changes in, 47–49
    documented, 33
    elaborating on, 29
    nonverbal, 26–27
    sharing, 16
    verbalizing, 54
    "writing," 33
Play
    as children's work, 190
    constructive (see Constructive play)
    exploratory (see Exploratory play)
    extending, 90
    and planning, 17, 19
    pretend (see Pretend play)
    purposeful, 17, 19, 112
    and recalling, 151
Play time, 162
Pointing or touching, 209
Praise, vs. encouragement, 32–33, 147
Preschoolers, and plan-do-review, 54
Pretend play, 77–78
Problem solving, 46–47, 115
    asking for ideas, 101
    follow-up support in, 101–3
    restating problems in, 101
    and social interaction, 100
    steps, 120–21
    use of another child in, 120–21
    use of team members in, 120
Props, 137–38, 209–14. See also individual props
    introducing, 53
Puppets, 211
Puzzle, 218

Q
Questions
    open-ended, 23, 25
    use of, 94–97

R
Recall
    choices, 157
    at mealtime, 154
Recall experiences
    active, 153
    with partner, 153
    planning and, 156
    representations of, 203–4

Recall games, 152. *See also individual games*
and children's ages, 208
making, 203
varying, 155
Recall journals, 223
Recall time, 3, 162, 233–34
activities, 153
and children's abilities, 150–51
as closure, 158
commenting on work time, 143
documenting accounts, 144
drawing meaning from, 132
and plan-do-review sequence, 132
props and games, 138–39
questions during, 138–39
responses, 140
sharing, 159
a summary, 230
supporting children during, 137
use of gestures in, 141–42
use of language in, 133–34
use of rephrasing, 140
using encouragement during, 147–48
Recall train, 222
Recalling, ways of, 134
Release forms, 199
Representations, 219–23
Rhymes, 217
Riding toy, 215
Rope, 218
Routine plans, 16

S
Samples, preserving, 119
Shell game, 218
Simon Says, 218
Small-group time, 8
Small groups, and planning, 19
Snake, 215
Social conflicts, 99–103
Social interaction, and problem solving, 100
Song or chant, 218
Spin the bottle, 217
Steering wheels, 211
Sticky notes, 213
Storage areas, labeling, 107
String a bead, 218
String or yarn, 213
Suggestions, offering, 54
Support, 80
acknowledging children's feelings, 100
acknowledging contributions, 96
from adults, 67
combining strategies, 146
encouraging problem solving, 97
strategies, 29, 32 (*see also* Adult interaction strategies)

Supporting Young Learners 1 (Brickman & Taylor), 185
Supporting Young Learners 2 (Brickman), 185

T
Tape, 213
Tape measure, 213
Tape recorder, 214
Taylor, L. S., 185
Teaching, art and science of, 80
Team planning, 181, 186–87, 209
time, 9
Telephones, 210
Television set, 214
Time limit, in interest areas, 113
Tours, 214–16
Toy area
assessing, 122–25
props, 124
Train, 215
Training for Quality (Epstein), 3
Transition strategies, 192
Transition time, 8, 121
Turn-taking, in play, 89

V
Vague plans, 16
Verbalizing, plans, 54. *See also* Planning time, as language experience; Plans
Video camera, 212
Videotapes, 118, 204
Visibility games, 54–55, 214–16. *See also individual games*
Visits to structures, 216

W
Walkie-talkies, 210
Weikart, David P., 4, 125, 185
Work time, 3, 7, 162, 233
activities, 115–16
carrying over activities, 148
duration of, 62, 121–22
as opportunity to interact, 121
reflecting on, 137
and social skills, 71
a summary, 229
Writing samples, using, 204
Writing tools, 220

About the Author

Nancy Vogel has taught in various early childhood settings, including High/Scope's Demonstration Preschool, several state-funded preschools, early childhood special education programs, and kindergarten programs. In addition, she has worked as a High/Scope field consultant, conducting a number of workshops for early childhood teachers and administrators. Nancy holds a

B.S. degree in Early Childhood Education from Bradley University, Peoria, Illinois. She currently lives in Michigan with her husband, Curt, and daughter, Ruth. The Vogels are expecting their second child in March 2001.

Related High/Scope® Resources

The Teacher's Idea Books

The Essential Parent Workshop Resource: The Teacher's Idea Book 4

If you are interested in presenting workshops for parents of preschoolers, you will be delighted with this collection of 30 original workshops. Presenters will find it easy to follow the workshop format, which includes intended goals, a list of necessary materials, an introduction and interactive opening activity, central ideas for discussion, scenarios for reflection and application of ideas, and follow-up plans that encourage parents to apply the information at home. Packed with handouts and charts, it's all you need for practical, dynamic parent workshops.

BK-P1137 $25.95
M. Graves. Soft cover, photos, 180 pages, 2000. 1-57379-018-4.

Planning Around Children's Interests: The Teacher's Idea Book 2

Like the others, the second book in this popular High/Scope® series is filled with practical teaching strategies and actual classroom examples of teacher-child interactions. All new, up-to-date, and fun for all, the ideas draw on children's interests as a rich resource for curriculum planning. An essential handbook for dedicated professionals.

BK-P1106 $25.95
M. Graves. Soft cover, photos, 171 pages, 1996. 1-57379-019-2.

100 Small-Group Experiences: The Teacher's Idea Book 3

Packed with suggestions teachers can use to provide 100 exciting small-group activities. Activities are presented in four sections: children's interests; new materials; the High/Scope® key experiences in child development; and community experiences. Chock-full of valuable ideas for introducing various concepts, activities, and materials to children in active learning settings!

BK-P1115 $25.95
M. Graves. Soft cover, photos, 220 pages, 1997. 1-57379-029-X.

Daily Planning Around the Key Experiences: The Teacher's Idea Book 1

Make each part of the daily routine a useful and focused learning experience for preschoolers and kindergartners with the practical, creative suggestions in this handbook. Provides specific ideas for each part of the daily routine, including suggested materials, questioning techniques, and ideas for small- and large-group activities.

BK-P1076 $19.95
M. Graves. Soft cover, 87 pages, 1989. 0-931114-80-2.

High/Scope's Preschool Manual and Study Guide

Educating Young Children: Active Learning Practices for Preschool and Child Care Programs

Written for early childhood practitioners and students, this manual presents essential strategies adults can use to make active learning a reality in their programs. Describes key components of the adult's role: planning the physical setting and establishing a consistent daily routine; creating a positive social climate; and using High/Scope's 58 key experiences to understand and support young children. Other topics include family involvement, daily team planning, creating interest areas, choosing appropriate materials, the plan-do-review process, small- and large-group times. Offers numerous anecdotes, photographs, illustrations, real-life scenarios, and practical suggestions for adults. Reflects High/Scope's current research findings and over 30 years of experience.

BK-P1111 $39.95
M. Hohmann & D. P. Weikart. Soft cover, lavishly illustrated, 560 pages, 1995. 0-929816-91-9.

Now available in Spanish. BK-L1016 $39.95

A Study Guide to Educating Young Children: Exercises for Adult Learners

The study guide you've been waiting for—a must-have workbook for High/Scope's latest preschool manual! Designed for early childhood college courses, inservice training, and independent study. Will increase your confidence and competence in using the High/Scope® Preschool Curriculum. Contains active learning exercises exploring the content of the manual in depth. Chapter topics parallel *EYC's.* Abundant, interactive exercises include hands-on exploration of materials, child studies, analysis of photos and scenarios in *EYC,* recollection and reflection about curriculum topics, trying out support strategies, and making implementation plans.

BK-P1117 $15.95
M. Hohmann. Soft cover, 275 pages, 1997. 1-57379-065-6.

Related High/Scope® Resources

Plan-Do-Review: Visiting High/Scope's Demonstration Preschool

These three videos are packed with tips and strategies for helping teachers make the most of the High/Scope® plan-do-review process. Here's your chance to visit High/Scope's Demonstration Preschool. You'll see how veteran High/Scope® teachers interact with children during these important times in the daily routine.

1. How Adults Support Children at Planning Time
BK-P1118 $19.95
Video guide included. Color video, 19 minutes, 1997. 1-57379-056-7.

2. How Adults Support Children at Work Time
BK-P1119 $19.95
Color video, about 25 minutes, 1997. 1-57379-057-5.

3. How Adults Support Children at Recall Time
BK-P1120 $19.95
Color video, about 19 minutes, 1997. 1-57379-058-3.

High/Scope® Extensions

Learn about the High/Scope® early childhood approach from High/Scope® consultants and trainers. Practical tips, suggestions, and updates for understanding and implementing the High/Scope® Curriculum and for training others to do so. Special features include **Classroom Hints, Ask Us, Network News, Trainer-to-Trainer, Computer Learning.**

BK-P1000 $30.95/year, overseas $33.95
N. Brickman, Ed. Newsletter of the High/Scope® Curriculum, 8 pages/issue, 6 issues/year. ISSN 0892-5135

Supporting Young Learners Series

Supporting Young Learners 2: Ideas for Child Care Providers and Teachers

Like its popular predecessor, this book is packed with practical strategies and tips for making an active learning program the best it can be. Contains over 50 *Extensions* articles that have been updated to reflect the latest thinking on the High/Scope® Curriculum. A must-have for early childhood professionals!

BK-P1105 $25.95
N. Brickman, Ed. Soft cover, photos, 328 pages, 1996. 1-57379-006-0.

Supporting Young Learners 1: Ideas for Preschool and Day Care Providers

Provides practical answers to the day-to-day questions that arise in early childhood programs. The selections, which originally appeared in *Extensions,* are updated and deal with these and other timely issues in developmentally appropriate education.

BK-P1083 $25.95
N. Brickman and L. Taylor, Eds. Soft cover, 314 pages, 1991. 0-929816-34-X.

Coming in 2001—*Supporting Young Learners 3;* parent information sheets and newsletters. Check our Web site, new releases, www.highscope.org for up-to-the-minute announcements!

Preschool Assessment Tool

High/Scope® Child Observation Record (COR) for Ages 2¹/₂–6

The High/Scope® Child Observation Record Kit includes all the materials needed for a full year of assessment for a classroom of 25 children. Includes a Manual, 25 Assessment Booklets, 4 sets of Anecdotal Notecards, 50 Parent Report Forms, and a Poster. Complete boxed kit.

BK-P1084SET $90.95
1992. 0-929816-40-4.

Individual kit components:

1. COR Manual. BK-P1085 $25.95
52 pages, 1992. 0-929816-41-2.

2. COR Assessment Booklets. BK-P1086 $40.95
24 pages, set of 25 booklets, 1992. 0-929816-42-0.

3. COR Anecdotal Notecards. BK-P1087 $7.95
Set of 25 cards/ring, 1992. 0-929816-43-9.

4. COR Parent Report Forms. BK-P1088 $12.95
Set of 25 forms, 1992. 0-929816-44-7.

5. COR Spanish Parent Report Forms. BK-P1089 $12.95
25 forms, 1992. 0-929816-45-5.

6. COR Poster. Lists major COR categories and items.
BK-P1090 $5.95
22" x 34", 1992. 0-929816-46-3.

To order these or any other High/Scope® products, contact High/Scope® Press: phone (800)40-PRESS fax (800)442-4FAX
To see a full listing of High/Scope® preschool products, visit our Web site: www.highscope.org

Related High/Scope® Resources

Preschool Key Experiences

High/Scope Preschool Key Experiences Series, Booklets & Videos

Language and Literacy

Learning to use language in all its forms is one of the most important areas of development for preschoolers. Using the ideas in this booklet, you can help preschoolers expand their conversational abilities and encourage them to discover the usefulness and fun of the written word by introducing six key experiences in language and literacy. The booklet includes both a list of materials and a teaching strategy checklist. The colorful, informative video focuses on how adults support and extend children's experiences in actual High/Scope classrooms and centers.

Book: BK-P1155 $9.95, Video: BK-P1156 $30.95, Set: BK-P1157SET $34.95
Book, soft cover, photos, 28 pages, 2000. 1-57379-097-4; Video, color, 60 min., 2000. 1-57379-098-2.

Creative Representation

Teachers, child care providers, and parents can use this easy-to-read booklet, and companion video, to learn how to recognize and support the six High/Scope® key experiences in creative representation. Included are examples of how representation occurs in children's play, strategies for promoting representation, lists of materials that encourage representation, and a creative representation checklist.

Book: BK-P1146 $9.95, Video: BK-P1147 $30.95, Set: BK-P1148SET $34.95
Book, soft cover, photos, 28 pages, 2000. 1-57379-030-3; Video, color, about 40 min, 2000. 1-57379-087-7.

Room Arrangement

Getting Started: Materials and Equipment for Active Learning Preschools

Provides detailed information on selecting materials and equipment for preschools and child care centers. Interest areas covered: art, block, house, toy, book, computer, music and movement, sand and water, woodworking, and outdoor. Includes sample diagrams of typical High/Scope® classrooms and lists of suggested materials, with quantities specified.

BK-P1116 $14.95
N. Vogel. Soft cover, 56 pages, 1997. 1-57379-055-9.

Videotapes

Adult-Child Interactions: Forming Partnerships With Children

Shows teachers at High/Scope's Demonstration Preschool interacting as partners with children throughout the daily routine. Part 1 introduces interaction strategies, demonstrates their use in two work-time scenes, and includes a teacher commentary on each scene. Part 2 contains additional classroom scenes without commentary, to encourage viewer analysis and discussion.

BK-P1104 $50.95
Video guide included. Color video, 60 minutes, 1996. 1-57379-022-2.

Supporting Children in Resolving Conflicts

This important new video will teach you six problem-solving steps you can use to help children in conflict situations. The problem-solving process is demonstrated with real scenes of successful conflict resolution from a New York City Head Start Center and from the High/Scope® Demonstration Preschool.

BK-P1130 rental $10, purchase $49.95
Video guide included. Color video, 30 minutes. 1-57379-042-7

Movement in Early Childhood

Round the Circle: Key Experiences in Movement for Young Children, 2nd edition, completely revised and expanded!

Young children learn through play, and their play is full of movement experiences. *Round the Circle* has been completely revised to present the *High/Scope Education Through Movement: Building the Foundation* program for young children, developed by Phyllis S. Weikart. This new edition presents eight *key experiences in movement* that help adults *engage, enable,* and *extend* children's active movement explorations. In addition, Weikart's teaching model provides a strong framework for encouraging and supporting young children's learning. Readers will appreciate the numerous *suggested activities, concrete guidelines,* and *effective teaching strategies* that are peppered throughout the book. Use this well-illustrated and easy-to-understand book to make the most of children's movement adventures!

BK-M1020 $24.95
P. S. Weikart. Soft cover, 176 pages, 2000. 1-57379-096-6.